# A Study of House Church in India

**Christian Heritage Rediscovered**

The Series, as the name suggests, is meant to focus on Christian Faith & Living vis-à-vis topics like Literature & Poetry, Indigenous Philosophizing, Ethical response towards Agriculture, Health & Healing, Science & Technology, Eco-feminist Theology, Sociological approach towards Human Rights, Law & Politics, Arts, History of Ideas, Ancient Civilizations, Cultural Contiguity, Religious Cosmologies & Mysticism, Footsteps of famous Theologians, World Peace & Harmony, Global Capitalism, Network Marketing, Cybertheology, Population & Demographics, Epigraphic Studies, Contextualized Education, and many others. We welcome a Mss. on any topic/s mentioned, whether they are original works, scholarly monographs, collections of conference papers, revised dissertations, or translations of historical documents. Through the Series we, the Publishers, are striving to put forward published works that may help Institutions, Academic Bodies, Researchers, Scholars and the World at large in furthering their respective knowledge and understanding on the concerned subject. We welcome your comments on our efforts and further suggestions on how we can foster the upcoming thought provoking theologically grounded books.

*Christian Heritage Rediscovered - 64*

# A Study of House Church in India

## Missiological Role of House Churches via Social Interdependence in the Urban Context

**Hyoshin Jeong**

CWI
Christian World Imprints™

First Published in 2018 by

**Christian World Imprints**(TM)
*Christian Publishing & Books from India*
H-12 Bali Nagar, **New Delhi-110015**
info@christianworldimprints.com
www.ChristianWorldImprints.com
Phone: +91 11 25465925

ISBN 13: 978-93-5148-271-0 ISBN 10: 93-5148-271-5

**Cataloging in Publication Data--DK**
Courtesy: D.K. Agencies (P) Ltd. <docinfo@dkagencies.com>

**Jeong, Hyoshin,** 1971- author.
A study of house church in India : missiological role of house churches via social interdependence in the urban context / Hyoshin Jeong.
pages cm. -- (Christian heritage rediscovered ; 64)
Originally presented as the author's dissertation (Ph. D.--Concordia Theological Seminary, 2016).
ISBN 9351482715
ISBN 9789351482710

1. House churches--India. 2. City churches--India. 3. Evangelistic work--India. 4. Church work with immigrants--India. 5. Christianity and other religions--Hinduism. 6. Hinduism--Relations--Christianity. I. Title. II. Series: Christian heritage rediscovered ; 64.

LCC BV601.85.J46 2018 | DDC 262.00954 23



Printed in India

For Junho
(See you soon!)

# Contents

# Acknowledgements

I wish to extend my thanks and appreciation to my research advisor, Dr. Robert H. Bennett. He taught me how to study academically and guided me pastorally throughout the research. To the other two readers, Dr. Klasus Detlev Schulz and Dr. Joshua A. Pagan, who devoted their time to read and make helpful comments on my work; I appreciate their patience and participation.

I thank the house church participants who shared their beliefs and impressions with me. A special word of thanks to Rev. Gerry Mohr and Rev. Jerry Winegarden who helped in reading and editing this work.

A special acknowledgement must be extended to Cynthia Johnson, who always helped me throughout the years of my PHD program.

Words cannot express my appreciation to my family. I thank my mother, Eunyoung Lee, and my three children, Junho, Noah and Yebin. They deserve special thanks for their willingness to endure dad's doctoral sojourn with love and gratitude. And finally, a special word of appreciation to my wife, Eunyoung Choi. This colosal work would never have been completed without her support, sacrifice, and supplications.

# Abstract

The purpose of this qualitative and scholarly work is to analyze and evaluate the house church as a mission strategy means for the Hindu migrants and locals living in the city. In this study, the house church in India is defined as an effective mission strategy mean for the Hindu migrants as well as locals. The research problem is to ascertain that whether the mission aspects of house church will make it possible to reach the migrants as well as the locals to evangelize and catechize them in the urban context in India. In other words, in what ways does the house church in the urban context evangelize and catechize migrants and locals into God's family?

This research starts by reviewing four core characteristics (interdependent relationship and leadership, house church model, worldview change, and obstacles) of house church from literature. It confirms that these four characteristics have not yet been fully explored in current academic literature. A descriptive-evaluative study, utilizing an ethnographic study based on interviews, was conducted using several pastors and leaders of house churches who are actively involved in church planting in cities of India.

This study found house churches as a proper mission strategy method to evangelize and catechize migrants and locals in the urban context in India; however, there are limitations to the house churches in this work. The house churches used in the present work are not representative of all house churches in India. Therefore, application of results from that aspect of the study to house churches in other parts of India and around the world must be undertaken with caution and care: 1. The practical definition of house church is needed to be understood in the light of various ecclesiological stances. 2. This study only shows the viewpoint of pastors and leaders of house churches. Therefore, it needs other viewpoint from the believers of house churches for further study. 3. Some of church planting theories from the literature review are not applicable to the house church planting. 4. Many research participants did not have their own realistic solutions for their difficulties (obstacles) in order to overcoming them. Nevertheless, the application and results may yet affect other cities since there can be many similarities between different cities in India.

# Illustrations

# Tables

Chapter 1

# Introduction

## 1. Missiological Research Concern

God has given the Christian church in India an awesome challenge: the evangelization of urban and rural communities. Many migrants are choosing to settle in metropolitan cities like Delhi, Chennai, Mumbai, Calcutta, Hyderabad and Bangalore.[1] Many of these migrants are from rural areas where Hinduism is the majority religion and Christianity is a minority. Mission work needs to be done among these groups. There is a need to evangelize urban migrants as well as locals in the city. Many low caste migrants moved from rural areas to the city. However, while family relationships among Hinduism is a great obstacle to reaching them with the gospel, nevertheless, urban migrants from low castes are easier to approach than those of a higher caste. Westernization and economic growth in India lead this group (urban low caste migrants) who are of traditional society and religion, to realize abroad world and other religions.

Indeed, these social and economic changes begin to influence the worldview of the migrants and locals in the city. This change of the worldview helps them to accept the gospel. Their possible rejection of the gospel is reduced because of this worldview change, while their previous worldview had rejected the gospel. In addition, house churches established in this urban context have an important missionary role for delivering the gospel to Hindus who have experienced this change of their worldview.

[1] In 1951, the urban population in India was 62 million people, 17% of the total population. By 2011, the urban population was 377 million, or 31 percent. By 2025, 42.5 percent of the population will be urban. "India's massive migration crisis," K. Laxmi Narayan, accessed January 10, 2015. Http://knowledge.allianz.com/demography/migration/?454/indias-massive-migration-crisis

## 2. Research Concern

Migrants to cities from rural areas or locals who hold a Hindu worldview are in a high context culture. Their identity is tied up with their family or the group to which they belong. Due to this basis, it would seem possible to conjecture that a house church might be a useful strategy to evangelize and catechize these high context people. Intimacy, caring, and community are traits of supreme importance to Indians, even as they move into new social changes such as westernization, secularism and individualism. In what way can the house church deal with an Indian's new social and economic change? Can it be a great opportunity for the house church to reach Hindu people who have experienced a major change in their worldview?

## 3. Missiological Rationale for Choosing this Research Concern

The rationale for this research concern is the reality that house churches have been used as effective missionary strategies in order to reach other countries where Buddhism,[2] Islam,[3] and Hinduism are major religions. In the case of India, house churches take an important place as a church planting model. However, research is needed now more than ever. It seems that Indian churches belonging in mainstream Christianity do not have much concern for the house church. The house church seems to be standing alone, apart from the mainline church. The house church in India is the place where mainly migrants or low castes are gathering for worship. Although the house church is in various difficult conditions for mission, it is continuously growing in that context. One of the problems is that there has been few research works to discover the inner or outer factors for the phenomenal growth of the house church in India. Since there have not been enough resources for extensive research, the researcher needs to determine specific methods for studying. One method would be to extract some contents which hold missiological meaning from the literature about the world house church movement in light of the researcher's ministerial experience in India. These contents are the categorized in terms of the possibility to apply those elements to the house church in India.

The rationale for this research concern is the personal researcher's ministerial experience as well as biblical evidences of the house church. The mission of God was revealed through gatherings in houses in the early Christian church. The New Testament describes how Christian faith was delivered through the household

[2] "5 Countries You Never Knew Were Buddhist," Historymakers: The Fuel of Missions Flame, accessed January 15, 2015. http://www.historymakers.info/blog/5-buddhist-countries-you-never-thought-about.html

[3] "Church Planting Movements among Muslim Peoples," Kevin Greeson, accessed January 15, 2015. http://www.missionfrontiers.org/issue/article/church-planting-movements-among-muslim-peoples.

relationship line. As the house church was the place for sowing the gospel to the souls then, so it will be sowed in the house church today.

## 4. Personal Ministerial Experience Guides the Research to this Research Concern

The researcher went to India in 2002 with his family as a Korean missionary. The researcher arrived at Trivandrum in Kerela and had completed his mission work in Youth With A Mission (YWAM) for one and half years. He then shifted to Bangalore City in 2003. He started mission work among the poor and a women ministry. He was also involved in a house church planting ministry with local pastors in Bangalore. When he suggested a conference for local house churches pastors in Banglore and Chikkubala District (Satellite city of Bangalore), more than one hundred pastors of house churches gathered. He then realized the importance of house churches as a strategy for the migrants in Bangalore. Most of the local pastors were coming from different rural areas in India, and their church members were also migrants from several rural areas. One thing of interest was that most of them had low caste background. On the other hand, some were in middle class, while others were in low class. Is the house church a plausible strategy for migrants as well as locals to use in the city to evangelize and catechize them into God's family? This question led the researcher to further studies of migrants of house churches in some cities of India.

## 5. The Research Concern over time as Described in the Literature

While the research of the house church movement has been studied in North America and China greatly, there has been a meager study of the house church movement in India. Even though there are a lot of house churches in India, the lack of academic concern makes her remain a loner, apart from the mainline church. The researcher categorized some viewpoints described in the literature about the house church toward research work in India.

First, there is a viewpoint that house church as church planting model come from contexts of religious persecution. One prominent research was conducted by Atul Y. Aghamkar among urban Hindus in Pune. He wrote *Insights into Openness: Encouraging Urban Mission* for suggesting the mission methods toward Hindus. He especially emphasizes that the role of laity is important to deliver the gospel to people among the urban Hindus in Pune. Many migrants in Pune city follow Hinduism.[4]

Relationship-centered approaching is effective with migrants or locals since one of their characteristics is relationship-centering. House Church can be a good strategy to approach the migrant for delivering the gospel through the relationship. Aghamkar supports the house church as a strategy in the India context because

[4] Atul Y. Aghamkar, *Insights into Openness: Encouraging Urban Mission* (Bangalore: SAIACS, 2000).

there are social objections and religious persecution toward Indian churches. He states that household evangelism and a house church model minimize the main hindrance and opposition for the church by avoiding the removal of individuals from their family and joint family system. Consequently, Aghamkar rightly argues that family coherence will enhance the growth of house churches and it always gives boldness for witness in the midst of opposition.[5]

Second, there is a viewpoint that sees the house church as a renewal movement. Wolfgang Simson who works as a strategy consultant within the DAWN International Network, wrote *Houses That Change the World.* His work is a remarkable contribution to the house churches in India. He feels that it is time to bring the church to the people, and not the people to the church. He proposes a meaningful idea, "A church not only has a message, but is a message."[6] He understood that the church itself can be a mission tool as a message. Wolfgang regards the house church as one of reformation: "reformations along the lines of theology by Martin Luther, reformation of spirituality of Schwartz, and a reformation of structure."[7] The house church can be the agency to reach unreached people and lead to revival in India.

Third, there is a viewpoint that sees the house church as a center of church planting in India. In his book *Church Planting Movement,* David Garrison sees, for examples, Victor Choudhrie as a forerunner of a house church planter in India. "In 1993, Dr. Victor Choudhrie, then a prominent cancer surgeon in India, surrendered to the Lord's calling to evangelize and plant churches among the peoples of Madhya Pradesh. Over the next eight years, God blessed his ministry. Today there is more than 4,000 churches in the state with more than 50,000 believers."[8] Choudhrie wrote *The Church in Your House.*[9] In his book, he proposes the church model of New Testament structure as a strategy for house churches that merges with the culture of the people and resonates with the will of God.

## 6. Recent Reports for the House Church Planting Project: Case Studies

This researcher sets forth two case studies (house church planting among the Lingayat and K-state) which are closely related, but cannot be explained in detail because of their confidentiality.

[5] Atul Y. Aghamkar, "Mission and Ministry of House Churches" *Class Lecture at SAIACS,* 01-22-2005.

[6] Wolfgang Simson, *Houses that Change the World: The Return of the House Churches* (Wayneboro, GA: Authentic, 1998), xii.

[7] Ibid.

[8] David Garrison, *Church Planting Movements: How God is Redeeming a Lost World* (Arkadelphia: WIGTake Resources, 2004), 36.

[9] Victor Choudhrie, *The Church in Your House* (English Edition, 2006).

### Case Study One: House Church Planting among the Lingayat

Baptist Press printed the following report in December 02, 2005.[10] Southern Baptist missionaries had planned to reach out to the Lingayat people in South India with the gospel. There were no other Christian workers for reaching them. In 1997, some researchers could count only 800 Christians and no churches among the Lingayats, a high-caste Hindu group that numbers 15 million. At that time, these Southern Baptist missionaries expected to see 18,000 believers in 1,000 house churches among this people group by 2006.

According to this report, several factors have played a role in sparking this church planting: Prayer, Lingayat witnesses, customized material, family evangelism, and training trainers. Even when the time came to leave the work entirely in the hands of Lingayat believers, their team had started house church planting among another people group just like the Lingayat. A team leader said, "About 50% percent of Last Frontier people groups are Hindu peoples. That is such a bloc of the Great Commission – one that's really neglected."

### Case Study Two: K State House Church Planting

In the case study of "K-State: Church Planting in a Responsive State" published in the Best Practice Institute Manual (page no. 41-42), over 600 house churches were started among Hindus in four years (2003-2007).[11] The author worked closely with leaders of this movement for entire four year period. The church planters used their own church planting method called *CPM methodologies,* because (a) they saw them as consistent with New Testament patterns for church planting and (b) because they found them to be effective in the Indian context particularly among Hindu peoples.[12]

Table 1. Numbers of House Church from 2003 to 2006

| Years | House Churches |
|---|---|
| 2003 | 17 |
| 2004 | 20 |
| 2005 | 224 |
| 2006 | 620 |

Source: "Best Practices Institute," accessed October 13, 2014. http://www.churchplantingmovements.com/images/stories/pdf/bpi-training-manual_20082.pdf

[10] "Gospel multiplies among India's Lingayat people so much that coordinators may leave," Mark Kelly, accessed October 13, 2014. http://www.baptistpress.com/22192/gospel-multiplies-among-indias-people-so-much-that-coordinators-may-leave

[11] "Best Practices Institute," accessed October 13, 2014. http://www.churchplantingmovements.com/images/stories/pdf/bpi-training-manual_20082.pdf

[12] Ibid.

In 2006, after 10 months, over 14,000 professions of faith were reported and approximately 1,100 baptized. According to this report, the most important key factor for church planting and its growth is the role and responsibility of national leaders: "National leaders are men with a great burden for the lost and a great vision… the house church model is allowing faster multiplication and attracts less persecution."[13]

The reporter also mentioned that some factors hinder growth. (1) Baptism is an issue. Immediate baptism is uncommon. This is in part due to tradition but also relates to hesitancy for lay leaders to baptize people. Hindus are only familiar with the priest performing special functions in the temple. Therefore, these new converts and new leaders are slow to accept this role of the lay leader. (2) Another problem is the discipling of new believers and development of leaders. There is no real way at present to track leadership development or multiplication. (3) There are doctrinal issues to be dealt with. This arises both from their Hindu background and from the denominational differences that exist. Though the Scriptures are available in the K-state language, many of these groups are non-literate. There are groups which will offer monetary or other enticements to conversion or to an affiliation with a group that is doctrinally incorrect according to Scripture. (4) The traditional church in the country is another problem. Much of the existing church today has lost its vision for evangelism and church planting. Many pastors want to see growth in their own congregations, yet reject house churches or multiplication. Often, leaders think that buildings are essential; new converts frequently have the idea that the church is the building.[14]

## 7. Research Context

Cities in India have increased rapidly. For example, Bangalore has the highest rate of increase in population in India.[15] Other cities also have increased in population. The reason for increasing population is the economic growth. Therefore many people shift to cities for economic benefits. As the population grows, the missiological concern has also grown for the migrants, who originate from a low caste. The role of the pastor for evangelizing the migrants and forming congregations is significant. The migrants have their own traditional background

[13] "Best Practices Institute," 142.

[14] Ibid.

[15] The steep rise in the population of Bangalore district has seen it top the population growth rate in the country. The Bangalore urban district has grown three times faster than the population of the state as a whole. Bangalore district's population ballooned 46.68 per cent over the past decade to around 9.59 million in 2011. The district today houses over 15.69 per cent of the state's population. This despite the thrust of the state on deflecting growth towards tier II and tier III cities in the state. Today, 4,378 persons cram every square kilometer space of the district. "Population boom: At 46.68%, Bangalore tops urban districts," Praveen Bose, accessed September 25, 2014. http://www.businessstandard.com/india/news/population-boom-at-4668-bangalore-tops-urban-districts/431302/

and are relationship center oriented. The role of a laity who has relationships with migrants is important to deliver the gospel to this group. The worship in house is efficient to the migrants in India.

On the other hand, overpriced land, building costs, and limited amounts of money make it impossible for a congregation to buy property and build or refurbish an edifice in which the people may gather for worship. Other cost-efficient ecclesial structures are needed.

## 8. Research Problem

While studies for the house church in North America and China are active, its study in India has not had much interest. The Indian Church has little concern about the house church since most house churches do not belong to any denominations. Some denominations do not allow forming a house church. This negative awareness of the house church discourages and weakens the mission aspect of the house church movement. Still, despites its weaknesses, house churches are now under way as a church planting mission model, even with the various obstacles.

Therefore, as the researcher looks carefully at the fields of the house church, and through the literature reviews which have already been studied, he also reviews the various problems and solutions related to worldview (other religions and other culture), leadership, and suffering (persecution). From this theoretical basis, he provided a house church planting mission model and interdependent relationship theory (to understand of relationship center approach) in order to assist in the development of mission work through the house church.

The major concern behind this research is the evangelical action by and to the urban migrant communities. This concern focuses on the following research problem: What aspects of the house church evangelize and catechize migrants or locals in the city into God's family?

## 9. The Statement of the Research Purpose

The purpose of this qualitative study is to analyze and evaluate the house church as a mission strategy for Hindu migrants and locals living in the city. In this study, the house church in India is defined as the effective mission strategy for Hindu migrants as well as locals.

## 10. Research Questions

The research problem is what mission aspects of house church make it possible to reach migrants as well as locals to evangelize and catechize them in the urban context in India. In other words, in what ways does the house church in the urban context evangelize and catechize migrants and locals into God's family? This research problem is guided by four research questions:

Grand Tour Questions

In what way can the house church in urban area effectively evangelize and catechize migrants and locals into God's family?

### *Research Question 1*

In what ways do interdependent relationships and leadership influence the house church to evangelize and catechize migrants and locals?

Operational Question 1

In what ways do you understand interdependent relationships in the house church? In what way do you understand leadership in the house church?

Operational Question 2

In your opinion, what are the results of the leadership and interdependent relationship in the house church?

Operational Question 3

In your opinion, in what ways do the roles of interdependent relationship influence people in the house church to reach migrants and locals to evangelize and catechize? In your opinion, in what ways do the roles of leadership influence the house church to reach migrants as well as locals to evangelize and catechize them?

### *Research Question 2*

What is a proper model for a house church model that will influence the house church to evangelize and catechize migrants and locals in the city?

Operational Question 1

Before you planted your house church, what was your idea about a model for a house church that influences evangelism and catechesis of migrants or locals in your city?

Operational Question 2

After you planted your house church, now what is your idea about a model for a house church that influences evangelism and catechesis of migrants or locals in your city?

Operational Question 3

In your opinion, what is an ideal model for a house church that influences evangelism and catechesis of migrants or locals in your city?

### *Research Question 3*

In what ways do house churches put their effort to transforming the worldview of the migrants as well as locals who hold a Hindu worldview in order to evangelize and catechize them in the city?

Operational Question 1

In what ways do economic migration and urban environment affect migrants to change their previous religious and cultural understanding? In what ways does the change of urban environment affect locals to change their previous religious and cultural understanding?

Operational Question 2

In what ways does your house church communicate with Hindu people in order to deliver the gospel and transform their worldview?

Operational Question 3

In what ways have Hindu migrants experienced their worldview transform after they have converted?

### *Research Question 4*

What kinds of obstacles (difficulties) may house churches confront when they evangelize and catechize migrants and locals into God's family?

Operational Question 1

What kinds of inner obstacles does your house church have when it evangelizes and catechizes migrants and locals into God's family in the city? In what ways does the house church overcome these obstacles? What elements of house church help it to overcome?

Operational Question 2

What kinds of outer obstacles does your house church have when she evangelizes and catechizes migrants and locals into God's family in the city? In what ways has the house church overcome these obstacles? What elements of a house church help it to overcome?

## 11. Preliminary Approach for Carrying out the Research

An important segment of the research design is an ethnographic study of a house church. Some urban house churches were selected. Semiformal interviews as qualitative research methodology were used. For this, the researcher had interviewed two house church pastors as a pilot study through *Skype* and face-to-face interview. He contacted 10 pastors or leaders to interview through *Skype*. He also contacted a person who was working as a partner for house church planting among the house church leaders to distribute the semiformal interview document to 24 persons to respond to it.

## 12. Delimitations

This study did not focus on the cell group or Meta church models.[16] Cell and Meta church groups are small groups of Christians who meet in someone's home on a regular basis for Bible study and fellowship. They are normally a structure of a congregation. In contrast, the concern of this study is a group of Christians who meet weekly in a house for the study of the Word, for prayer, for the breaking of the bread, for fellowship, and to evangelize migrants and locals.

This research dealt with leaders and pastors from house churches in cities of India. Therefore, application of results from that aspect of the study to house churches in other cities of other countries must be undertaken with caution and care. However, the application and results may yet affect other cities since there can be many similarities between cities in India. The field research design is primarily questions research. The research relies upon observations and interviews of the house church pastors or leaders.

[16] Carl F. George, *Prepare Your Church for the Future* (New York: Fleming H. Revell Company, 1991), 57.

Chapter 2

# Biblical and Theological Considerations

While there are other aspects of biblical consideration of the House Church Movement which could be examined, four aspects stand out as being worthy of in-depth examination because they directly affect the missiology of the movement: (1) social interdependence and leadership, (2) worldview and another religion – Hinduism, (3) church planting model, and (4) some obstacles from inside and outside of house churches. Each of these four aspects will be discussed in this chapter.

The belief in Scripture as God's Word is one of the distinctive traits of the house church. As Hian says, "The Bible is a family book, and Christians cannot neglect its focus on the family. When we turn to the biblical records, we shall discover that families feature prominently both as the recipients as well as the agents of salvation blessings."[17] The New Testament repeatedly reveals that the Christian faith spread along the lines of relationship. (e.g. Andrew and Simon Peter; James and John; Paul and his own kinsmen Andronicus and Junias). The beginning of the New Testament Church was the family unit and the family home. In New Testament times, the household was regarded as a basic political unit. The house could include not only family, but also slaves, freedmen, servants, laborers and sometimes business associates and tenants. Therefore, in the New Testament time we see the Christian faith moving from family to family and house to house. New Testament writers frequently used the Greek word *oikos,* translated in English as "house," "household," or "family." It is important to note that we find the New Testament usage of this word. Jesus and Paul recognized the

[17] Atul Y. Aghamkar, *God So Loves the City*, ed. Charles Van Engen & Jude Tiersma (Monrovia: MARC, 1994), 151.

importance of the family. Therefore, "Christ picked the family as the best model for the congregational life of His followers."[18]

A survey of Jesus' ministry, Acts, and the epistles reveals Christianity spreading through the conversion of households (*oikos*) and the planting of house churches in urban centers.[19] The spread of Christianity was rapid. Until approximately A.D. 250, Christians gathered in homes[20] or in renovated houses (*domus ecclesiae*) to study the word of God, to partake of the Lord's Body and Blood, to pray, and to evangelize the community.[21]

## 1. Jesus and *Oikos*

According to Allen Cabaniss, "The real home of Jewish worship was thus the Temple, even if performed in the synagogue."[22] This was said about the Jewish house. The household was the locus of daily activity and, though the Jews did not have statuettes (i.e., images of God), praying, chanting, reading and blessing were at the heart of Jewish life and home.[23] Although Christian worship was indebted to Jewish practices, Floyd Filson contends that the house church made possible "a distinctively Christian worship and fellowship from the very first days of the apostolic age."[24] The house in the ancient world was a sacred place and the sacrality of the house among the early Christians would have been unquestioned. Because of the sacred complexion of the house, both Jewish and Gentile converts to Christianity would have had no compunction about worshipping in a domestic place. The Church came to use the household as its organizational model.[25]

*Oikos* and *oikia* are joined by a common root and refer to the "house" and "household" (*familia*) respectively. *Oikos* can also be used more broadly as a way of referring to a community.[26] The distinctive expression of Hebrew *beth*

---

[18] Paul M. Miller, *Leading the Family of God* (Scottdale: Pennsylvania, 1981), 14.

[19] Glenn E. Hinson, *The Evangelization of the Roman Empire* (Macon, GA: Mercer University Press, 1981), 32.

[20] Calvin Guy, *Discipling the City: Theological Reflections on Urban Mission*, ed. Roger S. Greenway (Grand Rapids: Baker Book House, 1979), 28.

[21] Walter Oetting, *The Church of the Catacombs* (St. Louis: Concordia Publishing House, 1964), 26.

[22] Allen Cababiss, *Pattern in Early Christian Worship* (Macon, GA: Mercer University Press, 1989), 29.

[23] Mark B. Beesley, "At the Boundary of Place: Rethinking the Provenance of Early Christian Architecture" (PhD diss., The University of St. Andrews, 2010), 177.

[24] Floyd V. Filson, "The Significance of the Early House Churches." *Journal of Biblical Literature* 58 (1939): 109-112.

[25] Beesley, "At the Boundary of Place: Rethinking the Provenance of Early Christian Architecture", 177.

[26] According to Mark B. Beesley, the distinction between 'building' and 'community' is often rather nebulous. In the OT 'my house' refers to Israel itself, so that the NT exegesis reminds us of the equation of 'house of God' and the community. Ibid., 178.

*Israel* explains the common New Testament expression 'house of Israel' as the collective people (Luke 1:33 and Acts 7:46). It could also have the people and the city as its referent (Matt. 23:38).[27] Jesus did not intend the earthly Temple at all but something more ethereal. A concept intimately associated with "'Father's house," is that o*ikos* can also imply the Kingdom of God in John 14:2.[28] So far as the terminology is concerned, 'house' and 'household' followed typical Jewish parlance. House was a term used for dwellings of all kinds. It was also used of the Temple and it encompassed the whole community of Israel.[29] There is nothing particularly remarkable about the term itself, but it does claim a significant, albeit subdued, place in the Gospel's portrayal of Jesus of Nazareth. The house became an important backdrop for the life and work of Jesus.[30] The house played a more significant role in the life and teaching of Jesus within houses, though Jesus and his disciples attended both the Temple and synagogue.

The imagery of the *oikos* in the ministry of Jesus provided both a ready metaphor and a natural backdrop for His teaching. Jesus' teachings are replete with *oikos/oikia* imagery.[31] Many of His teachings in Luke contrast the household to the temple. This continued in Acts as well. According to John H. Elliott, the Gospel of Mark uses "house" and "family" as follows:

> ... link words for the combination of the separate sayings; more importantly, they are parts of a unifying theme for treating the issues of social division, demonic opposition and faithful obedience to the will of God as factors effecting membership in the household of Jesus.[32]

In the Sermon on the Mount (Matt. 5-7), Jesus refers to the Father fifteen times (thirteen as "your Father", once as "our Father", once as "my Father"). His purpose for coming to this world was to reveal the Father to the world (John 1:14, 18; 14:9) as well as to be the atoning sacrifice (Rom. 3:25; Heb. 2:17) so that many might be adopted into God's family (Eph. 1:5; Rom. 8:16, 23; 9:4; 1John 3:1). In Luke 15:11-32, Jesus illustrates the love the Father has for His lost children. In Matthew 13:38 as well as Luke 16:8 and 20:34-35, believers

---

[27] Ibid., 179.

[28] Leon Morris, *The Gospel According to John, The New International Commentary on the New Testament* (Grand Rapids, MI: Eerdmans, 1971), 638.

[29] Beesley, "At the Boundary of Place: Rethinking the Provenance of Early Christian Architecture", 180.

[30] Ibid.

[31] Oikia – Matt. 5:15; 7:24-27 (Luke 6:46-49); Mark 13:34-35; Luke 15:8, 25. Oiketes – Luke 16:13. Oikiakos – Matt. 10:25-26. Oikodespotes – Matt. 10:25; 13:27, 52; 20:1, 11; 21:33; 24:43; Luke 12:39; 13:25; 14:21. Oikodomeo – Matt. 7:24. 26; 16:18; 21:33, 42; 23:29; 26:61; Mark 12:1, 10; Luke 6:48-49; 11:47-48; 12:18; 14:28, 30; 17:28; 20:17. Oikodome- Mark 13:1-2; oikonomeo- Luke 16:2; oikonomia- Luke 16:2-4; oikonomos- Luke 12:42; 16:1, 3, 8; oikos- Matt. 10:6; 11:8; 12:4, 44; 15:24; Luke 6:4; 11:17, 24, 51; 12:39, 52; 14:23; 15:6; 16:4, 27; 18:14.

[32] Joh H. Elliott, *A Home for the Homeless* (Philadelphia: Fortress Press, 1981), 193.

are contrasted with the children of this age. Speaking to the crowds and to his disciples Jesus called them "brothers" and said, "And call no man your father on earth, for you have one Father, who is in heaven" (Matt. 23:9). Likewise, it is clear that Jesus presented his teaching in terms of the *oikos* (Luke 11:11; 15:11-32; Matt. 21:31). In addition to being a place for Jesus' teaching, the house was a place for working miracles,[33] fellowship,[34] and hospitality.[35] Recent scholarship has indicated a methodological theme within the Gospels that highlight the *oikos* (house or household) as strategic in the ministry of Jesus.[36] The context of the house provides a backdrop to well-known acts of Jesus such as His proclaiming the Good News of the Kingdom (Luke 8:30; 10:5-8), teaching (Mark 2:1-12; Luke 7:36-50; 10:38-42; 14:1-24), and healing (Mark 2:11-12; Luke 4:38-41).

## 2. Jesus' Ministries and Houses

Jesus' ministries involve a healing ministry to the disabled, teaching, discipleship training, reaching out to the Jews and Gentiles in relationship to house. In addition, the Scripture provides how Jesus ministered in the relationship network (the interdependent relationship). Capernaum[37] seems to be a special point of concentration in the Gospels. After Nazareth, Capernaum became the residence for Jesus.[38] All the Gospels agree that once Jesus began his public ministry, Capernaum appeared to be his preference for place of residence.[39] Many of the

---

[33] Matt. 9:23; Mark 5:35; and Luke 8:41.

[34] Matt. 9:10; Mark 2:15; and Luke 5:29.

[35] Luke 7:44-47.

[36] Robert Lee Turner, "Leadership Development Process of Select House Church Network in North America: A Case Study" (PhD diss, The Southern Baptist Theological Seminary, 2010), 18.

[37] Roger Gehring contends that the historical data from five verses of Mark (1:29, 33; 2:1; 3:20; 9:33) demonstrate that a significant amount of Jesus' healing and teaching ministry took place in and around the residence of Peter in Capernaum. He illustrates Capernaum and Bethany having some advantages as a base of operations for Jesus' outreach. During the time of Jesus, Capernaum was a town with a relatively large population and a substantial target group for Jesus' message of the coming kingdom of God. Capernaum was an economically flourishing as well as a political and militarily important Galilean border and garrison town. It was centrally located on an important trade route between Damascus and Caesarea with connections to Tiberias and Ptolemais. Capernaum's central location made it an ideal center for the missional outreach of Jesus and his disciples. The area was located far enough from the larger centers such as Sepphoris, Tiberias, and Jerusalem that Jesus was able to spread the message of God's kingdom at least initially without having to directly confront the political and religious leaders located in those cities. Like Capernaum, Bethany had a central location. It was close enough to Jerusalem and easily accessible for Jesus from there. At the same time, it was far enough away to provide the necessary distance from his enemies. Roger W. Gehring, *House Church and Mission* (Peabody, Massachusetts: Hendrickson Publishers, 2004), 37-43.

[38] Mark 2:1; Matt 4:14; 9:1. Jesus left his original home, Nazareth, and went and lived in Capernaum.

[39] Mark 1:2; 2:1; 9:33; Matt 4:13; 11:23; Luke 10:15; John 2:12; 6:17-59.

significant events in the life and ministry of Jesus took place in the town. Both the house of Peter was in Capernaum and the house of Martha and thus functioned as the center for Jesus' ministry. As we examine these two houses, one can find Jesus's ministerial methods and its model.

Interdependence Relationship and Leadership Model

Jesus carried out his own ministry through interdependent relationships among households and he saw the role of head of household as the leadership model of ministry. According to E. Haenchen, Jesus was "obviously dependent upon the hospitality of those who had a house, an income, and a job."[40] The house of Peter became the social and material basis for Jesus' missional ministry. It was the social basis of Jesus' ministry, as a source of coworkers (Peter, Andrew) and quite possibly as a 'network' of relationships that provide a source of evangelistic contacts – for example, the extended family of the *oikos* (Peter's mother-in-law and his wife), including friends of the family. It was the material basis in that it provided a meeting place for ministry activities such as preaching and healing and enabled mission journeys, as well as ministry on the home front.[41]

Del Birkey has studied the ministry method of Luke 10:1-11, where Jesus appointed seventy-two of His followers and sent them to every town and place he was about to go. Birkey sets forth the principle of interdependence in Jesus' leadership, that "the first principle was the small composite of the different teams, possibly for the sake of mutual accountability and support.... Third, if they did find such a person, they were to accept the hospitality of that house. Fourth, they were to remain in that home and build a base of operations while reaching those relationships that were connected to that particular home."[42]

Peter was the owner and head of his household, a head of the household and a fishing businessman. He had a secure and strong economic position in Capernaum. This allowed him to provide ongoing hospitality not only to Jesus but to all of the disciples as well. Thus, Jesus gained both the head of a household and with him the entire household for his cause, a household that was then available to him as an operational base for his missional outreach.[43] Besides, Jesus along with his disciples enjoyed the hospitality of Martha in Bethany during his

[40] E. Haenchen, *Weg Jesu: Eine Erklärung des Markusevangelium und der kanonischen Parallelen* (Berlin: Töpelmann, 1996), 109, quoted in Roger W. Gehring, *House Church and Mission* (Peabody, Massachusetts: Hendrickson Publishers, 2004), 42.

[41] Gehring, *House Church and Mission*, 42.

[42] Del Birkey, *The House Church* (Scottdale, PA: Herald Press, 1987), 50-51.

[43] Gehring, *House Church and Mission*, 41.

last stay in Jerusalem.[44] Martha appears in the role of the hostess in Luke 10:38-42. She was presumably a widow, a homeowner, and head of the household.[45]

Jesus sets forth the leadership model for the church in the house. Jesus compares church leadership to stewardship in a household (Matthew 24:45; Luke 12:45). He teaches his followers not to pull rank or to parade the power of patronage (Luke 22:25), but to regard one another as brothers (Matt. 23:8). In God's household as portrayed by Jesus, the key is not privilege or rank but love and service.[46]

### Jesus' Healing and Teaching Ministry in the House

Jesus taught not only in open-air settings, but in synagogues and houses as well. Much of Jesus' ministry of preaching the gospel and healing was spent in people's homes.[47] Jesus healed two blind men in a house at Capernaum (Mk 9:27-28). Although, a number of scholars like Bultmann maintain that Jesus only taught in the synagogues or in the open, Jesus practiced at least a sporadic teaching ministry in houses.[48] Jesus teaching ministry took place in and around the house of Peter in Capernaum. The teaching ministry of Jesus is much more clearly documented in Mark 9:33. In Capernaum and 'at home' Jesus has an instructional discussion with his disciples evolving out of their argument over who was the greatest. In the narrative about the temple tax in Matthew 17:24-27, a master-disciple conversation, that is, an instructional discussion, takes place in the house of Peter. According to Gehring, most of today's scholars take a position that Jesus himself actually taught catechism in the house.[49]

### Overcoming Persecution

Jesus did his ministry at the house in order to minimize the persecution. According to Roger W. Gehring, "Jesus' ministry can be divided into two periods: his public ministry and, following that, a period of time when Jesus, more or less in the role of a fugitive because of persecution, was forced to minister more

---

[44] Ibid., 43.

[45] I. H. Marshall, *Luke: Historian and Theologian* (Downers Grove, Ill.: InterVarsity Press, 1988), 451.

[46] Ekkehard W. Stegemann and Wolfgan Steggemann, Translated by O.C. Dean, Jr. *The Jesus Movement: A Social History of Its First Century* (Minneapolis, Fortress Press, 1999), 284.

[47] Matt. 8:14 (Mark 1:29; Luke 4:38); Matt. 9:10 (Mark 2:15; Lk 5:29), Matt. 9:23 (cf. Luke 8:51), Matt. 9:28; Matt. 13:1, 36; Matt. 17:25; Matt. 26:6 (cf. Mark 14:3; John 12:3); Mark 2:1; Mark 5:38; 7:17; 7:24; 9:33; 10:10; Luke 7:6, 36; 8:41; 10:38; 14:1; 19:5, 9, 46; 22:10.

[48] According to Gehring, a private home often provided the meeting place for religious and intellectual dialogue and instruction. Particularly in the Jewish and Christian setting, domestic houses were viewed as "die Urzelle der Zusammenkünfte von Meister und Jüngern (the basic cell for the assemblies of the master with his disciples)." Gehring, *House Church and Mission*, 29.

[49] Ibid., 38.

in private, most likely, at least in part, in domestic houses."[50] Jesus advised his disciples to escape from the persecution when they delivered the gospel in Luke 10:1-11. When Jesus appointed seventy-two of His followers and sent them to every town and place, according to Birkey, Jesus encouraged His followers not to confront those that rejected them. Birkey maintains that "the last principle for the disciples was the admonition to not spend undue time in an area where the message of the Kingdom was resisted."[51]

## 3. The House as Mission Outreach Model

Jesus looked at the social life of his time from the point of view of the household. According to Stegemann and Steggemann, "this does not merely shape the Jesus movement into the household form of the surrounding world. Rather, the model of discipleship tends to transform the model of the household."[52] Jesus makes the household vital to his mission strategy and vision of transformed community. Jesus used the household as a mission base in each village (Luke 10:5-10). He teaches his followers to view God as their Father (ten times in Matt. 6) and Jesus depicts himself as head of a household, with his disciples as household members (Matt. 10:25). Jesus stresses the concept of the familial fellowship of believers.[53]

Evangelical Triangle

During the period of residency in Capernaum, the house of Peter was available to Jesus as a center of operation for his ministry and outreach in the area surrounding the Sea of Galilee. Jesus concentrated on the areas of Capernaum, Chorazin, and Bethsaida (cf. Matt. 11:21; Luke 11:13-15). These three neighboring villages became the major focus for Jesus' ministry. In German scholarship, the term 'evangelical triangle' (*das evangelische Dreieck*)[54] was coined to describe this phenomenon. The three villages are only one to two hours by foot from one another. Chorazin and Bethsaida both are near Capernaum and so would have been easily and quickly accessible from Capernaum. Like Capernaum, the house of Martha in Bethany became a central location for Jesus' ministry. Jesus often came back from Jerusalem to Bethany (Mark 11:1, 11, 12, 15, 27; cf. Matt. 21:17) and stayed there for a time. Jesus, along with his disciples enjoyed the hospitality of Martha in Bethany during his last stay in Jerusalem (Luke 10:38-

---

[50] Ibid., 29.

[51] Birkey, *The House Church*, 50.

[52] Stegemann and Steggemann, *The Jesus Movement*, 277.

[53] Ibid., 278.

[54] This is a small geographic area containing the area between the biblical cities of Capernaum, Korazin and Bethsaida. We know from scripture that Jesus chose to make his home in Capernaum, on the northwest shores of the Sea of Galilee. He seems to have made this major change in ministry location in order to fulfill Isaiah 9:1. "The Evangelical Triangel," Jim Gerrish, accessed October 10, 2014. http://www.wordofgodtoday.com/evangelical-triangle/

39). The house in Bethany appears to serve as a meeting and teaching facility (John 11:19, 31; 12:1-9; Luke 10:38-42).[55]

### House as a Place for Discipline

During Jesus' lifetime, private houses were used for spreading the Gospel and for discipling the people. People worshipped Him at home (Matt. 2:11) when Jesus was born. Magi and shepherd came to Jesus and worshipped Him in the home. When we looked at the Bible, we see that Jesus used houses for healing and deliverance meetings (Matt. 8:14-16). Although there were synagogues, the temple, and some other places of religious importance, Jesus chose to celebrate in common, ordinary houses in accordance with the Jewish custom of Passover. He preached to crowds assembled in houses as well as in the open air and in the streets (Mark 2:1, 2). We can find Jesus' ministries in houses at Luke 5:17-20; 17:1; 19:1-10; Jn. 2; 4:53; Mark 1:29-34; 2:1; 7:24. The house of Peter was a place for Jesus and his disciples to cultivate their personal domestic faith life such as prayer, fellowship, and spiritual formation. Jesus trained his disciples to do house-to-house outreach (evangelism).[56]

### Promoting New Believers to Evangelize

Gehring answers the question of how those who led a sedentary lifestyle became followers of Jesus? He assumes many of those who came to hear Jesus in Capernaum returned home as his followers. As a result of the itinerant ministry of Jesus, a large number of people would have come to faith through his preaching. They would have remained in their vocations, and at home with their family in expectation of the coming kingdom.[57] Here, the church can promote the new believers to evangelize their family and reach out to their social network. Jesus sent His disciples to people's homes in order to announce that the kingdom was at hand (Matt. 10:12-14). He continues to invite and welcome people into his *oikos*. Jesus claims all who believe in Him as the Son of God and Savior are His siblings (Matt. 25:40; Mark 3:34; John 20:17), the seed of Abraham (Luke 13:16; 19:9; John 8:37), and his friends (John 15:14-15). All His children are united as one Body through the one Spirit (Eph. 4:4-6).

### Sedentary Life Style and Itinerary Ministry

Jesus' missional approach consisted of finding a house and a household willing to commit themselves to his kingdom message. With this house as a social and material basis, along with his newly recruited followers, Jesus attempted to reach the entire town of Capernaum, from there the surrounding area within

---

[55] According to Gehring, when Mary "sat at the Lord's feet listening to what he said," she took the same position as a pupil or disciple would have in the presence of his or her elementary teacher or scribe. Gehring, *House Church and Mission*, 44.

[56] Ibid., 46.

[57] Ibid., 44.

and beyond the evangelical triangle by traveling from house to house and village to village.[58] Indeed, Jesus recognized the importance of the family. During his earthly ministry, he often ministered in private homes, spreading the gospel through homes. For Jesus, the word 'church' always refers to people, not the church buildings. The house church is at the very center of Christ's plan for each believer. Thus, all the aspects of Jesus' ministry took place in homes, not in the temples or any other buildings. Throughout the ministry of Jesus, he consistently used the house church model by visiting people in their homes and ministering to them.

## 4. The Book of Acts

There is only limited information in Acts that provides day-to-day details of house churches, especially those house churches that were planted, cultivated, or encouraged by the Apostle Paul.[59] Nevertheless, the Acts do provide foundational understandings of how house churches were guided as the Gospel expanded from Jerusalem into the Gentile world.[60] The Acts provides the widest Scriptural scope of the existence and importance of homes within early church history.[61] In this section, biblical consideration on the topic of house church, centered on some selected texts, will be examined in relation to interdependence in the house church, persecution of the house church from another religion, and the house church as a conduit of proclaiming the gospel.

### Interdependence Relationship led by the Holy Spirit in the House Church: Acts 2:42-47

> 42And they devoted themselves to the apostles' teaching and the
> fellowship, to the breaking of bread and the prayers. 43And awe came
> upon every soul, and many wonders and signs were being done through
> the apostles. 44And all who believed were together and had all things
> in common. 45And they were selling their possessions and belongings
> and distributing the proceeds to all, as any had need. 46And day by day,
> attending the temple together and breaking bread in their homes, they
> received their food with glad and generous hearts, 47praising God and
> having favor with all the people. And the Lord added to their number
> day by day those who were being saved (Acts 2:42-47 ESV).

58 Ibid., 46.

59 Robert Lee Turner, "Leadership Development Process of Select House Church Network in North America: A Case Study" (PhD diss, The Southern Baptist Theological Seminary, 2010), 20.

60 Bradley Blue, "Acts and the house church," in *The Book of Acts in its First Century Setting, Vol. 2, Greaco-Roman Setting*, ed. by David W. J. Gill and Conrad Gempf. (Grand Rapids, MI: William B. Eerdmans Publishing Company, 1994), 120.

61 Turner, "Leadership Development Process of Select House Church Network in North America: A Case Study," 20.

As a result of the Holy Spirit's indwelling, believers fostered an awe that came upon every soul, continual praise of God, having favor with all people, and daily conversions to Christ. Verse 42 describes the early house church as devoting themselves[62] to the apostles' teaching and fellowship, to the breaking of bread and prayers. This echoes the unity of mind in Acts 1:14. The early house church's devotion to the four activities of the apostles' teaching, fellowship, breaking of bread, and to prayer reveals the interdependent basic work of the community of faith.[63]

The early house church was in interdependence relationship with sacrificial love through sharing the materials and spiritual need under the guidance of the apostle's teaching. The early house church was devoted to the fellowship. The fellowship in interdependence fulfills the need not only spiritually (by the apostle's teaching) but also physically. According to Ben Witherington,

> The term *koinonia* is found only here in all of Luke-Acts, though the idea is common. The term itself means a participation or sharing in common of something with someone else, in this case eating and praying. Thus, fellowship is not a very helpful translation, for fellowship is the result of *koinonia*, of sharing in common; it is not *koinonia* itself. *Koinonia* is an activity which can result in fellowship of some sort, and it can entail things like sharing not just spiritual activities such as prayer but also physical food or other goods in common.[64]

In other parts of the New Testament, *koinonia* can refer to the fellowship that believers have with each other because of the Holy Spirit (1 Cor 1:9; 10"16; 2 Cor 6:14; 13:13; Gal 2:9; Phil 1:5; 2:1; 3:10; Heb 13:16; 1 John 1:3). Thus, the term *koinonia* has a more practical meaning, such as the sharing of material possessions in the particular context (Acts 2:32-37; 45; Rom 15:26; 2 Cor 8:4; 9:13).[65] According to John Stott, "The early Christians met in homes and treated each other as family, sharing meals and possessions as well as more spiritual and verbal fare."[66] The connection between 'eating' and 'praying' could be a parallelism, deep physical and spiritual importance of two activities for life of the early house church. According to John B. Polhill, "the prayers were probably

---

[62] The phrase "devoting" themselves appears six time in Acts (1:14; 2:42; 2:46; 6:4; 8:13; 10:7).

[63] Darrell L. Bock, *Acts*. Baker Exegetical Commentary on the New Testament (Grand Rapids, MI: Baker Academic, 2007), 149.

[64] Ben III. Witherington, *The Acts of the Apostles; A Socio-rhetorical Commentary* (Grand Rapids, MI: William B. Eerdmans Publishing Company, 1998), 160.

[65] Luke Timothy Johnson, *The Acts of the Apostles* (Sacra Pagina Series, vol. 5. Collegville, MN: The Liturgical Press, 1992), 58.

[66] John Stott, *The Spirit, the Church, and the World: The Message of Acts* (Downers Grove, IL: InterVarsity Press, 1990), 161.

broader and involved primarily their sharing in prayer together in their private house worship."[67]

The early house church displayed an interdependence relationship in a sacrificial love for each other. This love was fostered by the gospel that had rendered them as 'one in Christ' (Gal 3:28; Eph 2:11). This unity within the house church "derives from and is guided by the gift of the Spirit that lies at the heart of its life together."[68] Darrell L. Bock notes that the outflow of that Spirit created a community that functioned with appropriate love and compassion toward those within the community that had material needs.[69] This early house church is not a mandated communism, but a voluntary selling and distributing of possessions to those within the community that were in need. It is evident from Acts 2:42-47 that particular attributes accompanied the initial life of the early church. A commitment of perseverance marked the early believers. This commitment is shown by their adherence to the apostles' teaching and to communion with each other. That communion exhibited itself in several ways: eating together, which could have involved a recalling of the death of Christ for their sins; praying together; having a view of all things in common; a willingness to hold possessions loosely in order to serve those who were in need; and expanding the role of the *oikos* as a place of religious activities.[70]

The House Church as Conduit of Gospel Proclamation: Acts 5:41-42

Peter and the apostles were continually using both the temple and individual homes as platforms for their teaching and preaching. Luke employs a Greek rhetorical construction in 5:42 called a chiasm, which is most easily pictured as an A-B-B-A pattern. John B. Polhill describes this pattern within this verse by stating, "In the temple (A) and in homes (B), the apostles taught (B) and preached the Gospel (A). The role of teaching was the task within the Christian fellowship and preaching was the public task in the temple grounds."[71] This pattern also underscores the fact that the content in both settings was essentially the same.[72] Indeed, Acts 5:41-42 describes the role of the house as the significant conduit of Gospel proclamation and Gospel growth within the early house church. The role of the house begins to emerge as parallel and eventually superseding the religious role of the temple. This is supported by the evidence that the content of apostolic

---

[67] John B. Polhill, *Acts*. The New American Commentary, vol. 26 (Nashville, TN: Broadman Press, 1992), 120.

[68] Ibid., 121.

[69] Darrell L. Bock, *Acts*. Baker Exegetical Commentary on the New Testament (Grand Rapids, MI: Baker Academic, 2007), 153.

[70] Turner, "Leadership Development Process of Select House Church Network in North America: A Case Study", 26.

[71] Polhill, *Acts*. The New American Commentary, 174.

[72] Roger W. Gehring, *House Church and Mission* (Peabody, Massachusetts: Hendrickson Publishers, 2004), 74.

teaching was consistently about Christ on both the temple grounds and in homes. This observation only underscores the fact that the apostles seemed to regard the home as a viable venue of corporate worship.[73]

Persecution from Other Religion: Acts 5:41-42

In the chapter five of Acts, the apostles are brought before the captain of the temple and the chief priests. They are explicitly told not to teach in the name of Jesus (5:28), but Peter and the apostles defy a command from the priests (5:29-32). The chief priests eventually defer to the wisdom of Gamaliel and set the apostles free but only after they are beaten (5:34-40). The Scripture clearly shows us the apostles' attitude about their suffering from other religious persecution. "Then they left the presence of the council, rejoicing that they were counted worthy to suffer dishonor for the name. And every day, in the temple and from house to house, they did not cease teaching and preaching Jesus as the Christ" (5:41-42).

Saul and Persecution of the House Church: Acts 8:1-3

The importance of the *oikos* is also seen in a tragic sense by the increasing persecution that depart from the idyllic reality of Acts 2:42-47, when the believers were enjoying at one time the 'favor of all the people,' to the Jewish rulers desiring to suppress the Gospel movement (Acts 4:17-18). Acts 8:1-3 shows us this transition in the life of the early house church:

> 1And Saul approved of his execution. And there arose on that day a great persecution against the church in Jerusalem, and they were all scattered throughout the regions of Judea and Samaria, except the apostles. 2Devout men buried Stephen and made great lamentation over him. 3But Saul was ravaging the church, and entering house after house, he dragged off men and women and committed them to prison (Acts 8:1-3 ESV).

Robert Lee Turner noted that "Ironically, the prominent 'point person' for this persecution would later become the 'point person' for the expansion of the Gospel into the Gentile world."[74] Saul had easy access to the believers because it was well established that home were the main gathering places for apostolic teaching and worship. Breaking into homes became the main method of finding believers to imprison or worse, to torture. The word 'ravaging' is found only here in the New Testament. The imperfect tense of the verb shows that the ravaging of the church was a continual action on the part of Saul. It was brutal action. The brutality upon believers was so ongoing and brutal that upon Saul's later conversion, the house church was said to experience 'peace' (Acts 9:31).

---

[73] Turner, "Leadership Development Process of Select House Church Network in North America: A Case Study", 27.

[74] Ibid.

## 5. House Churches in Pauline Writings

The existence and fruitfulness of house churches did not stay in Jerusalem. The Apostle Paul, who previously persecuted house churches, takes the mantle of Christ's commission (Matthew 28:18-20; Acts 1:8) to extend the Gospel's reach into the Gentile world. Paul gives us the most information about three geographical localities: Rome, Corinth, and the Colossae.[75]

Five House Churches for Gentile Mission: Romans 16:3-16

> 3Greet Prisca and Aquila, my fellow workers in Christ Jesus, 4who
> risked their necks for my life, to whom not only I give thanks but all
> the churches of the Gentiles give thanks as well. 5Greet also the church
> in their house. Greet my beloved Epaenetus, who was the first convert
> to Christ in Asia. 6Greet Mary, who has worked hard for you. 7Greet
> Andronicus and Junia, my kinsmen and my fellow prisoners. They are
> well known to the apostles, and they were in Christ before me. 8 Greet
> Ampliatus, my beloved in the Lord. 9Greet Urbanus, our fellow worker
> in Christ, and my beloved Stachys. 10Greet Apelles, who is approved in
> Christ. Greet those who belong to the family of Aristobulus. 11Greet
> my kinsman Herodion. Greet those in the Lord who belong to the
> family of Narcissus. 12Greet those workers in the Lord, Tryphaena and
> Tryphosa. Greet the beloved Persis, who has worked hard in the Lord.
> 13Greet Rufus, chosen in the Lord; also his mother, who has been a
> mother to me as well. 14Greet Asyncritus, Phlegon, Hermes, Patrobas,
> Hermas, and the brothers who are with them. 15Greet Philologus,
> Julia, Nereus and his sister, and Olympas, and all the saints who are
> with them. 16Greet one another with a holy kiss. All the churches of
> Christ greet you.

An important text arises near the end of Paul's letter to the church in Rome. This section of Romans points to possibly five house churches that are greeted: the home of Prisca and Aquila (v.5), those who belong to Aristobulus (v.10), those who belong to Narcissus (v. 11), and verses 14 and 15 contain probable members of two house churches. Thomas Schreiner contends that evidence for a house church in verse 14 is contained in the words "and the brothers and sisters" with them, suggesting that Paul names the five members of the church he knows of and then greets the rest of the church generally. Similarly, in verse 15, he greets the five persons he knows, then greets the rest of the church with and "all the saints with them."[76]

---

[75] Vincent Branick, "The house church in the writing of Paul" in *Zacchaeus Studies: New Testament*, ed. by Mary Ann Getty (Wilmington, DE: Michael Glazier Publishing, 1989), 58.

[76] Thomas Schreiner, *Romans*. Baker Exegetical Commentary on the New Testament (Grand Rapids, MI: Baker Books, 1998), 797.

Douglas Moo illustrates that the early house churches had great interest to the Gentiles, and that they included Gentiles as members of the church. Moo mentions the greetings and arrives at three themes: (1) A majority of the names are Gentile, which confirms the highly Gentile makeup of the church at Rome; (2) a significant amount of the names are those of slaves and freedmen, or the descendants of slaves/freedmen; (3) these greetings provide a glimpse of church organization in Rome by mentioning separate house churches.[77]

### Three Missiological Implications from Romans 16:3-16

Robert Lee Turner believes that three conclusions can be made from Romans 16:3-16 in missiological perspective. First, about cultural issues, he says that "house churches contained Christians who were from different stratums of culture. House churches in Rome apparently lived out the truth that everyone is 'one in Christ' (Gal 3:28; Eph 2:10-12)."[78] Second, the house church in Rome was a strategic model for reaching the Gentiles; he says, "this excursus by Paul provides credibility that multiplication of house churches was an intentional strategy toward Gospel expansion into the Gentiles world."[79] Third, house churches were in the network, with an interdependent relationship. He says that "Roman house churches were connected with each other and at times met as a whole."[80] The important factors in the early house churches from Turner's conclusions are: 1) that cultural aspects were accepted of house churches, 2) that house church were strategic models for Gentiles, and 3) that there was interdependence of relationship among house churches.

### The Role of Aquila and Prisca as a Missionary Model for House Church: 1 Corinthians 16:19

The Apostle Paul concludes his first letter to the church at Corinth as following. "The churches of Asia send you greetings. Aquila and Prisca, together with the church in their house, send you hearty greetings in the Lord" (1Corinthians 16:19). Aquila and Prisca[81] was an important couple in Paul's ministry. In Romans 16:3-5, Paul refers to them as his co-workers. They also accompanied Paul when he traveled to Ephesus, where they led Apollos to Christ (Acts 18:18-26), and where they still are at the time of Paul's writing to church at Corinth. Later they have another house church in Rome (Romans 16:3-5); then, in 2 Timothy 4:19, are back in Ephesus. According to Gordon Fee, "Aquila and Prisca's mobility and their patronage of house churches in Corinth, Ephesus,

---

[77] Douglas Moo, *The Epistle to the Romans*. The New International Commentary on the New Testament (Grand Rapids, MI: William B. Eerdmans Publishing Company, 1996), 918.

[78] Turner, "Leadership Development Process of Select House Church Network in North America: A Case Study", 31.

[79] Ibid.

[80] Ibid.

[81] Prisca is a variant of Priscilla.

and Rome indicate that they were well to do."[82] Robert Banks attests that the term *oikos* could refer to the quarters that Pricilla and Aquila occupied or to the household that was in their charge. If it means the latter term, then the home of Priscilla and Aquilla was the meeting place for some or all Christians in Ephesus.[83]

Woman Leadership in the House Church: Colossians 4:15-16

During his first imprisonment (Acts 28:16, 30), the Apostle Paul wrote, "To the saints and faithful brothers in Christ at Colossae" (Colossians 1:2a). This was a church that Paul had never actually visited, but he was writing in response to the concerns of Epaphras, who was an important teacher in Colossae (Colossians 1:7; 4:12). As he gives his final greetings, Paul writes "Give my greetings to the brothers at Laodicea, and to Nympha and the church in her house. And when this letter has been read among you, have it also read in the church of the Laodiceans; and see that you also read the letter from Laodicea"(Colossians 4:15-16). Nympha could have been a widower who hosted the church in her home or acted in a particular leadership role.[84] The fact that the church was in "her house" shows that Nympha had substantial financial means that enabled her to own her own home.[85] Nympha is one example of the significance of women in the life and mission of the early church. Lydia (Acts 16:14-15, 40), Prisca (1 Cor 16:19), Phoebe (Rom 16:1-2), Euodia and Syntyche (Phil 4:2-3), and Junia (Rom 16:7) are other Christian women that served in some capacity within New Testament house churches.

According to Robert Lee Turner, "it can be established that women, probably for the most part widows who had autonomous administration of their own households, hosted house churches of the early Christian movement. This fact itself does not necessarily mean that they had leadership in teaching or other spiritual responsibilities."[86] Colossians 4:15-16 highlights again the significance of women and Paul's desire that his communication be distributed through a geographical region (Laodicea) of house churches.

---

[82] Gordon D. Fee, *The First Epistle to the Corinthians*. The New International Commentary on the New Testament (Grand Rapids, MI: William B. Eerdmans Publishing Company, 1987), 836.

[83] Robert Banks, *Paul's Idea of Community: The Early House Churches in their Cultural Setting* (Peadbody, MA: Hendrickson Publishing, 2007), 31.

[84] F. F. Bruce, *The Epistles to the Colossians, to Philemon, and to the Ephesians*. The New International Commentary on the New Testament (Grand Rapids, MI: William B. Eerdmans Publishing Company, 1984), 183.

[85] James D. G. Dunn, *The Epistles to the Colossians and to Philemon*. The New International Greek Testament Commentary (Grand Rapids, MI: William B. Eerdmans Publishing Company, 1996), 285.

[86] Turner, "Leadership Development Process of Select House Church Network in North America: A Case Study", 33.

Interdependence in the House Church for Onesimus: Philemon 1:2

The Epistle to Philemon is closely related to Paul's epistle to the church in Colossae. They were both written by the Apostle Paul and from the same place, his imprisonment in Rome. The purpose of this personal letter is to appeal to Philemon about the treatment of Philemon's runaway slave, Onesimus (vv. 1, 2; Col 4:9, 17). Paul involves himself in this matter because Onesimus had come into contact with him, perhaps as a fellow-prisoner. Peter O'Brien asserts that perhaps Onesimus "had sought refuge in Paul's company because he had heard his name mentioned in the house of his Christian master and had now hastened to him for help in his trouble"[87] There is a significant progression within this greeting that will affect how Paul addresses this issue with Philemon. In Philemon 1:1-3, "Paul, a prisoner for Christ Jesus, and Timothy our brother, to Philemon our beloved fellow worker, and Apphia our sister and Archippus our fellow soldier, and the church in your house: Grace to you and peace from God our Father and the Lord Jesus Christ."

Paul addresses not only Philemon and his family members Apphia and Archippus, but also the church that met in his house. It is ironic that this matter seems to be a personal matter between Paul and Philemon but Paul seemingly chooses to involve the rest of the church.[88] Paul was depending on the house church for the issue of Onesimus, as well as the house church depending on Paul. This reveals the interdependent relationship between Paul and the house church.

## 6. Theological Considerations of the House Church

Although, the early house church does not give warrant to ongoing legitimacy to the modern house church movement,[89] biblical examples of house churches provides evidence for the existence of house churches in order to give continuing validity for the modern house church movement.[90] Therefore, theological aspects of the issues on house churches need to be considered in order to assist in the clarity of the missionary role of a modern house church for the church's existence. In this section, interdependence and network, leadership in the house church, and the strategic role of the house church toward other religions and Gentiles will be examined.

---

[87] Peter T. O'Brien, *Colossians, Philemon*. World Biblical Commentary, vol. 44 (Waco, TX: Word Books, 1982), 266.

[88] Richard B. Hays, *The Moral Vision of the New Testament: A Contemporary Introduction to New Testament Ethics* (New York, NY: HarperCollins, 1996), 57.

[89] Turner, "Leadership Development Process of Select House Church Network in North America: A Case Study", 21.

[90] Ibid., 36.

## Interdependence and Network in the House Church

The Greek word in the New Testament for church, *ekklesia*, referred in classical Greek simply to the assembly of the citizens of a city.[91] Robert Banks has distinguished the word *ekklesia* from meetings of the Jewish synagogue and the Hellenistic mystery cults. Banks' view of Pauline *ekklesia* encompassed three interwoven thoughts. First, *ekklesia* is a voluntary association, with regular gatherings of relatively small groups of like-minded people. Second, *ekklesia* has its roots in and takes some of the character of the household unit. Last, *ekklesia* is invested with supranational and supratemporal significance, a visible manifestation of a divine and eternal commonwealth.

The early house churches did not operate in a completely autonomous fashion but rather fostered relationships with other churches for the sake of the global mission.

Anthony C. Thiselton believes that Paul's greeting to the Corinthian church (1 Cors 1:2)

> reinforces the thought that the church at Corinth is not a self-contained autonomous entity: they are not a self-sufficient community; they are not the only pebble on the beach. Their lifestyle and practices are monitored by translocal fellow workers of Paul's (notably by Timothy, 1 Cor 4:17), and they are required to follow patterns of thought and lifestyle which characterize traditions or order in all the churches (1 Cor 7:17).[92]

The Early house churches did not operate in a completely autonomous fashion, but rather fostered relationships with other churches for the sake of the global mission.

Thiselton's comment provides a theological rationale for house church networks.[93] House church networks are comprised of house churches that are distributions of the local church. He further states, "It is possible to speak of the catholicity of the church of Paul's day, as well as its diversity. For its networks and shared commonality in Christ, in the Gospel, and in a common apostolic witness to Christ amounted to more than a loose federation of autonomous communities"[94] Recent scholarship has noted that the early churches existed in two forms: the

---

[91] Millard J. Erickson, *Introducing Christian Doctrine* (Grand Rapids, MI: Baker Academic, 2001), 340.

[92] Anthony C. Thiselton, *The First Epistle to the Corinthians.* The New International Greek Testament Commnetary (Grand Rapids, MI: William B. Eerdmans Publishing Company, 2000), 74-75.

[93] Ibid.

[94] Thiselton, *The First Epistle to the Corinthians.* The New International Greek Testament Commnetary, 75.

house church and the whole church at any given location.[95] Rad Zdero stresses the necessity of network on house church. According to him, "Sociologically, the idea and reality of belonging to an expanding global movement certainly added a sense of being part of something bigger than just one's own house church and gave people a bigger vision for what God was doing in the world at large."[96] He also illustrates interdependence that formed in the house church network; network practices that united these house churches together were behaviors such as traveling apostolic workers, the circulation of apostolic letters, and citywide gatherings of the individual house churches.[97] The livelihood of the house church movement was dependent on house church networks in order for them to increase their influence at local, regional, national, and international levels.[98]

The principle of simplicity that pervades the house church movement is strongly influenced by a theological metaphor of family. The aversion within the house church movement toward structures such as buildings and of potentially costly programs comes out of a commitment within the house church movement to do nothing that could lessen an emphasis on the supremacy of Christ[99] and the biblically redefined family. Believers are the family of God (1 John 3:1), birthed by Jesus (John 12:13), into the household of God (Eph 2:19), and with new brothers and sisters in Christ (Rom 16:2).[100] This strong commitment to the metaphor of the "family of God" places a behavioral emphasis on the mutuality (interdependence) connection and priesthood of all believers (Gal 3:27-29; 1 Pet 2:9-10; 1 Cor 14:26-27).[101]

Vincent Branick states how Paul has reinterpreted God's temple to apply to Christian gatherings in the sense of interdependence.

> The Christian gatherings under Paul may not have even looked like a religion to an outsider. The Christians had no shrines, temples, cult

---

[95] Peter T. O'Brien, *Colossians, Philemon.* World Biblical Commentary, vol. 44 (Waco, TX: Word Books, 1982), 59. Robert Banks, *Paul's Idea of Community: The Early House Churches in their Cultural Setting* (Peadbody, MA: Hendrickson Publishing, 2007), 42. Vincent Branick, *The House Church in the Writing of Paul in Zacchaeus Studies: New Testament,* ed. Mary Ann Getty (Wilmington, DE: Michael Glazier Publishing, 1989), 22-23, Wayne Meeks, *The First Urban Christians: The Social World of the Apostle Paul* (New Haven, CT: Yale University Press, 2003), 107-108.

[96] Rad Zdero, *The Global House Church Movement* (Pasadena, CA: William Carey Library, 2004), 49.

[97] Ibid., 49-51.

[98] Ibid., 114.

[99] John B. Polhill, *Acts.* The New American Commentary, vol. 26 (Nashville, TN: Broadman Press, 1992), 121.

[100] Steve Atkerson et al., *House Church: Simple, Strategic, Scriptural* (Atlanta, GA: NTRF Publishing, 2008), 86.

[101] Arthur L. Foster, "Dimensions of House Church Experiencing," in *The House Church Evolving,* ed. by Arthur Foster (Chicago, IL: Exploration Press, 1976), 7.

> statues, priests, or sacrifices. For Christians, Paul writes, the community is the temple: Do you not know that you are God's temple and that God's Spirit dwells in you? If anyone destroys God's temple, God will destroy him. For God's temple is holy, and you are that temple (1 Cor 3:16-17). One's whole life makes us worship and sacrifice: I appeal to you therefore, brothers, by the mercies of God, to present your bodies as a living sacrifice, holy and acceptable to God, which is your spiritual worship. Do not be conformed to this world, but be transformed by the renewal of your mind, that by testing you may discern what is the will of God, what is good and acceptable and perfect (Rom 12:1-2). The language of cult is there- 'sacrifice,' 'holy,' 'worship.' But Paul has reinterpreted it-in a way not dissimilar from the prophets-so that cult is not clearly distinguished from daily life. The Christian gathering as a sharing of gifts, as exercise of mutual 'edification,' was for Paul, then, an act of worship. Sacred space was not an issue. The assembly was its own sanctuary. Hence, even the family dining room was an appropriate place for the church.[102]

According to Steve Atkerson,

> The Scriptures are full of the "one another" commands. Church is to be about accountability, community, and maintaining church discipline (Mt 18:15-20). These ideals are best accomplished in smaller congregations where people know and love each other. Church is to be about relationships. A large auditorium of people, most of whom are relative strangers to each other, will not easily achieve these goals. Nominal Christianity is harbored as it becomes easy to get lost in the crowd. Churches that meet in homes best foster the simplicity, vitality, intimacy, and purity that God desires for His church.[103]

Although it has been overstated at particular points, this statement explains a ministry philosophy that evolves into house churches that are highly participatory. House church members will often eat, pray, handle Scripture, serve, and play together.[104] Frank Viola contends that "the elements of singing, sharing, eating, praying, playing, handling Scripture, and releasing gifts should find their way into participatory meetings in a spontaneous, interactive, participatory, and Spirit-led manner"[105] Turner points out that the participatory nature of the house church

---

[102] Vincent Branick, *The House Church in the Writing of Paul in Zacchaeus Studies: New Testament*, ed. Mary Ann Getty (Wilmington, DE: Michael Glazier Publishing, 1989), 104.

[103] Atkerson et al., *House Church: Simple, Strategic, Scriptural*, 87.

[104] Turner, 41.

[105] Frank Viola, *From Eternity to Here: Rediscovering the Ageless Purpose of God* (Colorado Springs, CO: David C. Cook Publishers, 2009), 400.

movement can have a tenor of idealism.[106] Rad Zdero acknowledges the relational hardships that can be endemic among house church members:

> Life as part of a house church or house church network can be exhilarating because of the close-knit nature of the relationships that are developed over time. However, the opposite is also true-when tensions and conflict arise, they can be significant. Everything is amplified in a house church that attempting to experience 'true community.' Along with this, come the more mundane realities of being in relationship to one another and doing things together, as we seek to deepen our relationship with God. These practical realities include spending quality and quantity time together, conflict resolution, decision making, children, money, baptisms, weddings, and hosting.[107]

Philip and Phoebe Anderson discovered that

> it is the commitment of house church members to love and care for one another in God's name which sets the house church apart from small group experiences outside the church. Neither sensitivity groups, nor encounter groups, nor therapy groups are founded on the premise which is basic to the house church: love incarnate is the Good News which is available to all women and men.[108]

The Andersons assert that human beings are made to think, feel, and act and that house church practices can have a significant impact on all three human components.[109]

## 7. Leadership within the House Church and Its Roles

The household instructions and the metaphor of church as household are viewed by some scholars as a blanket endorsement of authoritarian, hierarchical leadership patterns that often characterized Roman households and patronage relationships. David C. Verner charges that the Pastorals "directly and uncritically reflect the dominant social values of the larger society."[110] David Horrell asserts that a

---

[106] Turner, 41.

[107] Rad Zdero, *Nexus: The World House Church Reader* (Pasadena, CA: William Carey Library, 2007), 401.

[108] Philip Anderson and Phoebe Anderson, *The House Church* (Nashville, TN: Abingdon Press, 1975), 33.

[109] Ibid., 35-36.

[110] David C. Verner, *The Household of God: The Social World of the Pastoral Epistles* (Chicago, Calif. : Scholars Press, 1983), 145.

household model entails that "the eccliastical hierarchy mirrors the domestic and social hierarchy."[111]

In contrast to such misunderstanding, Andrew Clarke offers a more discerning view. According to him, New Testament revelation transforms the nature of relationships and does so without abruptly trashing all relationships and overthrowing the whole system.[112] Christians could not simply mimic existing family patterns, however, or apply them, unchanged, to church. The pursuit of status and power had to give way to a desire to serve and love.[113]

Clarke notes that "Paul's in exercise of leadership," stresses Christ's supremacy, not his own. Paul recognizes the legitimacy of multiple apostolic leadership and multiple overseers in local congregations, not one householder with absolute authority over a congregation. Paul, far from advocating stratification or authoritarianism, prefers tender appeals to harsh bullying. Paul is boldly "countercultural" in correcting those who prefer worldly concepts of power and control.[114]

The roles of leadership are another theological consideration of the house church movement. The issue of mediated authority is important throughout the epistles of the New Testament, though some believe that there is significant ambiguity in Paul's letters about church order and leadership in his Gentile churches.[115]

Edmund Clowney contends that

> our understanding of the government of Christ's church must begin with the Lord himself and his kingdom authority. He is the Head of the church; his rule is unique and incomparable. A second principle derives from the first. The church shows the organic life of Christ's body: it lives as an organism, not just an organization. The third principle is no less essential. The church is not like the kingdoms of this world, for it is organized for service, not dominion. All government in the church is stewardship: i.e., its leaders are servant-managers, who

[111] David Horrell, "Leadership Patterns and the Development of Ideology," *Sociology of Religion* 58, no. 4 (1997), 323-341.

[112] Andrew D. Clarke, "Serve the Community of the Church: Christians as Leaders and Ministers," *First-Century Christians in the Graeco-Roman World*, ed. by Andrew D. Clarke (Grand Rapids: Eerdmans, 2000), 247.

[113] David J. Feddes, "Caring for God's Household", *Calvin Theological Journal* 45 (2008), 285.

[114] Andrew D. Clarke, "Serve the Community of the Church: Christians as Leaders and Ministers," in *First-Century Christians in the Graeco-Roman World*, ed. by Andrew D. Clarke (Grand Rapids: Eerdmans, 2000), 246-51.

[115] Richard N. Longenecker, *Community Formation in the Early Church and in the Church Today* (Peabody, MA: Hendrickson Publishers, 2002), 85.

use their authority only to advance the interests of those they represent and serve.[116]

Paul did recognize the presence of local leaders (1 Thess 5:12-13) and asked his converts to 'respect' them and "hold them in the highest regard in love because of their work." These local leaders probably functioned as elders and deacons (Acts 11:30; 14:23; 15:2, 4, 6, 22, 23; 16:4; 20:17; 21:18; Phil 1:1; 1 Tim 5:1, 17, 19; Titus 1:5-6).[117] Turner states that leadership within the house church movement is usually expressed in implicit rather than explicit ways.[118]

Robert Banks delineated four principles of the Apostle Paul's use of authority. His observation provides the understanding of authority in the house churches. The principles of authority and decision-making have been summed up as follows: (1) Authority stems from God as revealed in Christ and as mediated through the Spirit. (2) The objective Word of God is the definitive expression of God's will, normative for all that precedes and follows. (3) God continues to speak and work authoritatively, not through coercion of people's personalitics, but by convincing their minds of the truth and warming their hearts with love so they can embrace it. (4) Authority is exercised through the service of others in word and deed, not through domination.[119]

A unique perspective on authority of the house church movement emphasizes the equipping gifts of Ephesians 4:11-13: "And he gave some to be apostles, some to be prophets, some to be evangelists, some to be the pastors and teachers, to equip the saints for the work of ministry, for building up the body of Christ, until we all attain to the unity of the faith and of the knowledge of the Son of God, to mature manhood, to the measure of the stature of the fullness of Christ." These ministries that equip the church toward Christian maturity are gifts from Christ that are different from the spiritual gifts elucidated in four other sections in scripture (Rom 12:6-8; 1 Cor 12:8-10, 28-30; 1 Pet 4:10-11). Ernest Best argues that "these gifts are not gifts made to people but gifts of people; people who have a particular role to play in the church."[120]

There are various views for the role of the apostle. Scholars contend that the apostle, along with the prophet, played a foundational but temporary role within

---

[116] Edmund P. Clowney, *The Church: Contours of Christian Theology* (Downers Grove, IL: InterVarsity Press, 1995), 202.

[117] Wayne Grudem, *Systematic Theology* (Grand Rapids, MI: Zondervan, 1994), 920-923.

[118] Turner, "Leadership Development Process of Select House Church Network in North America: A Case Study", 43.

[119] Robert Banks, *Paul's Idea of Community: The Early House Churches in their Cultural Setting* (Peadbody, MA: Hendrickson Publishing, 2007), 94.

[120] Ernest Best, *Ephesians*. International Critical Commentary (Dorset, England: T & T Clark Publishing, 2001), 388.

the first century church.[121] This role became more "marginalized in the Christian movement as their leadership role was taken over by the more stable teaching and ruling ministries"[122] Other scholars dispute the temporary interpretation of these gifts.[123] Peter T. O'Brien also believes that the gifts of apostle and prophet continue by commenting, "Evangelists, pastor, and teachers exercised their ministry during the apostles' time and subsequently, and were no doubt the church workers whom most of the readers had encountered."[124]

According to Harold W. Hoehner,

> There are three kinds of apostles mentioned in the NT: those who had been with Jesus in his ministry and had witnessed his resurrection (Acts 1:21-22); Paul, who was born out of season (1Cor 15:8-9); and those who received the gift of apostleship. The first two categories are to be regarded as offices, whereas the last is a spiritual gift to the church. In the present context the apostle refers to the third kind, the gift of apostle. There were people in addition to the original twelve who had not been with Jesus in his ministry and did not witness his resurrection but who are listed as apostles. To mention some, we cite Barnabas (Acts 14:4, 14; 1 Cor 9:5-7), James, the Lord's brother (1 Cor 15:7; Gal 1:19), Apollos (1 Cor 4:6, 9), probably Silvanus (1 Thess 2:6), Titus (2 Cor 8:23), Epaphroditus (Phil 2:25), and possibly Andronicus and Junia[s] (Rom 16:7). These had the gift of apostleship. It seems then that the main function of an apostle is to establish churches in areas that have not been reached by others (Rom 15:20). They are God's messengers to open up new territories for Christ.[125]

The role of the prophet is to communicate divine revelation. More specifically, it seems that prophecy is a gift that provides edification, comfort, and encouragement (1 Cor 14:3, 31), as well as for the purpose of understanding and communicating the mysteries and revelation of God to the church (1 Cor 12:10;

---

[121] Ibid., 389-390. Edmund P. Clowney, *The Church: Contours of Christian Theology* (Downers Grove, IL: InterVarsity Press, 1995), 255-268. Louis Berkhof, *Systematic Theology* (Grand Rapids, MI: William B. Eerdmans Publishing Company), 585. Malcolm B. Yarnell, "The Person and Work of the Holy Spirit," in *A Theology for the Church*, ed. by Daniel L. Akin (Nashville, TN: B&H Publishing), 604-685.

[122] Andrew T. Lincoln, *Ephesians*. World Biblical Commentary, vol. 42 (Nashville, TN: Thomas Nelson Publishers, 1990), 249.

[123] Markus Barth, *Ephesians* 4-6. The Anchor Bible Commentary, vol. 34A (New York, NY: Doubleday Publishing, 1960), 478. Harold W. Hoehner, *Ephesians: An Exegetical Commentary* (Grand Rapids, MI: Baker Academic, 2002), 541-542.

[124] Peter T. O'Brien, *Colossians, Philemon*. World Biblical Commentary, vol. 44 (Waco, TX: Word Books, 1982), 298.

[125] Harold W. Hoehner, *Ephesians: An Exegetical Commentary* (Grand Rapids, MI: Baker Academic, 2002), 541-542.

13:2; 14:6, 22, 30-31).[126] Ernest Best disagrees with this position because he believes that the letter to the church in Ephesus, "leaves no place for continuing prophetic activity in congregations" but he concedes that all the rest of the New Testament suggests that prophetic activity did indeed exist.[127] As Lincoln said, evangelists work both inside and outside the church by continually speaking the message of Christ's salvation.[128]

Pastors and teachers have elicited much scholarly discussion on whether this is two people or one individual. Marcus Barth believes that

> the wording is so ambiguous that is difficult to decide the exact character of the fourth group. Does it unite two lesser groups, i.e. "teachers" and shepherds," or is it composed of one ministry only, that is, of teaching shepherds, or of shepherding teachers? While sometimes in the NT "teachers" and "shepherds" (or the equivalent of shepherds) are mentioned separately, and at other occasions the titles "bishop" and "elder" occur, all these functions probably belong together.[129]

Pastors provide leadership through nurture, care, and guidance. It is probable that the pastor of Eph 4:11 fulfills functions located elsewhere in Paul's writings such as "to rule, manage" (1 Thess 5:12; Rom 12:8), "administration" (1 Cor 12:28), and "bishop/ overseer" (Phil 1:1) (Lincoln 1990, 251). Teachers, as addressed in this Ephesian context, communicated and interpreted tradition from the Old Teacher and earlier Christians (Rom 6:17; 1 Cor 4:17; Col 2:7; 2 Thess 2:15) as well as how those teachings influence life situations.[130]

According to Turner.

> the practical scope of the apostle and the prophet are not as clear as the evangelist, pastor, and teacher. Despite this concession there is no definitive biblical text that abrogates the gifts of apostles and prophets. It appears to do damage to the text by segmenting apostles and prophets from the rest of the gifts in Ephesians 4:11. There is nothing in the grammar or context that would logically dismiss the ongoing relevancy of apostles and prophets at the expense of the other gifts (evangelists, pastors, and teachers). The practice of modern apostolic ministry could be planting new works of the Gospel in unreached or hard to reach areas. Furthermore, there is still need of individuals who

---

[126] Ibid., 400.

[127] Best, *Ephesians*, 390.

[128] Lincoln, *Ephesians*, 249.

[129] Best, *Ephesians*, 438.

[130] Ibid., 391.

act prophetically by calling God's own people back to righteousness and alignment with His revealed Word.[131]

Practitioners within the house church movement interpret these people gifts as five different individuals who provide the foundational structure for the House Church Movement's. These individuals travel throughout a given network of house churches to equip them with vital competencies needed for Kingdom success.[132]

Wolfgang Simson contends that these five people gifts

> Function as a spiritual blood-circulation system by nurturing all house churches with the elements necessary to become or remain healthy and therefore to multiply. Those ministries are like sinews and joints, linking the various house churches together to be a whole system. Their ministry transcends the individual house church and serves the body of Christ like a spiritual gene pool, which the house churches of an area or a region, and sometimes beyond, can draw from.[133]

Turner illustrates that these individuals are trans-local and roam throughout a house church network to provide the appropriate equipping for individual house churches. Individuals who are gifted apostolically enable the house church to move forward and be committed to multiplying to new areas of the city where the gospel has not made an impact. They are always looking to take new territories for the Kingdom. Prophets challenge members of house churches to faithfulness to God's Word.[134]

Evangelists aid in the house churches' mission to reach the lost, but also equip house churches to keep the gospel central to everything they do. Pastors provide the warmth of community to the house church while equipping the house church to care for hurting people. Lastly, the teacher provides training for the house church in deepening the understanding of God's Word.[135] Michael Frost and Alan Hirsch provide the following figure to display the role, focus, myopia (possible barriers), and impact of each gifting in order to explain the contemporary expression of these particular gifts that function within the church.[136]

---

[131] Turner, 46.

[132] Larry Kreider, *House Church Networks: A Church for a New Generation* (Lititz, PA: House to House Publications, 2001), 99.

[133] Wolfgang Simson, *House that Change the World: The Return of the House Churches* (Wayneboro, GA: Authentic, 1998), 123.

[134] Turner, 47.

[135] Simson, *House that Change the World: The Return of the House Churches*, 98.

[136] Michael Frost and Alan Hirsch, *The Shaping of Things to Come: Innovation and Mission for the 21st Century Church* (Peabody, MA: Hendrickson Publishing, 2003), 48.

Table 2. A Comparison of Roles Mentioned in Ephesians 4:11

| Role | Definition | Focus | Myopia | Impact |
|---|---|---|---|---|
| Apostle | One who is sent | Urgency of tomorrow | Demands of today | Extension |
| Prophet | One who knows | Demands of today in light of tomorrow | Demands of today | Integration |
| Evangelist | One who recruits | Urgency of today | Demands of today | Expansion |
| Pastor | One who cares | Demands of today | Urgency of tomorrow | Nurture |
| Teacher | One who explains | Integration | Time | Understanding |

Source: This table is directly from Turner, "Leadership Development Process of Select House Church Network in North America: A Case Study", 48.

Frost and Hirsch, who give this Ephesians 4:11 gifting the acronym APEPT, conclude from their reading of Ephesians 4:12-16 that

> Paul actually sees APEPT ministry as the very mechanism for achieving mission and ministry effectiveness and Christian maturity. He seems to be saying that without the fivefold ministry pattern we cannot mature. If this is true, it is impossible to estimate what terrible damage the church has done through the loss, even active suppression, of this crucial dimension of New Testament ministry and leadership. But if we take these verses at face value, then it is our contention that the impact has been significant indeed. Perhaps the fact that APEPT has not been intentionally nurtured and practiced might have something to do with the immaturity we find in the Western church that inhibits fulfillment of its mission.[137]

The Strategic Role of the House Church toward Other Religions and Gentiles

The role of the house also played a strategic role in the expansion of the Gospel from Jerusalem into the Gentile world. An example of this can be found in Acts 16:14-15:

> [14]One who heard us was a woman named Lydia, from the city of Thyatira, a seller of purple goods, who was a worshiper of God. The Lord opened her heart to pay attention to what was said by Paul.[15] And after she was baptized, and her household as well, she urged us, saying, If you have judged me to be faithful to the Lord, come to my house and stay. And she prevailed upon us (Acts 16:14-15 ESV).

---

[137] Frost and Hirsch, *The Shaping of Things to Come: Innovation and Mission for the 21st Century Church,* 169.

This text is the first narrative of a household baptism. Luke uses the phrase a "worshiper of God" to describe Lydia. Darrell Bock claims that "this phrase often describes former polytheists who become worshipers of the God of Israel, adopt monotheism, and attend the synagogue but do keep the entire law (Acts 13:43)."[138] Household was used as a place for converting people from other religion. It also shows the geographical expansion of the Gospel movement from Jerusalem into the Gentile world. Furthermore, it shows the importance of homes as means of that Gospel expansion.

Acts 13:45-46, along with others within the Acts narrative (16:29-34; 17:1-9; 18:1-4, 7-8), support the fact that homes not only were places of worship, but that they played an important role in the Pauline mission.[139] Roger Gehring has emphasized that

> Houses served also as missional bases of operation. They provided the mission with co-laborers for outreach in the city and surrounding area. Houses offered Paul, his assistants, other itinerant missionaries, and fellow believer's room and board during their missional stay at any one location. At the same time, houses made significant contribution to the mission of Paul and his coworkers in their function as assembly places for missional proclamation, catechetical baptismal instruction, and Christian teaching. A hospitality-providing network of *oikos* was the basis that made possible Paul's letter writing ministry, so very important for his work of church planting and building. In addition, houses made missionary travel possible in that they provide necessary material and financial support for the trips. The house with its workshop and its network of relationships (extended family, clients, and association and business contacts) offered natural evangelistic contacts and conversation opportunities. Moreover, not only individual but also entire households were baptized, and this was one of the most significant factors contributing to the rapid spread of the gospel.[140]

Abraham Malherbe contends that sociological factors such as house church planting among important trade routes and the spread of Greek culture and language also contributed to the rapid expansion of the Christian movement.[141]

---

[138] Darrell L. Bock, *Acts*, 534.

[139] Turner, "Leadership Development Process of Select House Church Network in North America: A Case Study," 49.

[140] Gehring, *House Church and Mission*, 227.

[141] Abraham J. Malherbe, *Social Aspects of Early Christianity* (Baton Rouge, LA: Louisiana State University Press, 1977), 62-65.

Church Planting Missionary Model for the House Church

Kirk Hadaway asserts that a strong link is made by Jesus between His mission and the purpose of the church (Matthew 28:19-20; Luke 24:46-49; John 17:18; 20:21; Acts 1:8). This link, according to Hadaway, is that the "ultimate implication of the instrumental nature of the church is that mission is its very nature and function."[142] Furthermore, "experience tells us that a church that aims at ministry seldom gets to mission even if it sincerely intends to do so. The church that aims at mission will have to do ministry, because ministry is the means to do mission."[143] In this section, some theories that are used on the church's organizing principle in the modern house church movement will be examined.

## *Alan Hirsch's Incarnational Ecclesiology*

Incarnational Ecclesiology occurs when the identification of God with humanity becomes the essential signifier of a church's existence. This missional emphasis in ecclesiology has five implications. The first implication is that the church must always enter fully into the context in which it happens to find itself. Second, in reaching a particular people group the church will need to identify with them in all ways possible without compromising the truth. Third, the church must have a real and abiding presence among unredeemed people. Fourth, the church pursues a sending impulse instead of extracting people away from their unredeemed context. Finally, an incarnational ecclesiology enables people to experience Christ inside of their own culture.[144]

Incarnational ecclesiology runs counter to what has been labeled an attractional mode of church. In describing the attractional mode of the church, Hirsch states,

> The church bids people to come and hear the gospel in the holy confines of the church and its community. This seems so natural to us after seventeen centuries of Christendom, but at what price and to what avail have we allowed it to continue? If our actions imply that God is really only present in official church activities worship, Bible studies, and Christian youth meetings, ladies' fellowships-then it follows that mission and evangelism simply involves inviting people to church-related meetings.[145]

---

[142] C. Kirk Hadaway, Francis M. Dubose, and Stuart A. Wright, *Home Cell Groups and House Churches* (Nashville, TN: Broadman Press, 1987), 58.

[143] Alan Hirsch, *The Forgotten Ways: Reactivating the Missional Church,* 236.

[144] Frost and Hirsch, *The Shaping of Things to Come: Innovation and Mission for the 21st Century Church*, 37-41.

[145] Ibid., 41.

A commitment to an incarnational ecclesiology has caused Hirsch to promote what he terms "third place" communities.[146] A third place community is a setting outside of an individual's work and home by which he or she fosters relationships with unbelievers. This emphasis on incarnating into an unbeliever's culture, instead of extracting them out of it through church buildings and programs, gives Hirsch a significant degree of influence within the House Church Movement.[147]

### *Neil Cole's Missional Ecclesiology*

Neil Cole is critical of what he perceives as a theological propensity toward an emphasis on the Pauline epistles for understanding the nature of the church. Cole discusses three consecutive parables located in Mark 4 which provide principles that are foundational for understanding what he calls the organic nature of the church. Cole's treatment of the parables of the sower (Mark 4:3-20), the growing seed (Mark 4:26-29), and the mustard seed (Mark 4:30-32) led him to see the kingdom as simple, small, and spontaneous:

> Trying to multiply churches is starting at the wrong place. A church is a complex entity with multiple cells. We must go further down microscopically, to the smallest unit of Kingdom life if we want to start the multiplication process. If we cannot multiply churches, we will never see a movement. If we cannot multiply leaders, we will never multiply churches. If we cannot multiply disciples, we will never multiply leaders. The way to see a church multiplication movement is to multiply healthy disciples, then leaders, then churches, and finally movements- in that order.[148]

As Cole distilled attributes from this organic nature of the church, he synthesized them with principles derived from the widely read book, *The Spontaneous Expansion of the Church* by Roland Allen. The theological result is an

---

[146] Hirsch encourages the idea of small missional communities meeting in third places such as coffee shops, restaurants, and bars. A third place is a place of social interaction where relationships can develop and meaningful conversation entered with little risk. Having such gatherings drives missional minded people to think long and hard about the deepest necessities required for Christian community. Taking the party, of which we are a part, into the house of people who are outside of the church is not a new gimmick but a reclaimed expression of the early church. In fact, Jesus' incarnation is the greatest expression of missional endeavor. Jesus brought God's presence (the "party") into the house (the lives of his hearers) of those who were far from participating in the life of God. "Hirsch #3: Third Places," Tangence, accessed Octorber 30, 2014.http://tangence.wordpress.com/2008/07/02/hirsch-3-third-places.

[147] Turner, "Leadership Development Process of Select House Church Network in North America: A Case Study", 51.

[148] Neil Cole, *Organic Church: Growing Faith where Life Happens* (San Francisco, CA: Jossey-Bass, 2005), 98.

argument that movements of church planting must be incarnational (Phil 3:17), viral (1 Tim 2:2), transformational (Rom 6:17), and universal (1 Cor 4:16-17).[149] It is these principles that help us understand how the church's story "begins in Jerusalem, ends in Rome, and along the way visits nearly every commercial and political center around the Mediterranean: Antioch, Lystra, Iconium, Corinth, Philippi, Thessalonica, Ephesus and Athens."[150]

Turner analyzes Cole's theory as follow,

> The result for Cole is what he terms as the DNA that is needed in every part of church, from its smallest unit to its largest. This DNA within Cole's theological framework stands for Divine truth, Nurturing relationships, and Apostolic mission. Divine truth is rooted in the great commandment to "love the Lord your God with all your heart, and with all your soul, and with all your mind" (Matt 22:37-38). Nurturing relationships obey the second greatest commandment: "You shall love your neighbor as yourself" (Matt 22:39-40). Apostolic mission seeks to obey the great commission: "Go therefore and make disciples of all the nations, baptizing them in the name of the Father, and of the Son, and of the Holy Spirit. Teaching them to obey everything I have commanded you" (Matt 28:19-20). Though Cole does not deem himself as a leader in the House Church Movement, it is these principles that make him widely read and a person of reference in the House Church Movement.[151]

---

[149] Roland Allen, *Missionary Methods: St. Paul's or Ours* (London: Robert Scott Press, 1962), 147-150.

[150] Andy Crouch, *Culture Making: Recovering Our Creative Calling* (Downers Grove, IL: InterVarsity Press, 2008), 147.

[151] Turner, "Leadership Development Process of Select House Church Network in North America: A Case Study", 52-53.

Chapter 3

# Contributing Literature

## 1. Architectural Theory on the House Church

Roger W. Gehring says that for many years the subject 'house church' generated little or no interest among New Testament scholars. Only in the last twenty-five years has research begun to focus more closely on the architectural setting of early Christian gatherings and on its corresponding social and theological implication.[152] According to Bradly S. Billings, while the literary record points to the phenomena of the 'house church' in multiple localities across the Roman world, there is a paucity of archaeological evidence for houses large enough to accommodate the numbers involved, and no attested record of purpose-renovated or purposed-built meeting places is known until well into the third century.[153] Although there is a paucity of archaeological evidence, the 'three stage theory'[154] has come to represent something approaching a 'scholarly consensus' on the subject. L. Michael White adopts R. Krautheimer's periodization of the development of the house church up until the basilica. He makes significant progress in three ways as follow:

[152] Roger W. Gehring, *House Church and Mission* (Peabody, Massachusetts: Hendrickson Publishers, 2004), 1.

[153] Bradly S. Billings, "From House Church to Tenement Church: Domestic Space and the Development of Early Urban Christianity" (master's thesis, The University of Melbourne, 2010), 2.

[154] The 'three stage' theory is authoritatively set out in three sources: (1) R. Krautheimer et al, *Corpus Basilicarum Christianaum Romae* (5 vols; Rome: Pontifical Gregorian Institute, 1937-1977), and (2) elaborated with a comprehensive overview of subsequent scholarship by L. Michael White, *Building God's House in the Roman World: Architectural Adaptation among Pagans, Jews and Christians* (Baltimore: John Hopkins University Press, 1990) and (3) "The Social Origins of Christian Architecture," in *Texts and Monuments for the Christian Domus Ecclesiae in its Environment*, Vol. 2. (Valley Forge, PA: Trinity Press, 1997).

First stage (*Oikos ecclesiae*), 50-150 C.E. Christian community meeting in private homes of members and benefactors. Second stage (*Domus ecclesiae*), 150-250 C.E. Private homes renovated for dedicated Christian usage. Third stage (*Aula ecclesiae*), 250-313 C.E. Larger buildings, both private homes and public halls etc. renovated for Christian usage.[155]

White asserts that the old assumption of a genetic evolution from Roman houses to Christian basilicas is no longer tenable. He believes that the development of Christian architecture into the basilica is not some normative type of structure evolving from the pre-Constantinian house church, but rather a process of architectural adaptation and accompanying social factors.[156] Gehring states that White distinguished three basic possibilities: (a) the *house church* was defined as a private domestic house that remained architecturally unaltered. (b) A church house (*domus ecclesiae*) is a private domestic house that was physically altered and adapted in order to meet the social and/or religious needs of the group. (c) A hall church (*aula ecclesia*) refers to a larger, more formal, rectangular (private or public) hall that was used by Christians exclusively for social and religious purposes.[157]

## 2. Social Network Theory of Groups and Individuals in Roman Society

L. Michae White, in his article *Social Networks in the Early Christian Environment: Issues and Methods for Social History* attempts to show the relevance of network analysis by examining evidence for the social connectedness of groups and individuals in Roman society.[158] Billings also argues that the application of a relatively new approach in the sociological investigation of ancient communities, known as social networking theory, is applied to understand the social circumstances under which communities were formed and cohered around a common cultic practice or figure in the ancient world.[159] During the first and second centuries, the early Christians were a new social and cultic group, seeking to establish themselves in both the physical and social landscape of the urban area. They met in homes and continued to meet primarily in domestic space until at least such time as the first buildings dedicated to Christian use begin to appear in the archaeological record during the course of the third century.[160]

---

[155] L. Michael White, "Domus Ecclesiae-Domus Dei: Adaptation and Development in the Setting for Early Christian Assembly" (PhD diss., Yale University, 1982), 27-36.

[156] White, "Domus Ecclesiae-Domus Dei: Adaptation and Development in the Setting for Early Christian Assembly", 11-25.

[157] Gehring, *House Church and Mission*, 18-19.

[158] L. Michae White, "Social Networks in the Early Christian Environment: Issues and Methods for Social History," *Semia* 56 (1992): 23.

[159] Billings, "From House Church to Tenement Church: Domestic Space and the Development of Early Urban Christianity", 2.

[160] Ibid., 6-7.

Social network theory has been used for research on the early house church and its leadership. It is important to examine the groups and individuals who appear in the social network. White stresses the necessity of social network theory and its scope and application. According to White,

> Social network theory is not an integrated theory of social dynamics but a method or tool for analyzing social relationships which are constituent parts of larger societal groupings. He argues that the methodology is especially useful for interpreting and understanding the multiple relational structures between individuals and groups within highly diverse and highly mobile social environments, such as that of the Graeco-Roman city.[161]

### Primary Anchor

The group in which an individual's identity and sense of belonging was most acute is usually characterized by a single individual described as "the primary anchor," around whom other group members acquire their status and roles.[162] For most in the Graeco-Roman world, *paterfamilias* performed this function and the *familia* constituted the wider group in which meaning and belonging were primarily acquired. The family was primarily defined by a relationship of dependence, which encompassed all who depended on the husband (*dominus*) and wife (*domina*), whether biologically related or not. The *paterfamilias* exert the authority over the members of his household, including his own children.[163]

Beyond this, individuals belonged to multifarious other groups (religious, civil, commercial, political, etc.), each with its own social dynamics, and were in simultaneous contact with other individuals to whom they are linked by other social bonds such as kinship, trade, ethnicity and friendship, etc.[164] In some cases, a person other than the paterfamilias and a group other than the *familia* might become the primary anchor (e.g. the military, the Christian community). This might lead to transference of allegiance resulting in social dislocation with attendant consequences such as ostracization. In such cases, the primary anchor and the group in which identity was formed assumed special importance. At all times, in social network theory, the attributes and actions of individuals are of less consequence and importance than the relationships that exist between the individual and the group.[165]

---

[161] White, "Social Networks: Theoretical Orientation and Historical Applications," 23.

[162] James Moody & Douglas R. White, "Structural Cohesion and Embeddedness: A Hierarchical Concept of Social Groups," *American Sociological Review* 68 (2003): 103-127.

[163] Suzanne Dixon, *The Roman Family* (Baltimore: The John Hopkins University Press, 1992), 162.

[164] Billings, "From House Church to Tenement Church: Domestic Space and the Development of Early Urban Christianity", 19-20.

[165] Ibid., 20.

One consequence of a high incidence of density within a social network is a tendency toward consistency of behavior among the group members, together with a diminished capacity for deviation from established behavioral norms. Conversely, where the relational bonds are weak, the group may dissipate through conflict, experience assimilation, or be consumed by another stronger group.[166]

L. Michael White's Theoretical Question of Social Network

As White states, social network theory has been largely predicated on the examination of small, self-contained groups experiencing little change over time: "so what happens when a religious sect, largely of Jewish ethnic origins and highly committed to an apocalyptic worldview, finds itself living in and attempting to recruit from the population of a cosmopolitan Roman city?"[167]

> Should we think, as has been the tendency in the past, of a process of conversion to Christian away from Graeco-Roman paganism, or is there a more fluid dynamic at work, one of multiple points of connection between those gathered around a primary anchor such as the patron of a house church (or perhaps earlier an apostle or other charismatic leader, and later a bishop), gradually extending the reach of the group and its ethos and message through the agency of its ever increasing contacts to other individuals and into other networks, with a symbiotic process of assimilation occurring over the course of the two centuries until the Edict of Milan? Sample block quote.[168]

White's theoretical question above raises the issue of the process of conversion from another religion to Christianity. In his question, most of this process of conversion took place around a primary anchor as the patron of a house church.

The Significance and Role of Primary Anchor in the Social Network

In the Graeco-Roman world, a high degree of commitment and loyalty to the primary anchor, whether a leader or the exalted Christ mediated by a leader, must have been active. Groups gathered around a primary anchor, whether a person or something held in common, existed in every city of the ancient world, and are well known from both the epigraphical and literary record. According to L. Michael White, "Merchants, guilds, collegia, brotherhoods, and cults of all sorts flourished, especially in the major urban centers. There seems to have been a social need for people with a common bond to band together, and this need was most often expressed in organizations that had some sort of religious or cultic activity."[169] Such groups were often highly bonded; limited contact with

---

[166] Ibid., 20-21.

[167] White, "Social Networks: Theoretical Orientation and Historical Applications," 31.

[168] Ibid.

[169] L. Michael White, *The Social Origins of Christian Architecture*. Vol. 1, Building God's House in the Roman World: Architectural Adaptation among Pagans, Jews, and Christians, 59.

those outside the group was ensuring a high degree of commitment to established group norms. The sociological manifestation of this phenomenon was that, in most of the large cities of the empire, the population was fragmented into distinct communities, gathered around a familial or kinship bond, a common trade, or ethnicity.[170]

According to Florence Dupont, there was in fact little communication between the various different communities within Roman society. Communities, which could take the form of social and professional groupings... as well as of great families in which free men and slaves lived together, might come and go between the country and the city, their members never meeting anyone outside a narrow circle.[171]

Rodney Stark argues that the effect of social network and its contribution was that the church had grown through the social network in the persecution period. Stark shows how recognizing the effects of network ties among individuals in the Roman world, especially during times of crisis, can help to explain the numerical growth of Christianity in the second and third centuries. The application of social network found that religious cell groups or conventicles offered an important set of social links within the urban environment of the Roman world.[172]

### Social Network and Faith

Recent work in network theory as applied to processes of religious conversion holds that such conversions do not depend upon ideological appeal alone, but rather on the social ties between individuals. Recent work in the social, political, and economic structures of the Roman world suggests that new attention needs to be given to the interconnectedness[173] of life up and down the social ladder.[174]

White has evaluated that the social structures of the Roman world were undergoing change, either contemporaneous with or as a result of the emergence of Christianity. As a result, one begins to look at the way Christians came to be associated with networks of power and influence in the Roman world.[175] In any contemporary context of house church, like India and China, one needs to do research on how the house church associates with other networks in their own

---

[170] Hans-Josef Klauck, *The Religious Context of Early Christianity: A Guide to Graeco-Roman Religions* (Edinburgh: T & T Clark, 2000), 47.

[171] Florence Dupont, *Daily Life in Ancient Rome* (trans. Christopher Woodall; Oxford: Blackwell, 1992), 155.

[172] White, "Social Networks in the Early Christian Environment: Issues and Methods for Social History," 3.

[173] According to White, this interconnectedness was manipulated and enhanced by the noble women, most of whom carried the equivalent title "clarissima femina." White, "Social Networks in the Early Christian Environment: Issues and Methods for Social History," 10.

[174] White, "Social Networks in the Early Christian Environment: Issues and Methods for Social History," 3.

[175] Ibid., 6.

context. In high context culture, the religious affiliations were rooted deeply in traditional social relationships reinforced by strong ties within certain cliquish circles.[176]

White explains how Jewish and Christian groups established and attracted adherents as they made their way into the Roman urban settings. He says that the Christian message of immortal life through Jesus Christ offered a more satisfying and compelling response to the religious needs of the age than could its competitors.[177] In other words, the Christian message responded to some sense of need or of deprivation by contemporary people.[178]

Religious Recruitment

In this part, the research will deal with the transforming of worldview by faith on religious recruitment and its object (isolates or outsiders, such as migrants and widows), and the importance of leadership for religious recruitment within social network.

Recent work by Rodney Stark and William Sims Bainbridge points to certain inadequacies of a model of religious conversion or recruitment based solely on ideological appeal in response to some sense of need or deprivation, whether psychic or social. They argue that social bonds are often determinative of ideological attachment: "faith constitutes conformity to the religious outlook of one's intimates-membership spreads through social networks."[179] Conversion is understood in terms of psychic reorientation through intellectual assent and commitment to propositions and beliefs that satisfy such needs.[180]

Even if deprivation-appeal factors are operative in religious propagandizing, nonetheless new recruits will not be retained unless they are socially bonded into the group. Similarly, strong social bonds and intact social networks tend to reinforce existing commitments.[181] Social isolates, that is individuals who are themselves unattached to local networks, have little impact on overall success in diffusion. Such social isolates or outsiders would seem to be the most likely candidates for deprivation-appeal recruitment.[182]

Recruitment to new religious groups often moves through preexisting social networks, especially extended family units. These are particularly efficient because

---

[176] Ibid., 15.

[177] L. Michael White, "Adolf Harnack and the Expansion of Early Christianity: A Reappraisal of Social History," *The Second Century* 5 (1985): 115-117.

[178] White, "Social Networks in the Early Christian Environment: Issues and Methods for Social History," 20.

[179] Rodney and William Sims Bainbridge, "Networks of Faith: Interpersonal Bonds and Recruitment to Cults and Sects." *American Journal of Sociology* 85 (1980), 1394.

[180] Ibid.

[181] Ibid.

[182] Rodney and William Sims Bainbridge, "Networks of Faith: Interpersonal Bonds and Recruitment to Cults and Sects," 1379.

of the multiplicity of social contacts that can be accessed. In the context of the extended family structures of the Roman world, such insights become even more significant. Among the social structures that one finds most often are the economy of friendship and kinship and the popularity of clubs and collegial groups, often with religious overtones. But one of the most important social structures, both for the maintenance of the traditional religions and for the profusion of new cults, was the operation of patronage and clientelism.[183] Interpersonal relations are key to understanding the social structures. What is needed is a more complete sense of the dynamics of social networks in terms of theoretical orientation and in missiological application.[184]

## 3. Social Interdependence Theory

Till now, there has been no research work that applied social interdependence theory to house church study. Social interdependence theory is a good theory for defining the relationship between inner and outer circumstances of a house church. Therefore, in this part, the definition of social interdependence theory[185] and its types will be examined and the positive interdependence theory will be engaged in order to apply it to the house church.

According to David W. Johnson's definition of social interdependence theory, social interdependence theory is a classic example of the interaction among theory, research, and practice. The premise of the theory is that the way in which goals are structured determines how individuals interact, which in turn creates outcomes.[186] Social interdependence exists when the accomplishment of each individual's goals is affected by the actions of others.[187] There are two types of social interdependence, positive (cooperation) and negative (competition). Positive interdependence exists when individuals perceive they can reach their goals if and only if the other individuals with whom they are cooperatively linked also reach their goals and, therefore, promote each other's efforts to achieve

[183] Ramsay MacMullen, *Paganism in the Roman Empire* (New Haven and London: Yale University Press, 1981), 11, 125, 129.

[184] White, "Social Networks in the Early Christian Environment: Issues and Methods for Social History," 20.

[185] The historical roots of social interdependence theory can be traced to a shift from mechanistic to field theories in physics. "Field Theory in Social Psychology," Morton Deutsch, accessed October 30, 2014. http://www.institutovenezolanodegestalt.com.ve/Gestalteca_Articulos/Field%20Theory%20in%20Social%20Psychology%20-%20Deutsch%20Morton.pdf. Social interdependence theory has a long history and has been carefully formulated to explain cooperative and competitive relations among individuals. See. David W. Johnson, "Social Interdependence Theory," *American Psychologist* (2003): 936.

[186] David W. Johnson, "Social Interdependence Theory," 934.

[187] M. Deutsch, "A Theory of Cooperation and Competition," Human Relations, no. 2 (1949), 129-152. D. W. Johnson & R. T. Johnson, *Cooperation and Competition: Theory and Research* (Edina, MN: Interaction Book, 1989).

the goals. Negative interdependence exists when individuals perceive that they can obtain their goals if and only if the other individuals with whom they are competitively linked fail to obtain their goals; therefore, obstructing each other's efforts to achieve the goals. No interdependence results in a situation in which individuals perceive that they can reach their goal regardless of whether other individuals in the situation attain or do not attain their goals.[188]

**Figure 1.** Outcomes of Cooperation[189]

Psychological Processes

The psychological processes created by positive interdependence include substitutability (the degree to which actions of one person substitute for the actions of another person), inducibility (openness to being influenced and to influencing others), and positive cathexis (investment of positive psychological energy in objects outside of oneself).[190] These processes explain how self-interest is expanded to joint interest and how new goals and motives are created in cooperative and competitive situations. Self-interest becomes expanded to mutual interest through other people's actions substituting for one's own, through an emotional investment in achieving, and through an openness to being influenced so that joint efforts are more effective.[191] An emotional investment in achieving goals benefits others as well as oneself. It generalizes to caring and committed

[188] M. Stanne, D. W. Johnson & R. T. Johnson, "Social Interdependence and Motor Performance: A Meta-Analysis." *Psychological Bulletin,* no. 125 (1999), 133-154.

[189] D. W. Johnson & R. T. Johnson, *Cooperation and Competition: Theory and Research* (Edina, MN: Interaction Book, 1989), 6.

[190] M. Deutsch, *Cooperation and Trust: Some Theoretical Notes*, vol. 10, Nabraska Symposium on Motivation, ed. by M. R. Jones ( Lincoln: University of Nebraska Press), 275-319.

[191] "Social Interdependence Theory," Johnson & Johnson, accessed October 30, 2014. http://www.ceebl.manchester.ac.uk/events/archive/aligningcollaborativelearning/Johnson_Johnson.pdf.

relationships with those who are working for the same purpose and goals. Demonstrating the transition from self-interest to mutual interest is perhaps one of the most important aspects of social interdependence theory. Positive interdependence results in promotive interaction, negative interdependence results in oppositional interaction, and no interdependence results in the absence of interaction. Promotive interaction may be defined as individuals encouraging and facilitating each other's efforts to complete tasks, achieve, or produce in order to reach the group's goals. It consists of a number of variables, including mutual help and assistance, exchange of needed resources, effective communication, mutual influence, trust, and constructive management of conflict.[192]

Application of Social Interdependence Theory

Applications of social interdependence theory are required to operationalize positive (or negative) interdependence in order to create promotive (or oppositional) interaction that will lead to the desired outcomes.[193] In this continuing section, positive interdependence and promotive interaction will be examined.

### *Positive Interdependence*

According to David W. Johnson, knowing that one's performance affects the success of one's group mates seems to create forces for responsibility that increase one's efforts to achieve.[194] Positive goal interdependence is sufficient to generate higher achievement and productivity than are engendered by individualistic efforts. The combination of goal and reward interdependence tends to increase achievement more than does goal interdependence alone. There is evidence that positive interdependence tends to motivate individuals to try harder, use higher level reasoning strategies more frequently, and develops new insights and discoveries more frequently. Identity interdependence (i.e., defining oneself in terms of group membership) results in a greater willingness to take less from common resources and to contribute more toward the common good.[195]

---

[192] Ibid.

[193] David W. Johnson, "Social Interdependence Theory," 938. Operationalizations of positive interdependence have focused both on the relative efficacy of the ways in which it may be structured and on increasing the forces for responsibility through individual accountability procedures. Operationalizations of promotive interaction have included an emphasis on social skills and group processing. Although, the basic theoretical premise focuses on three variables (interdependence, interaction, and outcomes), the operationalizations of positive interdependence and promotive interaction have resulted in the emphasis of five variables (interdependence, individual accountability, interaction pattern, social skills, and group processing).

[194] Johnson, "Social Interdependence Theory," 938-939.

[195] Ibid., 938-939.

### *Individual Accountability and Personal Responsibility*

Positive interdependence is posited to create forces for responsibility that increase group members'feelings of responsibility and accountability for (a) completing one's share of the work and (b) facilitating the work of other group members. When a person's performance affects the outcomes of collaborators, the person feels responsible for their welfare as well as his or her own.[196] Failing oneself is bad, but failing others as well is worse. The shared responsibility created by positive interdependence adds the concept of "ought" to group members' motivation—one ought to do one's part, pull one's weight, contribute, and satisfy peer norms. Such feelings of responsibility increase a person's motivation to perform well.[197] M. Stanne, D. Johnson & R. T. Johnson note,

> Responsibility forces are increased when there is group and individual accountability. Hooper, Ward, Hannafin, and Clark found that cooperation resulted in higher achievement when individual accountability was structured than when it was not. Similarly, Archer-Kath, Johnson, and Johnson found that increasing individual accountability resulted in increases in perceived interdependence among group members.[198]

### *Promotive Interaction*

Positive interdependence is posited to result in promotive interaction, and negative interdependence[199] is posited to result in oppositional or contrient interaction. Promotive interaction is characterized by individuals engaging in actions such as providing each other with efficient and effective help and assistance and in exchanging needed resources such as information and materials. Promotive interaction requires the appropriate use of interpersonal and small group skills along with regular group processing.[200]

---

[196] T. Mastsui, T. Kakuyma & M. Onglatoco, "Effects of Goals and Feedback on Performance in Groups," *Journal of Applied Psychology* 72 (1987), 407-415.

[197] David W. Johnson, "Social Interdependence: Interrelationships among Theory, Research, and Practice," *American Psychologist* (2003): 939.

[198] Ibid.

[199] Negative interdependence typically results in individuals opposing each other's success. Oppositional interaction occurs as individuals discourage and obstruct each other's efforts to achieve their goals; individuals focus both on being productive and on preventing any other person from being more productive than themselves. Conditions of no interaction occur when individuals work independently without any interchange with each other; individuals focus only on being productive and ignore as irrelevant the efforts of others.

[200] Johnson, "Social Interdependence: Interrelationships among Theory, Research, and Practice," 939.

### Limitation for Applying the Social Interdependence Theory

Cooperative efforts tend to promote greater efforts to achieve, more positive relationships, and greater psychological health than do competitive or individualistic efforts.[201] The power of cooperation has been shown to depend on the presence of clear, positive interdependence (which includes individual accountability) that results in promotive interaction (which includes appropriate use of social skills and group processing). On the other hand, a number of conditions, such as inertia, resistance to change, economic conditions, prejudice, and cultural resistance, can preclude implementation or institutionalization of effective practices.[202]

## 4. Biblical Aspects of Interdependence as a Worldview

David W. Augsburger, in his book *Pastoral Counseling Across Cultures,* provides some interesting insights into our attitudes about dependence and independence.[203] In the Western worldview mindset, independence (an individual who has internal control and takes internal responsibility for his/her life) is considered healthy. Independence, assertiveness, and self-sufficiency are thought good, so those who lack such traits are considered in need of diagnosis and treatment.[204] In contrast, within a more "Eastern" worldview, a different attitude is found. Solidarity with one's social group is prioritized, so a more dependent person (an individual who accepts external control and accepts more of an external responsibility for life) is seen as healthy. Independence is seen as unhealthy.[205] Although, each of these worldview descriptions is a gross simplification, the simplifications do help us see problems with the two idealizations.

### The Biblical Ideal Model

The ideal church appears to model neither independence nor dependence. Rather, it describes a relationship of interdependence. First of all, Acts 4:32-37 describes a body of believers with great cohesiveness. They offered from their abilities and accepted help in their lacking. Sharing was a basic characteristic of their interaction. The early church was an interdependent body. Second, the description of relationships within the church can be seen in the 'one another' passages of the epistles of Paul, Peter, and John: Honor one another (Rom. 12:10), Live in harmony with one another (Rom. 12:16), Accept one another (Rom. 15:7), Instruct one another (Rom.15:14), Agree with one another (1 Cor. 1:10), Serve one another (Gal. 5:13), Bear with one another (Eph. 4:2), Submit to one another

[201] Ibid., 940.

[202] Ibid., 942.

[203] David W. Augsberger, *Pastoral Counseling Across Cultures* (Philadelphia, PA: Westminster Press, 1986), 87-91.

[204] Ibid., 87.

[205] Ibid., 88.

(Eph. 5:21), Forgive one another (Col. 3:13), Admonish one another (Col. 3:16), Encourage one another (1 Thess. 5:11), Offer hospitality to one another (1 Peter 4:9), Be humble to one another (1 Peter 5:5), Fellowship with one another (1 John 1:7), Love one another (2 John 5)

These (and there are others) show independence since they show capability to offer something to another person. Yet they also show dependence since they show we have needs that must be met by others. This is an interdependent body of believers.[206] Third, the body analogy of the church shows interdependence as well. In 1 Corinthians 12:14-31, one sees the church as a body united, yet made of individual parts or members. These members have abilities that other parts of the body need. Yet no member is so capable that he/she can do without the other members. The church in this analogy is an interdependent, interconnected membership.

### *David W. Augsburger's Assumption*

If interdependence is the ideal, then perhaps there are flaws with both the Western and Eastern ideals. David W. Augsburger contends that the flaws of the Western ideals on the four dimensions.

The first dimension consider church-planting. From Henry Venn, Rufus Anderson,[207] and John Nevius of the 19th century, the ideal for new churches was expressed in terms of the "3-selfs." New churches should be self-governing, self-propagating, and self-supporting, some add a "fourth self," "self-theologizing". On some level, this ideal is sound. If a new church maintains an inability to govern itself, to multiply itself, or support itself, it is dependent on others. This will hamper sustainability and growth. Certainly, dependence does not appear to be the Biblical ideal. However, it is quite possible that a genuine risk of the "3-selfs" is the mistaken assumption that the capability to act independently implies that independence is itself an ideal. But perhaps the utilization of each other's strengths (not just at an individual level, but at a church level) is a good thing.

The second dimension is community development. One of the major fears in community development is creating dependence in a community. Relief work tends to create dependence because it provides short-term help without skills and material transfer for long term betterment. Many involved in 'Community Development' see their work within the community as the transitioning from

---

[206] "Dependence, Independence, and Interdependence," Bob Munson, accessed September 20, 2014. http://www.bukallife.org/articles/Interdependence.pdf

[207] Shenk, Wilbert R. (1981). "Rufus Anderson and Henry Venn: A Special Relationship?" *International Bulletin of Missionary Research* **5** (4): 168–172. Though there is dispute as to who wrote about the idea first, the "three-self" method is attributed to both Anderson and Henry Venn. They both wrote about the need for creating churches in the missions field that were self-supporting, self-governing, and self-propagating.

a dependent community to an independent community. But perhaps, again, interdependence is a healthier goal, where different communities can share their strengths to support each other for the common good.

The third dimension is missions. This is an area where interdependence has been growing. Years ago mission organizations often sought to act as strictly independent agents. In other words, each organization has its own sending component, logistics component, literature component, member care component, and so forth. However, the sheer cost and redundancies created became unacceptable. Therefore, there has been a growing trend to specialize in areas of strength and to work with likeminded groups that have strengths that complement their own. This is sometimes described as collaboration. Even if one ignored interdependence as a Biblical ideal, it certainly is an economic ideal.

The fourth dimension is pastoral care. The tendency to promote independence has its potential flaws. Is it healthy to attempt to create independently minded individuals in a society that promotes social cohesiveness and, in fact, considers a high level of independence to be a mental or social malady? Is it good to always assume that guilt or shame (motivators toward social norms) are unhealthy? Would a society that maintains itself only through punishment and reward maintain long-term viability? Would it be preferable to develop people who feel an obligation to share from their strengths, or to be willing to accept help in their weaknesses? Wouldn't this be a healthy characteristic in almost any society?

In conclusion, Augsburger's assertion regarding interdependence will always be a difficult goal. Independence is fairly simple to understand, as is dependence. But to develop bonds of giving and receiving moves one away from any simplistic psychological model. It would challenge any culture, even as it appears to be a worthy and biblical goal to strive after.[208]

## 5. House Church Planting Model

### The Necessity of Church Planting: India Context

India has a population of more than 1.2 billion people; one of every six persons on earth lives in India. It is by far the most ethnically and linguistically diverse country on earth, with over 2,500 distinct people groups. Community and identity are based on caste as much as on race and language.[209] The world's least-evangelized peoples are concentrated in India. Of 159 people groups of over one million people, 133 are unreached. Hundreds more groups of fewer than one million are unreached. Also, 953 ethnic groups have populations greater than 10,000; of these, 205 have no church and little to no outreach from Christians. They can be found in every state, although they tend to be more concentrated in the north. There are 485 people groups with populations of over 10,000

[208] Munson, "Dependence, Independence, and Interdependence."

[209] Jason Mandryk, *Operation World* (Downers Grove, IL: InterVarsity Press, 2010), 405-407.

are unreached and unengaged, almost three quarters of the world's 639 people groups are in this category.[210] Mission, church planting and research initiatives in India have grown far beyond the humble beginnings of the 1960s, which were then largely controlled by foreign groups. Today, over 1,000 Indian mission agencies and church-based initiatives have sent out over 100,000 church planters, evangelists and social workers (many of them cross-culturally) and have planted tens of thousands of Christ-following congregations. Considerable thought and practice are now shaping an Indian Church and society that can follow Christ and live out the gospel in a contextualized fashion.[211]

These contexts in India demand resources, manpower, and effort. However, because of these needs of churches, both large and small are reluctant to enter the Indian context with church planting efforts. The demands bring various theories that involve laity in church planting. E. Stanley Jones exhorted his fellow missionaries in India, "Our business is not so much to do a job, but to create men who can do it."[212]

Peter Wagner also proposes the need of laity to be involved in church planting. Wagner says that "I believe the best way to introduce lay people to ministry is to help them discover, develop and use their spiritual gifts. This will take teaching, modeling, and practice."[213] Prosperly Bell Lyngdoh emphasizes on the importance of working together with young church planter as biblical model.[214] Ralph W. Neighbor also states, "There are very few things we actually do unless we work with someone who both informs and demonstrates for us."[215]

## House Church Planting Theory

Most research works for house church planting theory have focused on leadership development for the next generation and laity. These also assert that new converts need to be employed in church planting. Christian A. Schwartz points out that many churches hesitate to include these new Christians in evangelistic efforts because of their spiritual immaturity and their lack of knowledge (e.g., they might say something wrong).[216] One key role of a leader is to train the next

---

[210] Ibid., 414-415.

[211] Ibid., 408-409.

[212] E. Stanley Jones, *Christ at the Round Table* (New York: Abingdon Press, 1928), 194.

[213] C. Peter Wagner, *Church Planting for a Greater Harvest* (Ventura, CA: Regal, 1990), 117.

[214] Prosperly Bell Lyngdoh, "Church-Based Training for Lay Church Planters in India," 7. He says that Jesus taught the disciples many things, while at the same time Jesus was showing them by doing himself. By working together, pioneer church planters can directly help disciples by (1) telling them what to do (2) explaining them why they have to do it, (3) showing them how to do it, (4) doing it with them, (5) letting them do it by themselves, and (6) deploying them.

[215] Ralph W. Neighbor, *Where Do We Go From Here? A Guide Book for the Cell Group Church* (Houston: Touch Publication, 2000), 330.

[216] Christian A Schwarz, *Natural Church Development: A Guide to Eight Essential Qualities of Healthy Churches* (Carol Stream, IL: Church Smart Resources, 1996), 71.

generation of leaders for local congregations and new churches. Edgar J. Ellison writes, "Every leader's role is to prepare each ministry to be an equipping link to the next generation of leaders not only for the local church, but for new churches."[217] Prosperly Bell Lyngdoh argues that lay involvement in church planting produces the multiplication of churches. It becomes natural and spontaneous according to the leading of the Holy Spirit.[218] He points out the importance of lays and new converts to be part of the church planting ministry. Roland Allen, in his book *The Spontaneous Expansion of the Church*, writes:

> I mean the expansion which follows the un-exhorted and unorganized activity of individual members of the Church explaining to others the Gospel which they have found for themselves; I mean the expansion which follows the irresistible attraction of the Christian Church for men who see its ordered life, and are drawn to it by the desire to discover the secret of a life which they instinctively desire to share; I mean also the expansion of the church by addition of new churches.[219]

Christian A. Schwartz proposes that we should not stop new believers from getting involved in our evangelistic effort in planting new churches. Schwartz writes,

> The principle of energy transformation, however, sees the possibilities: new converts still have many contacts to "the world," still speak the "worldly" language, and have many thought patterns in common with their non-Christian friends. Instead of crying "Danger! Look out!" growing churches use these energies for the kingdom of God.[220]

David L. Mattson describes the important role of new churches for mission. He writes,

> Even though this new community may appear weak and lowly, it will carry out two important functions right from the start: (1) The Church will continue its role as the nurturing community. Especially at the beginning, it is likely that the believers will be confronted by almost irresistible pressure from the unbelieving community to conform to the traditional religion way of life. Without the support of fellow believers many new believers may fall away. Therefore it is important for believers whose commitment to the Christian faith has hardly gone beyond the verbal confession "Jesus is Lord" to begin dialogue

---

[217] Edgar J. Ellision, *Home Grown Leaders* (Pasadena, CA: William Carey Library, 1992), 119.

[218] Prosperly Bell Lyngdoh, "Church-Based Training for Lay Church Planters in India" (PhD diss., The Southern Baptist Theological Seminary, 2004), 4.

[219] Roland Allen, *The Spontaneous Expansion of the Church* (Grand Rapids: Eerdmans, 1984), 7.

[220] Christian A Schwarz, *Natural Church Development: A Guide to Eight Essential Qualities of Healthy Churches*, 71.

> with one another to work out the implications of the Scriptures for their daily lives. Many questions that did not occur to them at the beginning will have to be answered. (2) It is also the responsibility of the church, the body of Christ in the world, to continue the task of seeking and saving the lost. The Lord has clearly said that his search for lost sheep will continue, a task that must be carried out by his people on earth, namely the Church.[221]

It is significant to have partnership with new church planters. New church planters need to work with church planters who have experience. Thus, house church planting theory in the past had focused on the leadership development for next generation and stressed the role of laity and new converts for planting new church.

### House Church as New Expression in the Context

Eddie Gibbs asserts that the American church is morphing. He explains this "morphing" is the transition of the church to a new expression within the North American context.

> There is a growing realization among leaders committed to mission that the challenge will not be adequately met by adding new programs to ensure the local church's – or a denomination's – institutional survival. Such leaders are talking about an unfettered reimagining of the church, resulting in a comprehensive change in its self-understanding and its configuration.[222]

Robert Lee Turner argues that one example of this "reimagining" is the house church movement, which is growing in North America.[223] According to Deyoung and Kluck, the house church movement is not always the stereotypical "anticlergy, antiauthority, antiliturgy, antisermon, antibuilding, anti-most ways of doing church over the last 1,700 years."[224] The role of leaders and the autonomous nature of the house church are important for its multiplication. Turner argues that the house church multiplication occurs with leaders.[225] House church multiplication combined with its highly autonomous nature cannot be achieved without the

---

[221] Daniel L. Mattson, "Church Planting through Leadership Formation," *Missio Apostolica* 3 (1995): 80.

[222] Eddie Gibbs, *Churchmorph: How Megatrends are Reshaping Christian Communities* (Grand Rapids, MI: Baker Academic, 2009), 16.

[223] Robert Lee Turner, "Leadership Development Process of Select House Church Network in North America: A Case Study" (PhD diss, The Southern Baptist Theological Seminary, 2010), 1.

[224] Kevin Deyoung and Ted Kluck, *Why we Love the Church: In Praise of Institutions and Organized Religion* (Chicago, IL: Moddy Publishers, 2009), 179.

[225] Turner, "Leadership Development Process of Select House Church Network in North America: A Case Study", 2.

development of individuals who will lead these emerging faith communities.[226] Eventually, the role of leadership and autonomous nature is the core of the house church method as a new expression in the context.

### Five Strategy Steps Proposed by Rad Zdero Toward Establishing the House Church Model

House church trends take place in various countries with rapidly growing people movements like India. Rad Zdero suggests five strategic steps (deliberate, rapid, small, saturation-focused, and volunteers-led) to help house church movement.[227]

(1) Missiological studies have concluded that church planting movements are customarily preceded by a deliberate strategy to begin new disciple-making communities.[228] An example of this was the formation of 3500 house churches (totaling 70,000 people) in one Indian state in the late 1990s as the result of an intentional planting strategy.[229]

(2) House churches need to blueprint themselves with a healthy emphasis on evangelism, the goal being to multiply their house church by two or sending a team to start a new one. Multiplying house churches typically grow large enough to form a second group within 6-9 months.[230]

(3) Currently around the globe, explosive Christian conversion growth from church planting movements is characterized by the reproduction of multiplying house churches and cell groups of no more than 10-30 people.[231] According to Rad Zdero, it is known that smaller churches experience a proportionally higher growth rate than larger churches: 1-100 member church (63% growth in 5 years), 100-200 (23%), 200-300 (17%), 300-400 (7%), and over 1000 (4%). In other words, churches tend to plateau in numbers as they get larger, making the necessity of continually sending out groups from existing churches to start new ones. Given their mobility, flexibility, simplicity, and low

---

[226] C. Kirk Hadaway, Francis M. Dubose, and Stuart A. Wright, *Home Cell Groups and House Churches* (Nashville, TN: Broadman Press 1987), 203.

[227] "Launching House Church Movements," Rad Zdero, accessed April 10, 2014, http://www.missionfrontiers.org/issue/article/launching-house-church-movements

[228] David Garrison, *Church Planting Movements: How God is Redeeming a Lost World* (Midlothian, IL: Wigtake Resources, 2004), 34.

[229] James Rutz and Victor Choudhrie, "House Church Explosion in India," House-2-House Magazine, Issue 2, 2002, accessed April 10, 2014, http://www.house2house.com/files/MAG_issue_2.pdf

[230] Wolfgang Simson, *House that Change the World: The Return of the House Churches* (Waynesboro, GA: Authentic, 1998), 107.

[231] David Garrison, *Church Planting Movements*, 35.

cost, small house churches are the most strategic choice in reaching the masses.[232]

(4) Every neighborhood, apartment complex, work setting, and educational institute should be considered as a potential area for a new house church.[233]

(5) The weight of responsibility and leadership for emerging house church movements should be placed squarely on the shoulders of grassroots volunteers, so-called "lay people." Current research shows that the extent to which rapid church planting movements are birthed depends on the degree to which indigenous non-professionals (lay people) are encouraged, trained, and released.[234]

### House Church as A Home Fellowship Missionary Model

This model focuses on church planting and mission. Del Birkey considers the house church a "missionary model" for contemporary mission and church planting.[235] He especially saw it as a home-fellowship missionary model. Birkey provides the examples of it around the world and asks this question: how is the home-fellowship "missionary model" strengthening the gospel's advance in Two-Thirds World environments? As examples for answering his own question, he mentioned as follows; China's Charismatic House Churches, The Base Ecclesial Communities of Latin America, The "New Testament" Church of Nepal, Burmese Believers and a Dispersed Church, We Do Not Need Our Church Buildings Anymore in Vietnam, A Small Beginning in Sri Lanka, A Mombasa Model, and A Spanish 10,000 by 2000 Vision.[236]

### Implications for Mission Strategy toward Contemporary House Churches

Birkey set forth some meanings of house churches in the strategic aspect of mission. (1) The house church structure was the working model during the first few centuries of the church's missionary advance.[237] (2) Simple structures generally work better than complex ones. Reed E. Nelson also proposes that it is better not to set up a new structure if an existing one can be used; it is wise to seek for correspondence between local societal patterns and ecclesiastical patterns, and rationality should not exclude spontaneity. He argues that minimalist structure will help avoid stifling the creativity, spontaneity, and celebration that

---

232 "Launching House Church Movements."

233 Robert Fitts, *The Church in the House: A Return to Simplicity* (Salem, OR: Preparing The Way Publishers, 2001), 55-60.

234 Garrison, *Church Planting Movements*, 35.

235 Del Birkey, "The House Church: A Missiological Model," *Misssiology: An International Review*, Vol. XIX, No. 1 (1991): 69.

236 Ibid., 75-77.

237 Ibid., 77.

are the hallmarks of successful movements.[238] (3) The church in difficult places of our world is a lesson to the affluent church in the easy places. The simple but dynamic small-group "missionary model" remains the basic working prototype for outreach and sustaining power, and possesses an inherent ability for discipline and self-correction.[239]

### Some Typical Obstacles for Establishing a House Church Model

Rad Zdero set forth some obstacles for establishing a house church model:

First, there exist many versions and even distortions of a biblical house church. There are various groups out there: the glorified Bible study, the post-evangelical, the charismatic (Latter Rain and Word Faith influence), the radical wing (Gene Edwards influence), the fundamentalist, those who use house church merely as a tool for evangelism, the 'us four no more' club, etc. The lack of cohesion is perhaps symptomatic of a lack of direction and vision.[240]

Second, some of these groups tend to be very reactionary and rabid against the institutional church; they carry "a Bible in one hand and a rock in the other." Thus, many house churches are quite independent. Part of this may be due to abuse they have experienced in traditional churches at the hands of a controlling leadership. On the other hand, some Christians in conventional churches become defensive when the topic of house church is raised because of ignorance and personal negative encounters with well-meaning but not-so-nice house church folks. These tensions will not help the rest of the Body of Christ get on board with what God seems to be doing through the emerging house churches.[241]

Third, there also do not seem to be any local churches, denominations, or mission groups particularly devoted to starting house churches, although some are starting to make room for it by being involved in such endeavors. This probably comes from a combination of the inertia of traditional ways of doing church, ignorance of what house churches are in the eyes of most Christians, and/or fear of the reactionary nature of some house churches.[242]

### Toward a Desirable Model for Planting House Churches for Cities in India

House churches have been planted in cities like England's urban centers among the poor. In China, a congregation can gather in the house without registering with the government if their number is below hundred. Now, houses churches are in the unban-centers in China. House churches in India have also

[238] Reed E. Nelson, "Five Principles of Indigenous Church Organizations: Lessons from a Brazilian Pentecostal Church." Missiology: An International Review Vol. 17, No. 1 (1989): 50.

[239] Birkey, "The House Church: A Missiological Model," 78.

[240] Rad Zdero, *The House Church Movement* (Pasadena, California; William Carey Library, 2004), 111.

[241] Zdero, *The House Church Movement*, 111-112.

[242] Ibid., 112.

rapidly spread out around the country because their characteristics, especially, family/relative/community-centered, are very much in line with Indian society.

According to Havie M. Conn, "the Muslim city offers some advantages to the model (of house churches)."[243] He says that cities offer a greater degree of freedom than villages or the country, where close-knit social and kin ties tend to discourage change and experimentation. For example, in Algiers, an Arab Muslim city of over two million, relatively liberal policies permit greater freedom for house churches than for groups outside the capital. In places like Lebanon, Jordan and Egypt, this social group is found to be the most receptive to Christianity.[244] Therefore, theoretical research on house churches is demanded for applying a desirable model for house church planting.

This researcher believes that the house church theology must be based on the *mission Dei*. This means that the house church itself should be planted strategically, with focus on its essence (church) rather than its form (house). On this point, the theological foundation of urban house church planting is so crucial. In this study, the researcher also will review the desirable urban house church through the study of an urban church planting model. Furthermore, the missionary church model for the urban mission suggested by Schulz's article, *Toward a Missionary Church for the City*, will be analyzed in this study including the possibilities to apply its values to the urban house church planting.

The Necessity of the House Church in the City

In the twenty-first century the need for urban church planting is growing. In 1984, D. Barrett predicted "We will live in a world of seventy-nine supercities (fifty-nine of them in developing countries), each with over four million inhabitants in A.D. 2000. Our urban population will increase by 1.6 million people per week. Poverty in our urban areas will continue to expand, producing a 'planet of slums'"[245] Barrett's prediction was right. According to Barrett, supercities are urban agglomerations with over 4 million inhabitants. Megacities are those with over 1 million. He predicted then that the number of supercities would go to 79 and the megacities to 433 in A.D. 2000. In 2014, the number of supercities had actually grown to 108 and the number of megacities to 527 around the world.[246]

Klaus Detlev Schulz also stresses the reason why the city needs the church. He said,

---

[243] Harvie M. Conn & Manuel Ortiz, *Urban Ministry : The Kingdom, the City & the People of God* (Downer Grove: InterVarsity Press, 2001), 247.

[244] Ibid., 247.

[245] David Barrett, *Cosmos, Chaos and Gospel: A Chronology of World Evangelization from Creation to New Creation* (Birmingham, Ala.: New Hope, 1987), 84.

[246] "Major Agglomerations of the World: All agglomerations of the world with a population of 1 million inhabitants or more," accessed November 17, 2014. http://www.citypopulation.de/world/Agglomerations.html

> the city demands resources, manpower, and efforts that should be initiated by the church, both the church at large and the local churches. The city of today brings together the "ends of the world," the Jerusalems with the Samarias and Judeas; all that traditional foreign missions stood for is now right at our doorsteps. There is thus a need for a communal effort, a church that nourishes, equips, and supports any urban mission outreach. In this way, the church will express its solidarity with those individuals who stand in these front line situations.[247]

### Theological Considerations toward the Urban House Church Planting

Some theological considerations for urban house church planting and its possibility of applications need to be examined. Schulz criticizes the "three-self formula" in order to rebuild the theological consideration on church planting. According to Schulz, "Although this formula expresses a certain human logic, its scriptural support is less clear." Schulz rightly points out that the Church and local congregations remain dependent on God and His Word, but human goal such as three-self formula (self-serving) remain independent of church.[248] Schulz proposes some theological considerations for overcoming human standards such as the three-self formula which has been applying to the church planting for more than a century. He doesn't neglects human standards for the church planting. He says, "Nevertheless, it must be acknowledged that human ingenuity and hard work are crucial in church planting. Human standards are applied to bring a church planting project to a close. There must be an exit strategy for the withdrawal of foreign mission presence"[249]

Some theological considerations for church planting proposed by Schulz will be examined in order to rethink church planting. First, "theologically speaking, a church must be considered planted once faith comes about and the believers meet together to be nurtured and strengthened through the Gospel."[250] Second, "Church planting efforts should focus on establishing communities that identify themselves with the objective realities of the Word and Sacraments."[251] The basic principle of church planting: "if the Church is able to guarantee those activities as they are set in the definition of the Church, then the missionary goal of church planting has in essence been accomplished."[252] Third, Church planting efforts

---

[247] Klaus Detliv Schulz, "Toward a Missionary Church for the City" in *Missio Apostolica,* Vol. XI, No. 1 (May 2003): 5.

[248] Klaus Detlev Schulz, *Mission from the Cross: The Lutheran Theology of Mission* (St. Louis: Concordia Publishing House, 2009), 20.

[249] Ibid.

[250] Ibid., 21.

[251] Ibid., 207.

[252] Ibid.

need to distinguish between the dispensable and the indispensable issues. No longer should church planting efforts focus on creating replicas of the church body back home or on that entity which sponsors the project.[253] What is indispensable is that the community is raised on essential elements of the Christian faith. Church planting includes an obligation to the proclamation and teaching of all essential elements of the Christian faith as found in Scripture. Fourth, Church planting efforts include the goal of raising up an indigenous, independent church body. The regional church body should raise up her own indigenous clergy to continue and sustain the proclamation of the Gospel and the administration of the Sacraments.[254] Fifth, Church planting should engage the four-self formula (self-propagation, self-governing, self-supporting, and self-theologizing) so that the church planted may teach itself the Gospel and Sacraments wherever its location may be.[255] Sixth, Church planting strategies should entertain a certain degree of latitude that leaves time for development and growth. (1) One can plead the avoidance of a paternalistic approach to church planting that rigorously and legalistically imposes foreign structures upon indigenous Christians.[256] Therefore, church planters can plan to lead a young church on a path to a responsible maturity. (2) A rigorous imposition of these guidelines may result in disastrous consequences. A premature withdrawal of support may disrupt the missionary and pastoral activities of a congregation and so offset the work of the Gospel.[257] These theological considerations guide us to establish criteria for the house church planting in order to start a practical study on house church planting in an urban context.

Principles of Urban Church Planting

How may the church participate in God's mission in order to planting the house church in the city? A response is offered through the existing church (congregation) of Schulz's concept for urban mission.

## *Principles of Urban Church Planting*

The researcher will examine some principles of urban church planting developed from ideas of Klaus Detlev Schulz's urban mission research work. Schulz focuses three aspects for the urban church planting as principles: (1) team effort (Romans 16:1-16) and Communal task (Acts 13:2-3). (2) Individuals always maintained a close relationship to their sending congregation (Acts 14:27), so they became

[253] Ibid.

[254] Ibid.

[255] Ibid., 208.

[256] The American model for church planting consists to a great extent on the understandable concept of finding loose individuals and collecting them into fellowship which are like surrogate families. This does not work very well in a traditional society where natural families are already the basic structure. Evangelical Dictionary of World Missions (2000), s.v. "Strategy in Mission."

[257] Klaus Detlev Schulz, *Mission from the Cross: The Lutheran Theology of Mission*, p. 208.

part of that church in delivering their gift of compassion to a mission field city like Jerusalem (Acts 11:30). (3) Today's mission efforts should utilize already existing Christian communities into which, through appropriate mission efforts, individual believers are incorporated. Schulz emphasizes these principles so that the lost may be led on their path to salvation in the spiritual nourishment of the preached and administered Word, and in the communal fellowship with the Triune God and the believers.[258] Thus, the church planter in the city should consider incorporating in the local urban congregation to plant new house churches.[259]

### *House Church Planting in the City as an Indigenous Mission Model*

An indigenous mission model has been proposed because of the shift in position and role of a missionary. Traditionally, missionaries preached, baptized, and planted churches. They generally held leadership positions. They were curbing the process of building indigenous churches and leadership. Schulz quotes Tom Steffen's word that "missionaries should work themselves out of a position from the outset."[260] He criticizes the paternalism of the missionaries, in which these paternalistic attitudes have strained relations between young churches and foreign missionaries. As a result, some local churches declare a moratorium on mission, a stop to foreign missionary presence. Christians wanted to assess their national situation apart from foreign intervention so as to emerge with a renewed and better sense for a mission of their own.[261] The missionary task of this indigenous model is the church planting. Schulz's main question for this model is "*what type of a church should be planted.*"[262] To respond to this question, this researcher will deal with Schulz's new approach to church planting.

### *Assimilation or Adoption as a Strategy for Urban House Church Planting*

Schulz suggests that assimilation or adoption should be offered, where possible, as an alternative to new mission efforts struggling apart from already extant worshipping communities.[263] He believes that existing churches become crucial havens for the mission concept of assimilation. But Schulz did not forget to mention about the realities on existing churches. He says that these churches become functional again for outreach. They often do not receive the support they deserve. He says that inevitably and sadly, urban missions must become an enterprise of volunteering individuals, rather than an extension of the corporate

---

[258] Ibid.

[259] Ibid., 6.

[260] Klaus Detlev Schulz, *Mission from the Cross: The Lutheran Theology of Mission*, 9.

[261] Ibid., 9-10.

[262] Ibid., 20. See. 205.

[263] Ibid., 6.

essence of the church that celebrates a worshiping and vocational life in the broader community.[264]

## *Modesl for Urban House Churches: "Place where" model? Or "Inside out" model?*

Schulz set forth the concept of "a Place where" model from George Hunsberger's[265] criticism. Hunsberger compares today's church to a service club that offers programs and activities so that people look at it as "a place where" they would go to be served. This is called "a place where" model. The church projects itself as an organization that caters to special interests, and that very often in superficial ways. In this model, Church is perceived as a vendor institution where members are reduced to consumers and its leaders to production mangers. Therefore, in this model mission becomes just one activity among many.

Mission is more than a mere accessory action to all other activities. The worshipping community should perceive worship as part of the mission of the Lord. Schulz also brings forward the concept of the "Inside out" model from Thomas Schattauer to suggest that worship signifies the missionary activity of the Triune God to His believers. He argues that the visible act of worship of this community – what is called liturgy space-enacts and signifies the reconciling movement of God towards the world. With that perspective there is no separation between liturgy and mission.[266]

According to Conn, in Paul's understanding, the taproot of mission was the glory of God and its display and acknowledgement in global worship. Mission was not the ultimate goal of the churches Paul planted. Nor was the goal church growth. Worship is. Missions, then, exist because worship doesn't. God's glory fuels our mission and draws our worship. Worship is not a mere function of the church; it is her ultimate purpose.[267]

Schulz, however, does not simply neglect the "a place where" model for church planting. He says that the concept of the church as the "a place where" remains crucial and necessary, as both the traditional terms "*mission ad extra*" and the "*mission ad intra*" denote; this perspective validates the visible realities of preaching and the sacraments to which people must be brought and through which they are assimilated into a fellowship.[268]

---

[264] Ibid.

[265] George Hunsberger follows Hokendjke's *missio Dei* concept. Although he brought his own criticism of "place where", he reduced the mission of church itself. On the other hand, as Schulz brought the characteristics of church, which the church is apostolic, in the Nicene-Constantinopolitan Creed, he criticized Hunsberger's idea of *missio Dei.*

[266] Schulz, "Toward a Missionary Church for the City", 7.

[267] Conn & Ortiz, *Urban Ministry: The Kingdom, the City & the People of God,* 141.

[268] Schulz, "Toward a Missionary Church for the City", 9.

Indeed, the lifestyle of the church becomes the centripetal drawing point, pulling the Gentile peoples to itself and, beyond it, to God. Thus, the planting and nurturing of the church is part of its missionary calling to the world. The church's exemplary existence is to be a missionary magnet drawing inside those whom Paul calls outsiders (Col 4:5; 1Thess 4:12; 1Tim 3:7).[269] Merging with this centripetal role of the church as the God-centered magnetic drawing point for the Gentiles is the God-centered centrifugal role of the church.[270]

The Four Classical Activities Toward Planting a House Church in the City

Schulz believes that these four classical activities - *Martyria and Kerygma, Koinonia, Leitourgia, Diakonia* - provide us a helpful yardstick to measure the character and nature of the inner city church.[271]

## *Martyria and Kerygma (Confession and Witness)*

*Kerygma* provides another connection between urban mission then and now. In the Greco-Roman city the announcement call to worship was the responsibility of the herald (Keryx). Similar to the town crier of later centuries, the herald was a messenger vested with public authority. His news (kerygma) carried the weight of the one who commissioned him. His demands were those of the urban king or the god whom he represented before the city. Twice Paul uses the term, *herald,* to refer to his appointment by God to preach (1Tim 2:7; 2Tim 1:11). And repeatedly the verb form invades his language to describe his message and its declaration. The object of the heralding was the "good news" (euangelion, 2 Cor 11:4; Gal 2:2; 1Thess 2:9; Phil 1:15; Col 1:23).[272]

## *Koinonia (Fellowship)*

If it is from kerygma that Christian faith is taught, it is within the setting of *koinonia* that it is caught. This word was not uncommon in the urban context of the Greeks. But in the Hellenistic world, koinonia was much less than a dream. Class and status divided the honorable and the humble, those with wealth and property from those without it, master from slave. In this setting, the church offered, and still offers, a community the urban world cannot match. It was, and still is, to be a family, Jew and Gentile "foreigner" both now part of "God's household" (Eph 2:9).[273]

---

[269] Conn & Ortiz, *Urban Ministry: The Kingdom, the City & the People of God*, 145.

[270] Ibid., 146.

[271] Schulz, "Toward a Missionary Church for the City", 11.

[272] Conn & Ortiz, *Urban Ministry: The Kingdom, the City & the People of God*, 152.

[273] Ibid., p. 153.

## *Leitourgia (Liturgy)*

*Leitourgia,* in extrabiblical Greek, was a term originally used to denote specific services performed by the public benefactor for the urban public welfare. In the Bible, it becomes worship, mission as the celebration of God before the nations (Ps 107:21-22), and the people of God assembled for worship on Mount Zion (Is 56:6-8).[274]

## *Diakonia (Care/services)*

*Diakonia* exemplified that communal ministry of love. In the city life of the empire, the term was often used of the work of slaves. In the kingdom of God, *diakonia* is transformed by Jesus' service on the cross (Mk 10:45), the compulsion of the messianic servant's "I must" (Mt 16:21; Lk 24:26). Human ideas of greatness and rank are reversed again as Jesus the Lord, who was the servant, becomes the object of our joyful and patient service in suffering (Rom 12:11; 14:17-18). Apostles become servants (1 Cor 3:5; 2 Cor 11:23), and the freedom of sonship demands that we "serve one another in love" (Gal 5:13). Through gifts of service and the ministry of mercy the church grows in maturity (Eph 4:7-16). Giving, not receiving, becomes the blessed reward for those who help the weak (Acts 20:35).[275]

In addition to the four activities of the existing local visible congregation extension, Conn adds one more activity – ***dikaioma*** (justice).[276]

House Church Planting in the Challenges of the Urban Setting

According to Charles Van Engen, while there is increasing interest in planting and growing house churches in the city, too few of them seem to have a strong missional intention to be God's agents of the transformation of the city itself.[277] Many evangelistic, church-planting efforts do not deal with the entire scope of evil in the city. Therefore, urban churches need to be equipped for its missionary purpose toward the world.

## *Urban Setting and its Challenges*

What kinds of challenges is the church faced with today in the urban setting? There are some challenges from the population explosion, from the socioeconomic gap,

---

[274] Ibid., p. 151.

[275] Ibid., p. 153.

[276] Ibid., p. 153. Diakaioma – To his people who came through the city's gates, he had cried of old, "Do what is just and right" (Jer 22:3). Christian masters, themselves under their Master in heaven, are exhorted, "Grant to your slaves justice and fairness" (Col 4:1). Elder-bishops are to be sought who exhibit justice mixed with their self-control and love of what is good (Tit 1:8). And Christians are to fill their minds with everything that is noble and pure, lovely and honorable – and just (Phil 4:8).

[277] Charles van Engen, *Mission on the Way: Issues in Mission Theology* (Grand Rapids: Baker Books, 1996), p. 93.

and from the public arena. Urban populations will continue to grow at almost twice the rate of national growth, and large cities at a rate three to four times as high. Does the church show any indication of interest in these expanding urban centers? There is a socioeconomic gap in the urban setting. Millions of rural-to-urban migrants were ripe for new ideas (transforming the worldview), including religious teaching. Urban church planting is needed in the slum for the poor and for the working classes. A Church program is needed for the working class. The House church model needs to design itself for meet these challenges among migrants, the poor and the working class.[278]

### *House Church Planting and Diakaioma (Justice) in the Public Arena*

Across the globe, urban realities require that Christianity develop an agenda that addresses more than church planting or evangelism. The problem of evil is an important issue in urban contexts. Children and youth encapsulate these challenges of rapid urbanization on more than simply a private level. Children are exposed to danger such as poverty, prostitution, unwanted pregnancy, and homelessness. The church faces a new urban generation. How do we respond to their needs? Is entrance into the urban public sector a legitimate role for the church in its institutional form? What is the calling of the church? Where does the limited competence of the church end?[279] What is the responsibility of the people of God in this public sector?

According to Conn, "Individualism led churches to turn most naturally to charities and voluntarism to respond to urban needs."[280] The motivating compassion of Christ, coupled with the acculturated individualism of a middle-class church, produced large-scale religious philanthropy and organized charity programs for the city, such the rescue mission, the Salvation Army "slummers," cheap hotels for the impoverished, shelter homes for women and children, the settlement house, and the "institutional church" movement.

According to Schulz, "urban church planting will have to become holistic." He asserts that the inner city church must address the communal life with a broader scope that might include forms of expression from which it would rather prefer to disassociate itself.[281] Charles van Engen supports scholars' idea above as follows.

> The church is not a social agency - but is of social significance in the city. The church is not city government - but is called to announce and live out the kingdom of God in all its political significance. The church is not a bank - but is an economic force in the city and is to seek the

---

[278] Conn & Ortiz, *Urban Ministry: The Kingdom, the City & the People of God*, 21.

[279] Ibid., 23.

[280] Ibid.

[281] Klaus Detliv Schulz, "Toward a Missionary Church for the City", 12.

> economic welfare of the city. The church is not a school - but is called to educate the people of the city concerning the gospel of love, justice, and social transformation. The church is not a family - but is the family of God, called to be a neighbor to all of those whom God loves. The church is not a building - but needs building and owns buildings to carry out its ministry. The church is not exclusive, not unique - but is specially called by God to be different in the way it serves the city. The church is not an institution - but needs institutional structures to effect changes in the lives of people and society. The church is not a community - development organization-but the development of community is essential to the church's nature.[282]

## 6. Worldview

In this section, the researcher reviewed some books which grasp the worldview of migrants in urban context and Hinduism. This literature review is divided into three parts: Literature Review on General Worldview, Literature Review of Worldview on the People Group (Urban migrants, locals, and tribes), and Literature Review of Worldview on Hinduism.

Literature Review on Culture, Worldview and the Gospel

Many house churches are planted in other religious and cultural contexts. It is important to understand the worldview and culture in order to deliver the gospel to regions which have a different culture. Charles H. Kraft discusses some issues on Worldview in his book, *Anthropology for Christian Witness,* such as reality, perception and mental mapping. Kraft gives various aspects of worldview's element, characteristics of worldview, functions of worldview and some perspective on worldview. Kraft also speaks about God, culture and human beings on the theme of worldview in a missiological perspective. It is about how the seeds of the gospel change the local culture's worldview. The Christian worldview is planted to change the deep worldview level.[283]

There are those who speak of a Christian worldview, but there is no single Christian worldview. If there were, Christians would need to have a single approach, both to things like moral values and to things like time, space and categorization. Jesus had a worldview. It consisted of His Kingdom perspectives integrated into His first-century Hebrew worldview. Our missionary task is to follow His example by integrating those same perspectives into our cultural worldview.[284]

Sherwood G. Lingenfelter illustrates this in his book, *Transforming Culture: A Challenge for Christian Mission*. The major question of his field study is: "Is

[282] Charles van Engen, *Mission on the Way: Issues in Mission Theology,* 93-94.

[283] Charles H. Kraft, *Anthropology for Christian Witness* (Maryknoll, NY: Orbis Books, 1996), 65.

[284] Ibid., 67-68.

it possible to bring a truly transforming gospel, or are we always limited to reproducing our own cultural reflection of Christianity wherever we carry the message?"[285] Lingenfelter assures us that missionaries have succeeded in bringing a biblically informed worldview, but one that is thoroughly contaminated by their culture. His study is very much adjustable to research on hierarchical societies such as Africa, Asia (e.g., India and Sri Lanka) in order to find out the Worldview aspects on missiological issues such as Social Order, Interpersonal Relationship, Authority and Family, Authority and Community.[286] These missiological issues, which are formed by local worldview, take place in India. Indeed, it should be considered how the gospel faces other religious worldviews and their cultural context.

Literature Review on Worldview of the People Groups
(Urban Migrants, Locals, and Tribes)

### *Worldview Transformation*

It is a tough mission task to deliver the gospel to a different religious context and another cultural context without syncretism. This is especially complicated in an urban context where migrants and tribes from different regions gather in a city. Migrants in the city experience their worldview being transformed. As their worldview transform, the churches need to approach them to deliver the gospel. Paul G. Hiebert reveals how insights from anthropology can help missionaries communicate biblical content without syncretism in his book, *Anthropological Reflections on Missiological Issues*. For this, he proposes the theory of critical contextualization.[287] Hiebert presents global trends that missionaries must understand in order to reach key groups. He helpfully discusses spiritual warfare and power encounters with other religions, such as Hinduism and Animism.[288] He believes that worldview can be transformed. A. Scott Moreau analysed Paul Hiebert's proposal,

> He grounds his understanding of transformation in the biblical language of conversion which, he notes, includes both an initial turning from sin (repenting) and the process of walking in a lifelong discipleship relationship with God through Christ. It is both point and process. Repentance (the initial turning) results from a radical

[285] Sherwood G. Lingenfelter, *Transforming Culture: A Challenge for Christian Mission* (Grand Rapids, MI: Baker Academic, 1998), 12.

[286] Ibid.

[287] Paul G. Hiebert, *Anthropological Reflections on Missiological Issues* (Grand Rapids, MI: Baker Academic, 1994), 75-92.

[288] Ibid., 203-213.

> paradigm shift; discipleship (the process) more often results from the normal process of growth and development as a follower of Christ.[289]

For Hiebert, the core contents of worldview transforming are repentance and discipleship.

Charles Edward Van Engen, in his book *Mission on the Way: Issues in Mission Theology* sees a biblical view toward the cities in order to get the Christian worldview for the urban mission. It helps us to construct a theology of mission of the city. It suggests how to construct our understanding for the frame of worldview in Cities. For this, his emphasis is on biblical text, urban context and faith community.[290] The churches also need to emphasize these same three elements to the Hindu migrants through repentance and discipleship as they are experiencing their worldview transforming in the cities.

### *Hindu Migrants in Urban Context*

*The Changing Face of World Missions: Engaging Contemporary Issues and Trends* (Pocock, et. al) provides information on the growth of international migration as a population trend capturing the attention of missiologists. Throughout its various data we can reflect on the worldview of migrants. Migrants who migrate in search of employment constitute the vast majority of the increase in global migration.[291] Missiological studies need to respond to this migrant phenomenon. Understanding the worldview of migrants is a first step. Research work is also need on how economic migration impacts the migrants themselves, transforming their worldview.

Louis J. Luzbetak, *The Church and Cultures: New Perspectives in Missiological Anthropology,* provides thoughts for a culturally sensitive ministry and witness. He introduces non-anthropologists to a wealth of scientific knowledge directly relevant to pastoral work. He focuses on a burning theological issue: contextualization, the process by which a local church integrates its understanding of the Gospel with the local culture/worldview.[292] For this great mission task, we should find a biblically faithful way to integrate the biblical worldview and the local worldview.

*The New Era in Religious Communication* by Babin and Iannone presents some elements of worldview on religious life, such as the way of beauty or the symbolic way, with the family as the cradle of the symbolic way. Its research will be helpful to apply on the house church family in India in order to find

---

[289] A. Scott Moreau, Paul G. "Hiebert's Legacy of Worldview", *Trinity Journal* 30NS (2009): 229.

[290] Charles Edward Van. Engen, *Mission on the Way: Issues in Mission Theology* (Grand Rapids, MI: Baker Academic, 1996).

[291] Michael Pocock, Rheenen Gailyn Van, and Douglas McConnell. *The Changing Face of World Missions: Engaging Contemporary Issues and Trends* (Grand Rapids, MI: Baker Academic, 2005), 22-44.

[292] Luzbetak, Louis J. *The Church and Cultures: New Perspectives in Missiological Anthropology* (Maryknoll, NY: Orbis Books, 1988).

their religious life style.[293] By using this book, we can conduct research work on what aspects of Christianity are still influenced by other worldviews or religions, especially Hinduism. One great task in the church is how to stem Hinduism influence in Christianity in order to escape syncretism.

The thesis of the book, *Communicating God's Word in a Complex World: God's Truth or Hocus Pocus?* is that contemporary communication of the biblical message can be modeled after the way the writers of Scripture utilized earlier texts and restructured them for their contemporary audience. Shaw and Van Engen contend that "Communication of the Gospel takes the entire proclamation process (the original communication, the communicators, and the present-day audience) into account. This entire process is impacted by knowing God, which in turn is informed by all of the relevant contextual data. The objective in writing this book is to apply theological, communicational, and anthropological principles to the hermeneutical process in order to provide appropriate and relevant messages for the people who hear the word of the Lord."[294]

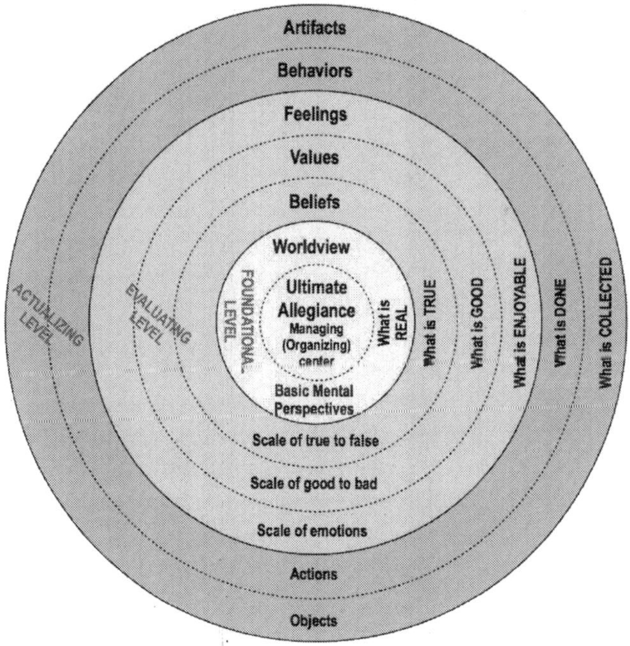


**Figure 2.** The Golden Circle.[295]

---

[293] Pierre Babin, and M. Iannone. *The New Era in Religious Communication* (Minneapolis: Fortress Press, 1991).

[294] R. Daniel Shaw and Charles E. Van Engen, *Communicating God's Word in a Complex World: God's Truth or Hocus Pocus?* (Lanham, Maryland: Rowman & Littlefield Publishers, 2003), xiv.

[295] "The Golden Circle," accessed November 19, 2014. http://gregandmeg.net/wp-content/uploads/2013/05/Bunkowske-model.jpg

In his book, *Receptor-Oriented Gospel Communication*, Eugene W. Bunkowske contends that successful communication is the linking of speaker and hearer for concept sharing. It involves ideas, code, encoding, decoding, noise, and feedback as well as questions of communication channels, and the medium for message sharing.[296] As in the above diagram, it is important to understand what worldview is in the center of the cultural skin. If not, we will never be able to communicate with people of backgrounds different from ours because the wellspring from which life itself flows is at the core of our way of life, our culture. Therefore, Christian mission need to be equipped with understanding of the worldview of the different culture in order to proclaim the gospel effectively.

The major task of Christian mission is communicating the gospel of Jesus Christ. Communication is not only by words, but holistic, that is, by life, words, and deeds. This is especially true in communicating with tribal people. The book, *Tribes in Transition: Indian Christians Reflect on the Original Inhabitants of the Land: A SAIACS Consultation* has a lot of quality information about knowing the worldview of Indian tribes. F. Hrangkhuma brings the main question for mission to tribal people in India: How can we establish a church where they will feel at home, and own the church as their very own, and not the missionary's?[297] The tribes of India need the transforming presence of Jesus Christ in their midst. God uses us as his communicational tools.

Atul Y. Aghamkar points out the lack of study for the migration of tribals in India. He questions why people are moving toward cities in India. He presents the 'push factors' that push people out of their original location and the 'pull factors' that pull people into the cities.

> One of the push factors is economic. Some people migrate to improve their standard of living while others just to survive. Natural calamities also force people to migrate to cities. With religious fundamentalism, communal and religious riots force certain communities to safer dwelling places, often in cities. Government policies and legislation also move people city-wards. Furthermore, many people left their traditional occupations to find other employment. Male migration comes first in Indian cities. Over a period of time, these male migrants bring their wives and children along. Soon the whole family comes to settle down in the city. Migration is changing to family, clan and even sub-caste group migration. More people migrate as a group rather than as individuals. Industrial growth pulls people to key urban centers like Bangalore. The influence of mass media also increases

[296] Eugene W. Bunkowske and Richard French, *Receptor-Oriented Gospel Communication* (Fullerton, CA: The Great Commission Resource Library, 1989), 13.

[297] F. Hrangkhuma, Padmini Chand, and Beulah Wood. *Tribes in Transition: Indian Christians Reflect on the Original Inhabitants of the Land : A SAIACS Consultation* (Bangalore: SAIACS, 2004), 11.

migration. Through radio and television urban ideas, values, and lifestyles are projected. In cities higher and professional education is available easily. All major cities of India are noted for their educational institutions to which many rural people send their children to cities. Like this, push and pull factors promotes the people move to the cities of India.[298]

Aghamkar brings some questions on the missiological reflections of migration in India. "What will it take to reach tribal communities in our cities with the gospel and plant churches among them? What kind of church do tribal migrants need? What kind of leadership structure? What could equip them to share their new faith with their own people in the city?"[299] His questions on the migration in an Indian city like Bangalore can be used in the research of the house church.

### *Worldview on Hinduism*

The origins of Hinduism are uncertain, but we do know that it is an ancient religion with roots in India.[300] It has no single founder but numerous sacred texts. The earliest are known as the Vedas, which date back to at least 1000 BC. Perhaps the most famous Hindu in recent history was Mahatma Gandhi (1869-1948). Using Hindu principles of nonviolence, he led India in a mass passive protest of British rule, which ultimately ended in the British withdrawal from the subcontinent.

---

[298] F. Hrangkhuma, Padmini Chand, and Beulah Wood. *Tribes in Transition: Indian Christians Reflect on the Original Inhabitants of the Land : A SAIACS Consultation*, 48.

[299] Ibid., 53.

[300] The term 'Hindu' has been used in at least four ways. The first definition was geographic-given to India by the invaders of India" the Turk, Persian and Arab Muslims, and the British rulers. 'Hindu' was the Persian word for 'Indians,' and was originally used of peoples living beyond the Indus River, not followers of a particular religion. David Ludden, ed., *Contesting the Nation: Religion, Community, and the Politics of Democracy in India* (Philadelphia: University of Pennsylvania Press, 1996), 7. The second definition is socio-religious. The most common description which Hindus give to their religion is sanatana dharma, 'eternal religion'. This refers to what is sometimes called Brahmanical Hinduism, a highly sophisticated worldview for categorizing all of life that emerged by the tenth century B.C. "Brahmanical Hinduism" lumped all mankind into a single category and then subdivided this category into a color-coded system of separate species and subspecies, genuses and subgenuses; and then ranked these hierarchically according to innate (biological, cultural, and ritual) capacities and qualities. Robert Eric Frykenberg, "Constructions of Hinduism," in *Christians and Missionaries in India: Cross-Cultural Communication since 1500* (Grand Rapids & Cambridge: Eerdmans, 2003), 527. The third definition of Hinduism was a product of the West's encounter with the Indian civilization. European scholars translated the Vedas and defined Hinduism in terms of these ancient texts. They invented Hinduism as an exotic religious tradition that stood in contrast to the rational religions of the West. Paul G. Hiebert, "The Christian Response to Hinduism," in *Missiology for the 21st Century: South Asian Perspectives*, Hedlund, Roger E., and Paul Joshua. *Bhakiaraj* (Delhi: ISPCK/MIIS, 2004), 325.

Hinduism is often described as a polytheistic religion. Indeed, it is said that there are over 330 million gods in Hinduism. In reality, Hinduism teaches what scholars call pantheistic monism, a religious philosophy that teaches that everything shares in the entire divinity of the universe (*Brahman*). The souls of human beings share in this divinity. They thus survive after the death of the body and transmigrate until they are reincarnated in a different (human, animal, or plant) body. The cycle of soul transmigration and reincarnation is determined by a force called *karma* (deeds in one's present life determine one's status in the next); this cycle or process is called *samsara*. The overall goal of a Hindu is to be released from this cycle (*moksha*) and be reunited with the universal world soul (*atman*).[301]

### Christian Response toward Hindu Teaching

While Hinduism teaches that the entirety of creation is divine (Brahman), Christianity teaches that God is separate from creation (Ps. 33:6, 9). Hinduism teaches that there are multiple deities though they are all part of the one unified whole. But Christianity teaches there is one God, although there are three persons in the one divine essence (Deut. 6:4; John 15:26). Because it associates anything in creation with the divinity, Hinduism sees Jesus as just one god among a multitude of others. In Christianity, Jesus is true God, the second person of the Trinity, one with God the Father and God the Holy Spirit (1 Cor. 8;4-6). Hinduism teaches that humans can, through their own merits, obtain salvation or release from the cycle of reincarnation. Christianity teaches that all have sinned and fall short of the glory of God, but Christ took our sins upon Himself for our forgiveness and salvation (Rom. 3:22-24; 1 Peter 2:24). Hinduism teaches that there are numerous deities, represented by a multitude of idols, worthy of worship and devotion, but God forbids us to worship idols; these images do us no good (Ex. 20:3-5; Jer. 10:5). Hinduism also teaches that each one of us has numerous lives. Christianity teaches that we die only once (Heb. 9:27-28).[302]

Through the centuries, the gospel of Christ has had only limited response among the highly-developed religions of India. India, greatly influenced by Hinduism, has proved especially resistant to the Christian faith. Hinduism's advocate often feels that its faith is superior to what it perceives as the simplicity of the message of Christianity. Hinduism's faith is diverse, tolerant, paradoxical, multifaceted, and complex. It has been called the most difficult to understand of all religious and also the most fascinating.[303] Thus, Hinduism remains a challenge for Christianity in India. Christian missions must take note of and plan for evangelizing among the Hindu people in India.

---

[301] Adam Francisco, "Being A Hindu," The Lutheran Witness, September 2014, 17.

[302] Ibid.

[303] Terry, John Mark, Ebbie C. Smith, and Justice Anderson. *Missiology: An Introduction to the Foundations, History, and Strategies of World Missions* (Nashville, TN: Broadman & Holman, 1998), 363.

John R. W. Stott in his book, *Christian Mission in the Modern World* suggests dialogue as a communication tool for the understanding of other religions. He cites some places of dialogue in evangelism: Hindus in India,[304] Muslims, and the industrial areas of Britain in order to give examples of dialogue in different context. Indeed, in the contexts of India, using critical themes such as authenticity, integrity, and sensitivity, in dialogue with Hindus brings out their worldview.[305]

Lesslie Newbigin states the dialogue with the Hindu in his book, *The Open Secret: An Introduction to the Theology of Mission*. He says that the Christian needs to go to meet their neighbor of another religion on the basis of his commitments to Jesus Christ.[306] A confession of faith is the starting point of their truth seeking.[307] Christians will be in the same position as the other partners in dialogue. The purpose of dialogue for the Christian is obedient witness to Jesus Christ, who is not a property of the church, but the Lord of the church and of all people. He is glorified as the living Holy Spirit takes all that the Father has given to humankind and declares it to the church as that which belongs to Christ as Lord. In this encounter the church is changed, the world is changed, and Christ is glorified. For the delivery of the gospel, the common place (contextualization) can be found for the dialogue. Dialogue is a useful tool for understanding the Hindu people's worldview in order to deliver the gospel.[308]

Ruth Tucker has given us some insights on the various worldviews in her book, *Another Gospel: Cults, Alternative Religions, and the New Age Movement*. Especially, she discusses transplanted Hinduism. It shows us how Hinduism has influenced other religions.[309] Indian Christianity has some of its form borrowed from Hinduism. Some parts on this book will help one see the elements of Hinduism on Christianity in India. For example, one of the elements of Hinduism on Christianity is Yoga so called Christian Yoga.[310]

Yoga is one of the practices of Hinduism.[311] Ronald M. Enroth helps us see what Yoga really is in his book, *A Guide to New Religious Movements*. People treat

---

[304] John R. W. Stott, *Christian Mission in the Modern World* (Mumbai: F.C. Durham for Gospel Literature Service, 1978), 99-102.

[305] Ibid., 94-98.

[306] Newbigin, Lesslie. *The Open Secret: An Introduction to the Theology of Mission* (Grand Rapids, MI: William B. Eerdmans, 1995), 164.

[307] Ibid., 165.

[308] Ibid., 168.

[309] Ruth Tucker, *Another Gospel: Cults, Alternative Religions, and the New Age Movement* (Grand Rapids: Zondervan, 2004), 267-284.

[310] "Outstretched in yoga worship: A Christian approach to yoga," Susan Bordenkircher, accessed October 10, 2014. www.christianyoga.us

[311] According to Adam Francisco, "Meditation and yoga have become common forms of stress release in our society, with classes offered at numerous colleges and fitness centers." Adam Francisco, "Being A Hindu," *The Lutheran Witness*, September 2014, 17.

Yoga as a sport even in India among Christianity. As Enorth says, Yoga reveals the meaning of salvation through physical exercises. It also presents the mechanical path to salvation. As a result, it is about salvation in Hinduism. Yoga will be a sample research model in order to find out other elements of Hinduism on Christianity in India.[312] But, how can we define it in Christianity?

The book of Timothy C. Tennent, *Christianity at the Religious Roundtable: Evangelicalism in Conversation with Hinduism, Buddhism, and Islam* is about interreligious dialogue in an evangelical perspective. Tennent has compared the worldview between Christianity and Hinduism regarding the Doctrine of God and Doctrine of Creation. He also tries to explain the contextualization of these doctrines, whether some elements of Hinduism can explain Christianity in order to deliver the gospel to the Hindu world.[313] It is complicated, but it is challenging for mission. How can the gospel spread and explain the truth from and to another worldview?

The book of Paul G. Hiebert, *Understanding Folk Religion: A Christian Response to Popular Beliefs and Practices* includes the theory of critical contextualization that can help to define the elements of Hinduism related to Christianity. Hiebert's *Understanding Folk Religion* provides sound theoretical understanding, comprehensive elucidation of the characteristics of folk religions, and fundamental biblical and theological principles for practical application in ministry. In the light of theological response to folk religion, it deals with dangers to avoid, such as syncretism – combining elements of Christianity with folk beliefs and practices in such a way that the gospel loses its integrity and message.[314] In the light of missiological response to folk religion, Hiebert encourages Christians to apply the theory of critical contextualization to the other cultural and religious contexts in order to deliver the gospel. Hiebert says that Critical contextualization remains an ongoing process that will not end until we all stand around the throne of God and join that great throng of believers from every language, tribe, and nation, and worship the Lamb who was slain for the salvation of all people.[315] The theory of critical contextualization helps Christians to realize whether local churches in other cultural and religious contexts can maintain their biblical identity.

---

[312] Ronald M. Enroth, *A Guide to New Religious Movements* (Downers Grove: InterVarsity Press, 2005).

[313] Tennent, Timothy C, *Christianity at the Religious Roundtable: Evangelicalism in Conversation with Hinduism, Buddhism, and Islam* (Grand Rapids, MI: Baker Academic, 2002), 37-86.

[314] Paul G. Hiebert, R. Daniel Shaw, and Tite Tiénou, *Understanding Folk Religion: A Christian Response to Popular Beliefs and Practices* (Grand Rapids, MI: Baker, 1999), 378.

[315] Ibid., 392.

## Neo-Hinduism[316]

In his article, *The Christian Response to Hinduism,* Paul G. Hiebert explains the emergence of Neo-Hinduism as a new worldview which is supported by most of Hindu Indians. The environment of Neo-Hinduism leads them to confront and reject to the Christianity.[317] It makes Christianity difficult to conduct its mission in India. Understanding of Neo-Hinduism helps us find how to build a proper mission strategy among people who hold its worldview. Hiebert deals with the Hindus diaspora in order to explain this new emerging worldview. He then suggests that Christians need to respond to this new worldview in order to the deliver the gospel to them. He also proposes that churches need to approach them with a critical contextualization form of the church such as Indian indigenous church and churchless Christians. The Indian church can respond to the new Hindu worldview with their form of churches since it contains a similarity with the Hindus in order to have dialogue and spread the gospel.[318] Indeed, understanding of the Neo-Hinduism worldview can be a way to approach Hindu people for the delivery the gospel today.

According to Vinoth Ramachandra's book, *Faiths In Conflict?,* "A web of crisscrossing influences covers our planet, producing hybrids like Tandoori pizzas and ninja ballets, Silicon valleys in Bangalore and Zen monasteries in

---

[316] Neo-Hinduism is a new form of Hinduism as an Indian response to the confrontation of Christianity and the Enlightenment in the last decades of the nineteenth century and the beginning of the twentieth century. Neo-Hinduism was created by the Hindu revitalization movements (conversion movements, accommodation movements and revitalization movement by cultural collusion). Conversion movements made people change their allegiances to the new ideology (when the British introduced the Enlightenment, some Indians adopted a modern secular scientific worldview. Most of these came from high Hindu caste. When missionaries brought the Gospel, others became Christians in Western based churches). Accommodation movements made people adopt many of the elements of the new religion or culture, but reinterpret these in terms of their old worldviews. Revitalization movements by cultural collision made people look to the past, and seek to revive it through a new synthesis based on the old religion, but accommodating elements of the new. The Hindu revitalization movements were the result of India's encounter with the West. On the other hand, Neo-Hindu scholars were inspired by the recognition given to the Vedas and Upanishads by European scholars. They sought to create doctrines and institutions on the basis of the old texts, and organized Neo-Hinduism as a modern, formal 'high' religion. They rejected undesirable customs, such as idolatry and untouchable, as degenerate accretions to pure Vedic religion. They popularized their teaching by linking these to the great epics, the Mahabharata (with its Bhagavad Gita) and the Ramayanam, which are at the heart of popular Hinduism. On the other hand, these movements emerged out of the success of Christianity in winning untouchables. Hindu leaders became anxious about the landslide of the lower sections of Hindu society to Christianity, which, they said, weakened the solidarity of the society. Paul G. Hiebert, "The Christian Response to Hinduism," 325-327.

[317] Hiebert, "The Christian Response to Hinduism," 327.

[318] Ibid., 332.

California."[319] This mixing of cultures is also fraught with tension and conflict. Far from blending and mingling together, new barriers are emerging between peoples. At the heart of the conflict is religious belief. Ramachandra examines the complex interaction of some major world faiths, including Hinduism and Christianity. He looks at the distinctiveness of the Christian message in a world of many faiths, and asks if a truly tolerant, pluralistic society can ever emerge from a rejection of universal truth-claims.[320] Ramachardran's work is relevant to Hiebert's idea about a Neo-Hinduism worldview.

## 7. The Obstacles of a House Church

### Women's Leadership in Cultural Aspect

House church is not merely a result of social phenomena. It mixes with the structural figure of house which Paul Yonggi Cho suggested in his book, *Successful Home Cell Groups.* Younggi Cho illustrates how home cell groups developed and how home cell groups have brought about not only phenomenal growth, but also intimate fellowship and involvement. He describes his ministerial principle of home cell groups, the programs of home cell groups and some obstacles of home cell groups. Especially, he deals with women leadership of the small group in the cultural aspect.[321] In the case of Korean culture, men are offended by women leadership in leading Bible study and small groups in the beginning of Korean Christianity. Its cultural impact still remains in the church in Korea. Paul Younggi asserts that it is one of biggest problems among the small group in his church that needs to be overcome.[322] Like Korean church, women of house churches in India have also great opposition in their cultural position. How can they overcome it and get a training for developing their leadership?

Craig Ott and Gene Wilson write about role inequities in the church. Women make up an important part of the church-planting force, whether they are married or work alongside their husband. They also face some unique challenges. Some religious systems, particularly in Muslim and tribal cultures, have distinct patterns of worship and practice for women that tightly restrict cross-gender communication. The Apostle Paul worked in meaningful partnerships with women assistants such as Priscilla (Acts 18-19), Euodia, and Syntyche (Phil. 4) and with local workers such as Lydia (Acts 16), Nympha (Col. 4:15), Phoebe,

---

[319] Vinoth Ramachandra, *Faiths in Conflict?* (Secunderabad: OM, 1999), 9.

[320] Vinoth Ramachandra, Faiths In Conflict?, 75-85.

[321] Robert Banks, *Paul's Idea of Community: The Early House Churches in their Cultural Setting* (Peabody: Hendrickson Publishers, 2007), 124-126. According to Banks, there were cultural restrictions that placed upon women by Paul: Concerning dress (1 Cor. 11:10, 14, 15), within marriage (1 Cor. 11:7 - 16), and during church (1 Cor. 14:34-35). This kinds of cultural restriction is for the virtue of the church.

[322] Paul Yonggi Cho, *Successful Home Cell Groups* (Plainfield, Logos International, 1981), 32.

and others (Rom 16) in an age when women were rarely found in leadership positions.[323]

### Cultural Relationship's among Individuals

According to Younggi Cho, another cultural problem in the small group of the church is cultural relationships among individuals. Korea is a borrowing culture.[324] Church members in small groups borrow money from other members of the group. Sometimes it becomes a great obstacle for the small group ministry.[325] India is a relationship-center culture. They may therefore have some great inner obstacles about relationship among the House Church members for cultural reasons.

### Common Obstacles in Small Groups

Clyde Reid mentions the internal core contents which small groups dealt with in the church. His illustration in his book, *Group Alive-Church Alive: The Effective Use of Small Groups in the Local Church* can be applied in the house church as well. Reid provides the important basic elements of the group's life. He uses the social science called 'group psychology' for his analytical study. Reid says that the intensive group experience is the most significant social invention.[326] His book starts with the concept that small groups have "exploded" into every part of our social order – institutional and organizational, corporate, educational, and religious. He deals with the nature of a small group, leadership, and common problems of small groups.[327]

Some common small group problems can be identified. There are problems which grow out of conflicts in expectations about the group such as, (1) differences

---

[323] Craig Ott and Gene Wilson, *Global Church Planting: Biblical Principles and Best Practices for Multiplication* (Grand Rapids, Michigan: Baker Academic, 2011), 318.

[324] See. Sherwood Lingenfelter, *Transforming Culture* (Grand Rapids, Baker Book House, 1992), 83-105. Each culture understands the borrowing differently. Borrowing brings relationship problem in some cultures, but not in others. Therefore, some cultural issues of house church in every culture need to reflect on their own culture with biblical instruction and solution.

[325] Youggi Cho, *Successful Home Cell Groups*, 37.

[326] Clyde Reid, *Group Alive-Church Alive: The Effective use of Small Groups in the Local Church* (New York: Harper and Row, 1969), 7.

[327] Ibid., 93. According to Reid, common problems in small group are conflicts in expectations about the group, differences in understanding of the contract, leadership competition, and relation to authority. He also outlines a few additional group problems that arise with some regularity: 1. Groups can occasionally be hurtful because of it. 2. It is also possible for a group to be warm, concerned, and sensitive but completely self-centered. 3. A common problem in groups is the existence of a small power clique. 4. The discrepancy between the purpose of a meeting and the setting is a common problem. Many church buildings are constructed as formal settings that they do not encourage the kind of personal, informal encounter we now feel is essential for religious growth. This conflict simply calls for us to be aware of the setting we choose for a particular type of meeting, especially for small-group meetings. Ibid., 103.

in understanding of the contract,[328] (2) leadership competition, and (3) relation to authority.[329] In addition to these, when a small group has discussion, two different groups may appear: one group dominates that discussion, the other has apathy in the discussion. This small group has to make a very difficult decision because of these two kinds of people.[330] It is very common for an individual to attempt to dominate a group. The group may be afraid to interrupt him, or fear his anger if they oppose him. How to deal with this dominator in a small group (house church)? Reid contends that there is only one way to deal with the dominator, that is, tell him openly how members feel about his behavior, how it affects members. Members simply share honestly with him how his behavior affects members.[331] There are reasons for apathy in small groups. The small groups may become apathetic if they feel the subject they are discussing is not important or that they have an unimportant task, or members may become apathetic if they feel that the task is important, but that they do not have the resources or the ability to deal with it.[332]

### Relationship between Institutional Church and House Church

Victor Choudrie, in his book *The Church in Your House,* brought some issues which house churches must solve. Some of the contents of his book seem to view negatively toward the traditional church (structural church).[333] However, he asserts the need of theology for the house church and demands a renewal of the traditional churches. He tries to compare between two different church models: house church and traditional church (structural church). He also has emphasis on what a church should change and not change. Choudrie provides and carefully deals with vital issues in the house church movement, such as biblical basis, history and culture, leadership, worship, baptism, Lord's Supper, and women's ministry. However, his book has some conflicts with traditional and organizational churches because the author recognizes them as counterparts to the house church. Some leaders in the house church movement recognize the traditional church, but with a negative view. That influences the congregation of the house church. How can they overcome their negative perspective toward the structural church? How can they build their own house church theology? The task is that a house church needs to be balanced with the traditional church. The purpose of Choudrie's book is to start a critical dialogue for a radical restructuring

[328] The contents of contract are that purpose of group, meeting time and place, proposed sized of group, composition of group, and level of group interaction (business matters, discussion of ideas and personal sharing), leadership pattern, and group discussion. Ibid., 44.

[329] Ibid., 93.

[330] Ibid., 94-95.

[331] Ibid., 96.

[332] Ibid., 97.

[333] Victor Choudhrie, *The Church in Your House* (English Edition 2006), 1-9.

of the church, to remove the stranglehold of extra-biblical structures, and to restore the original New Testament model that merges with the culture of the people and resonates with the will of God.

According to Prosperly Bell Lyngdoh, early Christians faced the severity of persecution, and they were thrown out of temples and synagogues. For their own safety Christians met in their homes. The Gospel spread to the entire Roman Empire and beyond. This biblical example is good for the house church movement as it reminds us of the relationship between institutional structure (temple and synagogue) and house church in the early church.[334]

## Obstacles of Leadership

At least two dimensions impact leaders as they strive to carry out their leadership in the house church. One is lack of leadership training for the house church, the other is financial difficulty for his living.

### *Lack of Lay Leadership Training*

Lyngdon observes that the lack of lay leadership training is a very serious handicap for the house church planting ministry.[335] Pioneer workers are called not only to reach people with the Gospel, but also to equip God's people for their meaningful life together as well as service to others. He says that there are no other alternatives but to equip the lay people for the work.[336]

### *Financial Difficulty of Leadership*

Turner says that "The house church multiplication occurs with leaders who get little or no financial compensation for developing leaders within their respective network. Most of leaders that are trained have families and full time jobs while leading the various aspects of house churches."[337] Here are some questions that one should respond to about the financial obstacles for the leader in a house church: How do the leaders of house churches overcome their financial difficulty? Are they receiving any support from the house church or individuals? Do they have a secular job for their living? Are there any difficulties for leaders because they carry out both a secular job and leadership in house church? In what way does the financial difficulty impact their leadership in the house church?

## Some Obstacles that House Churches face toward Evangelism

First, some people understand the house church as a process toward building the church edifice. Glenn Earl Schaeffer proposed that the house church is a plausible model to evangelize and catechize urban Caucasian Canadians in

---

334 Prosperly Bell Lyngdoh, "Church-Based Training for Lay Church Planters in India," 14.

335 Ibid., 16.

336 Ibid.

337 Robert Lee Turner, "Leadership Development Process of Select House Church Network in North America: A Case Study," 2.

Toronto.[338] However, there are some obstacles for the house church to reach them. Schaeffer's study revealed that the house church is not usually considered a long-term solution. The goal of most congregations is to eventually build an edifice church in order to accommodate the growing worshipping community and to enhance their ability to evangelize and catechize the community. For this, he brought questions to consider: (a) How long do you plan to stay in this house church? (b) Is it a permanent situation? (c) Will it be tolerated for five, ten or twenty years?[339]

Second, Schaeffer argues that some people (especially low context people) desire privacy and the opportunity to choose who they want to get close to, but the worshipper is close to almost all participants in a house church. For this reason, the house church is not for everyone.[340]

Third, there is a danger of heresy. House churches often attract individuals who are *individualists* who are looking for a group that allows them to express their own individuality. These individualists have the potential of undermining the cohesion of the house church community, especially if they are promoting "all kinds of strange teachings" (Heb 13:9). A house church that becomes a haven for the propagation of false doctrines is doing a disservice to the Lord and his church (1Tim 1:3-11; 6:3; Rom 16:17-19). In order to counter the impact of these false doctrines, there needs to be high context communication in the house churches so that cohesion and uniformity in the group are developed.[341] This cohesion and uniformity might be achieved by the house church participants working towards doctrinal unity based on a thorough study of the Word of God and by implementing a liturgy that is rooted in the universal church. The location and people of the house church might change, but the creeds, confession, and liturgical practices remain constant and the congregation remains rooted in the doctrine and life of the universal church.[342]

Fourth, house churches are unable to provide space for expanding ministries and outreach. The house church community might decide to move to a larger building or set up many small house church centers where they carry out specialized ministry and mission work in the community.[343]

Fifth, some people seem to prefer certain settings. Some people prefer the anonymity of a large church and find that choirs, organs, and the historically-based liturgical traditions enrich their worship of God. Others less concerned for these things look for a church that provides an intimate setting where they

---

[338] Glenn Earl Schaeffer, "A Study of the House Church and Its Relevance for Planting Churches in the Greater Toronto Area" (PhD diss., Concordia Theological Seminary, 1996), 315.

[339] Ibid., 317.

[340] Ibid., 318.

[341] Ibid., 319.

[342] Ibid.

[343] Ibid., 320.

are known and loved by others, but yet teaches the Word of God in its truth and purity.[344] The use of a variety of ecclesiastical structures is helpful to the *missio* because they provide different environments in which the Holy Spirit can minister to a wide range of people.[345]

Sixth, a potential danger with the house church model is its overemphasis on horizontal relationships between people. Due to its small size, the house church community can focus so much on the development of relationships between people that the relationship between God and people is neglected.[346]

One of Glenn Schaeffer's research questions in *A Study of the House Church* is, what might deter a low context urban Caucasian Canadian from joining a house church?[347] To answer this, Schaeffer brought some responses from his research work. Low context people tend to be achievement-oriented. Therefore, the general attitude of these achievement-oriented house church participants was that the house church was a temporary structure.[348] The long-term expectation is that the congregation will own an edifice church to accommodate all the new worshippers. In this context, the house church is considered the first step towards a larger facility.[349] A result of Schaeffer's research is that many people in the house church believe that the house church is a temporary structure of church.

## The Lesson from the Past: How can the House Church Overcome the Obstacles?

### *Theological and Practical Aspect*

Sociologist Rodney Stark states that the Christian response to social conditions such as poverty, disease, and ostracism greatly facilitated its eventual triumph. Stark argues that Christianity became particularly attractive in the wake of large scale calamities such as plague, natural disasters, or military defeat because its theodicy provided a theological structure for explaining and accounting for them, its eschatology provided hope at an individual level, while on a pragmatic level the Christian concern and care for the poor, sick, and helpless won sympathy, support, and converts.[350]

### *Social Network*

In social network theory, L. Michael White observes that the attributes and actions of individuals are of less consequence and importance than the relationships that

---

344 Ibid., 322.

345 Ibid., 321.

346 Ibid., 322.

347 Ibid., 3.

348 Ibid., 171.

349 Ibid., 172

350 Rodney Stark, "Epidemics, Networks, and the Rise of Christianity," *Semeia* 56 (1992): 159-175.

exist between the individual and the group. One consequence of a high incidence within a social network is a tendency toward consistency of behavior among the group members together with a diminished capacity for deviation from established behavioral norms.[351] Consistency of behavior as Christians caused their faith. This faith led them to overcome the obstacles and pressure from outside. In addition, while groups organized around trade, ethnicity, and religion were present in most cities in the Roman Empire, the Roman authorities were often deeply suspicious of any association that was perceived to operate out of their control and so potentially threaten the social and political order.[352] In the case of India, the Hindu government or Hindu political groups are deeply suspicious of house churches as a threat to their Hindu religious and political order. For this reason, they menace house churches in India.

### *Overcoming Obstacles from Outside: China*

Those who join the TSPM (Three-Self Patriotic Movement) are wary that, if they remain outside the movement, they will be accused of being opposed to the government. TSPM made it clear that Christians must identify not only with the culture but also with the political philosophy of the country.[353] Love of country is placed ahead of love of church. That emphasis creates a dilemma for many house church Christians. Therefore, they may refuse to join the TSPM, yet they do love their country, and they are fully prepared to serve in their communities and follow the government in all secular affairs. But they do not believe that the church should be involved in political activities. Remembering past history, they fear that once again the church might be used for indoctrination classes and accusation meetings. They also believe that pastors should be chosen by church members on the basis of spiritual qualifications rather than appointed and supported by the Chinese government.[354] These experiences of Christian in China raise the case of India: how can the house churches communicate and respond to the Hindu government?

### *Changing Missional Direction*

The world house churches are transitions in leadership and missional direction. According to Jong Keol Yoo, today Chinese Protestant house churches are faced with a pastoral leadership crisis.[355] Daniel Kim observes that the house churches

---

[351] L. Michael White, "Social Networks: Theoretical Orientation and Historical Applications," *Semeia* 56 (1992): 32.

[352] Bradly S. Billings, "From House Church to Tenement Church: Domestic Space and the Development of Early Urban Christianity," 28.

[353] David Adeney, "Springtime for the Church in China," *Christianity Today,* June 18, 1982, 30.

[354] Ibid.

[355] Jong Keol Yoo, "Training Chinese House Church Leaders: Factors Influencing Leadership Development Strategies" (PhD diss., Southern Baptist Theological Seminary, 2005), 101.

are in a period of transition: (1) from emphasizing evangelism to pastoral care, (2) from seeking miraculous signs to biblical truth and apologetics, (3) from short-term to long-term leadership training, (4) from rural areas to cities, and (5) from Han people to cross-cultural mission.[356] These changes demand more trained, mature leaders than ever before. We need to examine in what way other house churches around the world are changing their missional direction. In China, for example, migration to the cities for economic survival has caused a rural church 'leadership drain'. The urban house churches do not have enough trained pastors to care for the new rural immigrants and new seekers from student and intellectual groups.[357]

## *Overcoming Obstacles of Theological Differences*

The house church should overcome theological obstacles from different denominations. For example, in 1984, Alan Munden criticized the house church movement from the Anglican Church's stand point. Munden believed that people are unaware of the important issues which are at stake over the doctrine of the church, ministry and sacraments. He views the house church movement as a schism, saying "Schismatic groups have appeared throughout the history of the church. We should take notice of how others dealt with them, and also re-evaluate our own position without totally condemning the new movements."[358] He says that "Since the issue is primarily a matter of ecclesiology, we should think through our doctrine of the church."[359] Although, the house church was understood as a schismatic group from some denominations in the beginning, most denominations have begun their own house church. Therefore, house churches should reevaluate in the light of each theological dimension.

## *Overcoming Dissatisfaction with Leadership*

Each denomination accepts the house church movement as a mission phenomenon. Gary Alexander says, "Communal or not, charismatic or not, home churches are every bit as much the church of God as the most established denomination. And they might very well be the wave of the future."[360] However, Alexander interviewed Christians in terms of the reason why they do not want to go to churches. The reason was dissatisfaction with pastoral leadership. They

---

[356] Daniel Kim, "The Effective Missionary Strategy for the Chinese House Church," *The Chinese Church and Missions* 10 (2001): 93-94.

[357] Jong Keol Yoo, "Training Chinese House Church Leaders: Factors Influencing Leadership Development Strategies," 102.

[358] Alan Munden, "Encountering the House Church Movement: A Different Kind of Christianity," *Anvil* 1 (1984): 213.

[359] Ibid., 212.

[360] Gary Alexander, "House Churches Your Hope for the Future? " *Christian Life*, January, 1982, 32.

would say, "We love the people, but we're really not unhappy with our own pastor."[361] Therefore, they meet every Thursday night to share their faith at home with a different group. Alexander argues that this dissatisfaction with pastoral leadership led those Christians to the house church in the North America in the 1980s. The questions arise: what is the difference of leadership between these two: institutional and house church leadership? Are there any dissatisfactions of house church leadership from house church members? If yes, what are they?

### *Overcoming False Teachers*

House churches are susceptible to false teachers because of the lack of instruction and Christian literature. It is easy for Christians to be led astray by false teachers. For this reason, some house churches face dangers and divisions. House church leaders are afraid that their fellowship may be infiltrated by a false teacher. For example, some house churches teachers like Witness Lee have placed so much emphasis on miracles and healing that they have failed to realize the importance of having a faith that is truly grounded in the knowledge of Christ as he is revealed in the Scriptures. Divisions also arise because some believe they should join the local committee set up by the TSPM; others believe such an attachment would involve compromise. For these reasons, the greatest need is for biblical materials and pastor-teachers who can lead new believers into the knowledge of the truth.[362]

### *Overcoming Restriction of Being House Church Members*

In the Reformation era, one of characteristics for churches influenced by the new movement seems to have been to seek high spiritual standards. John Howard Yoder states that in our day many have found that hard to do in large churches with low membership standards. He argues that some churches, such as Anabaptists, suggested that only churches with high standards could practice the high moral and spiritual standards the Bible requires. Yoder believes that Martin Luther opposed them bitterly and advocated a state church open to anyone. However, in his 1526 essay, *The German Mass*, Luther reveals that he himself would have rejoiced to participate in a small, face-to-face fellowship.[363] In the case of house churches, do they open their door to every one? Or is there any restriction to enter the door to house church? If they have some restriction to become a member of house church, what is the reason for that?

### *Overcoming Disadvantages of Small Groups*

In the context of North America, Christianity has experienced a distinct small-group movement since 1954. This means North American Christianity has been

---

[361] Ibid.

[362] David Adeney, "Springtime for the Church in China," 30.

[363] John Howard Yoder, "Martin Luther's Forgotten Vision," The Other Side, April, 1977, 66.

under the influence of the small group movement.[364] We can look at the house church as comparable to a small group. There are some potential cautions for small groups. These can be applied to the house church. According to Warren Bird, (1) today's small groups may lack the stability of yesteryear's networks of family and church; (2) They may be more concerned with the emotional state of the individual than with spiritual formation; some are prone to accent subjective experiences more than objective truths. Some scholars point out the weakness of the small groups that can be applying to the house church.

> J.I. Packer believes that when churches encourage people to join small groups, "it is not so much thought of as a way of seeking God as much as seeking Christian friends. The vertical axis is not emphasized as much as the horizontal axis." Wuthnow argues that the Bible studies for small groups do little to increase the biblical knowledge of their members. Hestenes says, "Small groups easily become too faddish or too psychologically oriented whenever they are not grounded in the authority of Scripture or the centrality of God, and in the need for redemption, conversion, and the transforming power of the Holy Spirit."[365]

Warren Bird also set forth that another potential pitfall is spiritual abuse. He points out numerous examples of churches and groups that control, manipulate, and misuse power in a way that could be called spiritually abusive. Bird points out the weakness of small groups. He says that small groups have a tendency toward weak teaching, confusion of purpose, lack of leadership, and even such mundane concerns as inadequate childcare.[366] In what way can the house church overcome the disadvantages that small groups have?

---

[364] Warren Bird, " The Great Small-Group Takeover," Christian Today, Febuary 7, 1994, 26.

[365] Ibid., 29.

[366] Ibid.

Chapter 4

# Research Design

The purpose of this qualitative study is to analyze and evaluate the house church as a mission strategy for work with Hindu migrants as well as locals living in the city. In this stage of the study, the house church in India is defined as the most effective mission strategy for the Hindu migrants and locals. This chapter will address the following questions regarding this study: (1) the nature of study, (2) limitations of the research, (3) delimitations of the research, (4) a description of how the study carried out, (5) the sources to be used and how they were used, and (6) how the data collected was analyzed.

## 1. Nature of the Study

This study was an ethnographic study based on interviews to be conducted with pastors or leaders of the house churches which are actively involved in church planting in cities of India. The ethnographic study best fits the type of research being considered under this proposal since there are not many research studies on house churches in cities of India (even though Atual Y. Aghamkar had done his research work on mission toward Hindus of cities). This research is confined to house churches in cities of India. It had aspects of being an ethnography study as well as being a phenomenological study by virtue of its descriptive nature.[367] It is

[367] Ghada Abu Shosah, "Employment of Colaizzi's strategy in Descriptive Phenomenology: A Reflection of A Researcher," European Scientific Journal 70 (2012): 31-43. P.F. Colaizzi process for phenomenological data analysis. 1. Each transcript should be read and re-read in order to obtain a general sense about the whole content. 2. For each transcript, significant statements that pertain to the phenomenon under study should be extracted. These statements must be recorded on a separate sheet noting their pages and lines numbers. 3. Meanings should be formulated from these significant statements. 4. The formulated meanings should be sorted into categories, clusters of themes, and themes. 5. The findings of the study should be integrated into an exhaustive description of the phenomenon under study. 6. The fundamental structure of the phenomenon should be described.

also expected that this is a qualitative study, since no quantitative data is expected to be collected.

The intent of this study is to examine the possibility of a house church as a mission strategy means through research in the relationship between some variables represented by research questions. In order to accomplish the goal of the proposed research, qualitative method research design was employed to guide this process. In the qualitative method of the study, interviews were used. The objective is to gather adequate data to create categories. The reason this research uses qualitative methods is that its scope of research is not broad. According to Mengsteab, "redundant information may not have value to the proving or disproving of the hypothesis."[368] Overall, a qualitative methods approach is considered more appropriate in this study. The reason is that a body of literature in house church exists, the variables are known, and there are existing theories that need explorations.

## 2. Description of How the Study was Carried Out

The conduct of the study started by contacting local house church leaders and pastors to interview. The researcher has already been working with pastors and leaders of house churches in Bangalore and Chikkibalapura district (near a rural area of Bangalore) as a partner for planting house churches. The researcher selected a few people who worked and studied with him at previously at a seminary in India as a mediator to assist the procedure of the interview.

The researcher arranged for interviewing the pastors or leaders who are serving the house churches in cities through the internet media tool called *Skype*. He arranged ten interviews to be conducted. Then interview questions to be answered were distributed to twenty four pastors (or leaders). The researcher had already conducted interviews with two pastors as protocol questions. He analyzed these interviews for forming follow-up protocol questions. These interviews were conducted as time-permitted since there is a time difference between USA and India.

The researcher took notes during the actual interviews themselves. In order to protect the identities of those who offered to participate in the interviews, names of the informants is de-identified in the final dissertation using a matrix approach. Once the interviews were completed, the researcher started to analyze the data.

For any questions where there was a high degree of coherence of the responses, the reasons for this coherence is discussed. Likewise, for any research

---

7. Finally, validation of the findings should be sought from the research participants to compare the researcher's descriptive results with their experiences.

[368] Yohannes A. Mengsteab, "Effective Urban Congregations: A Study of Ministry Factors That Contribute to the Effectiveness of a Lutheran Church –Missouri Synod Urban Congregation" (Ph.D. diss., Concordia Theological Seminary, 2008), 81.

questions for which there is a low degree of coherence of responses, the reasons for this lack of coherence is discussed. For this study, the following were the research questions and operational questions, along with protocol questions:

This research problem is guided by four research questions: What mission aspects of house church make it possible to reach the migrants as well as the locals to evangelize and catechize in the urban context in India? In other words, in what ways is the house church in the urban context evangelizing and catechizing migrants and locals into God's family?

Grand Tour Questions

In what ways is the house church in urban settings evangelizing and catechizing migrants and locals into God's family?

### *Research Question 1: Interdependent relationship and leadership in the House Church*

In what ways do an interdependent relationship and leadership influence the house church to evangelize and catechize migrants and locals?

Operational Question 1

In what ways do you understand an interdependent relationship in the house church? In what way do you understand leadership in the house church?

Operational Question 2

In your opinion, what are the results of the leadership and an interdependent relationship in the house church?

Operational Question 3

In your opinion, in what ways do the roles of an interdependent relationship influence people in the house church to reach migrants and locals to evangelize and catechize? In your opinion, in what ways do the roles of leadership influence the house church to reach migrants as well as locals to evangelize and catechize them?

*Protocol Question 1.* In what ways can you describe the interdependent relationship between the pastor (leader) and congregations?

*Protocol Question 2.* In your house church, what are the contents of interdependent relationship between the pastor (leader) and congregations? In other words, what are the factors that promote their interdependent relationship in your house church?

*Protocol Question 3.* In your opinion, what are the benefits of an interdependent relationship between pastor (leader) and congregations?

*Protocol Question 4.* In your opinion, how does the interdependent relationship between the pastor (leader) and congregation influence the house church members to reach migrants or locals in order to evangelize?

*Protocol Question 5.* In your opinion, what is the practical meaning of "house church" in light of the interdependent relationship between the pastor (leader) and congregation?

### ***Research Question 2: House church planting model in the city***

What is a proper model for a house church model that will influence the house church to evangelize and catechize migrants and locals in the city?

Operational Question 1

Before you planted your house church, what was your idea about a model for a house church that influences to evangelize and catechize migrants or locals in your city?

Operational Question 2

After you planted your house church, now what is your idea about a model for a house church that influences to evangelize and catechize migrants or locals in your city?

Operational Question 3

In your opinion, what is an ideal model for a house church that influences to evangelize and catechize migrants or locals in your city?

*Protocol Question 1.* Before you planted your house church, what was your idea about a house church? At that time, what kind of house church had you planned to establish?

*Protocol Question 2.* After you planted your house church, did you change your idea about a house church? If yes, what made you change your idea about a house church?

*Protocol Question 3.* In what way can you describe your house church model in the present? What are the notable differences before and after the house church plant?

*Protocol Question 4.* What is your future plan for your house church? What is your future model for house church?

### ***Research Question 3: Worldview Change***

In what ways do house churches put their effort to transform the worldview of the migrants as well as locals who hold a Hindu worldview in order to evangelize and catechize them in the city?

Operational Question 1

In what ways do economic migration and urban environment affect migrants to change their previous religious and cultural understanding? In what ways does the change of urban environment affect locals to change their previous religious and cultural understanding?

Operational Question 2

In what ways does your house church communicate with Hindu people in order to deliver the gospel and transform their worldview?

Operational Question 3

In what ways have Hindu migrants experienced their worldview transform after they have converted?

*Protocol Question 1.* In what ways does the economic migration and urban environment affect the migrants and the locals to change their previous religious and cultural understanding?

*Protocol Question 2.* How do you deliver the gospel to the Hindu immigrants and the Hindu locals who join your house church?

*Protocol Question 3.* How does the house church lead the migrants or locals in the spiritual aspect? What kinds of programs does your house church have in order to support the spiritual needs of immigrants and locals?

*Protocol Question 4.* What kinds of cultural elements from Hinduism does your house church have? How does the congregation in your house church respond to the elements of Hinduism in their lives? What do you think about Yoga? What do the congregations of the house church do on the Hindu festivals?

### *Research Question 4: Obstacles*

What kinds of obstacles does a house church confront when they evangelize and catechize the migrants or locals into God's family?

Operational Question 1

What kinds of inner obstacles does your house church have when she evangelizes and catechizes the migrants and locals into God's family in the city? In what ways does the house church overcome these obstacles? What elements of house church help her to overcome?

Operational Question 2

What kinds of outer obstacles does your house church have when she evangelizes and catechizes the migrants and locals into God's family in the city? In what ways has house church overcome these obstacles? What elements of house church help her to overcome?

*Protocol Question 1.* What were the inner difficulties in your house church? How did you overcome (deal with) them?

*Protocol Question 2.* What were the outer difficulties in your house church? How did you overcome (deal with) them?

*Protocol Question 3.* In your opinion, how do you describe the house church as a mission tool evangelism during persecution?

## 3. A Description of Data Analysis

The sources used are interview responses to the protocol questions which were formulated as part of the research questions. Notes were taken during each interview, with these notes used in reconstructing the interviews. It is anticipated that each interviewee was asked all eleven operational questions and their responses recorded. Responses from the interviewees was collated for each the operational questions to the research questions. The degree of coherence in the responses of the various interviewees was determined. Based on their response, an attempt is made to find common threads in the responses of the interviewees. The results are discussed from Chapter 5 to Chapter 8 of the dissertation for each of the research questions queried.

Chapter 5

# Research Finding 1: Interdependent Relationship

This study started with the research problem: in what ways do the house churches in Indian urban areas evangelize and catechize migrants and locals into God's family? In the literature review, some scholars in the studies for house church have provided some theories: archeological theory and social network theory. In Archeological theory, R. Krautheimer and Bradly S. Billings provided us the archeological development process for the early house church. Its development process helps us to narrow down our range of understanding between the house church and the modern church building. In Social network theory, L. Michael White studied the early house church, especially the concept of primary anchor, which is the core term of social network theory provided a significant understanding for house church leadership. It is also important how the primary anchor influenced individuals in their conversion process. As Rodney Stark declared in the literature review, the effect of a social network and its contribution was that the church had grown through its social network during the persecution period. The main results from the application of social network theory are the transforming of one's worldview by faith, the importance of leadership for religious recruitment by a social network, and the significance of interpersonal relationships. In the literature review, David W. Augsburger supports interdependent relationship theory as an ideal biblical model. He views this theory as alternative model for overcoming the Western worldview of independence. In this chapter, the researcher analyze the interview data with applying interdependent social theory in order to find out what factors influence to evangelize migrants and locals in India.

## 1. Interdependent Relationship and Leadership in the House Churches

This section deals with data regarding how interdependent relationship and leadership influence the house church to evangelize and catechize migrants and locals

Understanding the Relationship between the Pastors and the Believers

Under the research question 1, operational question 1 is: In what ways do you (research participants) understand an interdependent relationship and leadership in the house church? What are the factors that promote interdependent relationship between the pastor and the believers in the house church?

In order to respond to these questions, the contents that research participants expressed regarding the relationship between the pastors and the believers are categorized as below. As seen in the diagram (Figure 3) four nodes (leader and follower, father and children, spiritual caregiver, friend) were categorized under the theme, Understanding of the Relationship between the Pastors and the Believers. The theme is closely related, not only to their relationship, but also their roles that promote their interdependent relationships. Even though there is no direct expression for some research participants (Non-response) regarding the relationship between the pastors and the believers, their descriptive contents for the interdependent relationship between pastors and the believers belong to the category of Father and Children.

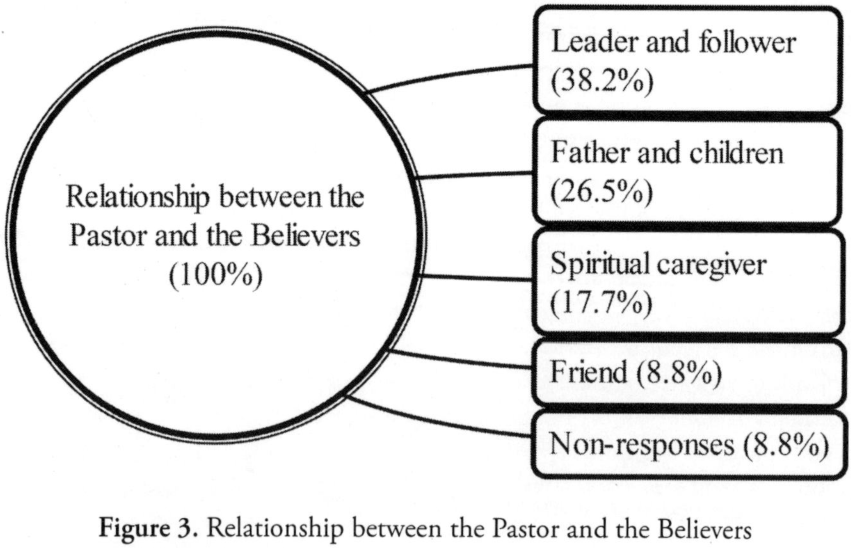


**Figure 3.** Relationship between the Pastor and the Believers

### *Leader and Followers*

The data shows that 38.2% of research participants understood the relationship between pastor and believers in the house churches as 'Leader and Follower.' (RP01, RP03, RP06, RP07, RP13, RP15, RP19, RP25, RP26, RP30, RP31,

RP34). In particular, some emphasized the spiritual dimension when they expressed the pastor as the leader. "Leader is the spiritual head" (RP6), "Leader is considered as spiritual head" (RP07), "A spiritual Leader. I lead the people and they follow me" (RP19).

Participants considered the relationship between the pastor and believers as a relationship between leader and follower that expresses trust, a partner relationship for common goal, and advisor relation for problem-solving.

First of all, the trust relationship between the pastor and the believers in the house church begins with how the believers understand about the role of the pastor. RP01said, "My house church had not structure led by one boss, but interdependence relationship between the leaderships becomes the model for the interdependence relationship model of the congregation in the house church." RP25 said,

> Since the church is the body of Christ, pastor and believer are part of the body of Christ, there is no head of the church, but Jesus Christ. Pastor is a part of Church, just as all the other parts of the body, just as the entire believers are the part of the body of Christ. Since pastor and believers are all parts of the body of Christ, and definitely all parts of the body depends on each other to function effectively according to the will of God. Since Christ has pastors and believers as a part of the body, so eventually the pastor and believers are depending on each other to function effectively.

Thus, their interdependent relationship starts with this understanding of the believers about the pastor. More concretely, research participants who understood the relationship between the pastor and the believers as 'leader and follower' said that building a trust relationship improves their understanding of their interdependent relationship between the pastor and the believers. RP01 said, "Trust among individuals increase interdependence relationship." RP33 said, "By maintaining the good will, people see me as a leader. Trust is built."

Second, participants think a leader should propose clear common goals to the believers. This promotes an interdependent relationship between pastor and believers. RP26 said, "Leader is motivator who lead the believers toward common goal." RP31 said, "(Pastor is) leader. I have a certain vision about people in extending God's kingdom in this world. As a leader, I lead my people in the right direction towards God."

Third, participants see the pastor as a leader who gives advice for problem-solving:

> RP03,
>
> When they face some kinds of hostile situation at home; they come and share with us first. They may not go around getting people's

> opinion. They share with me different aspects; they have liberty to share about their not only spiritual life, but also parental reaction. Through their sharing, they get solution for themselves. They look at for more of counsels, how they get the solution from the problem. They look at the guider the person who can become a guru, master. Believers understand us as leader, although we are not wearing formal clothe like mainline church pastors.

RP12 also stated the pastor is a leader; he emphasized the role of the leader as the mentor who meets the believers regularly.

We need to give attention to what are the main factors that promote these interdependent relationships between the pastor and believers. The main three factors are shown in the diagram: Interdependent relationship model, Proposal for house church ministry model, and Problem-solving of house church.

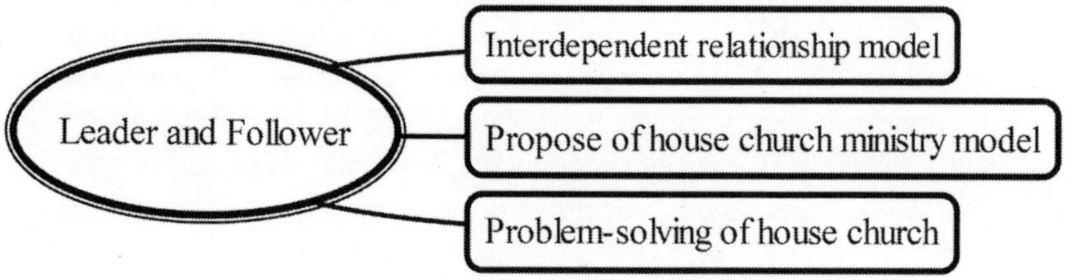


**Figure 4.** Leader and Follower

Interdependent Relationship Image of House Church that Propose to the Believers Promote Interdependent Relationship

Proposing interdependent relationship image of house church promotes the interdependent relationship between the pastor and believers. It is categorized by three sub-factors. Research participants (RP01, RP03, RP13, RP15, RP26, RP25, RP31, and RP32) understood these three sub-factors to promote an interdependent relationship between the pastor and the believers: Multiple roles of leaders, the roles of the believers, and spiritual dimension of interdependent relationship. In other words, an interdependent relationship image of the house church appears in the multiple roles of leadership, the roles of the believers, and spiritual aspect of the interdependent relationship.

First of all, according to the study's data, it was found that research participants counted multiple roles of leaders as proposing interdependent relationship image. RP01, RP03 and RP25 expressed that a house church is not led by one leader. "My house church had not structure led by one boss…" (RP01), "In house church, there is no one big leader. There are few leaders. There is not one pastor" (RP03), and "there is no head of the church, but Jesus Christ" (RP25).

As RP03 mentioned, the pastor alone could not solve individual's problems in the house church, "in the house church, there is no one man who can solve the all the problems of the individuals come for the fellowship." Therefore, it needs cooperation of several leaders in the house church.

RP01 stated multiple roles of leaders in the house became a model of interdependent relationship for the believers. "Several leaders take in charge of multiple roles in the house church. My house church had not structure led by one boss, but interdependence relationship between the leaderships becomes the model for the interdependence relationship model of the congregation in the house church." Thus, multiple roles of leaders are a factor promoting interdependent relationship in the house church.

RP25 emphasized on the need of interdependent relationship in the house church for effective function of their relationship.

> Since the church is the body of Christ, pastor and believer are part of the body of Christ, there is no head of the church, but Jesus Christ. Pastor is a part of Church, just as all the other parts of the body, just as the entire believers are the part of the body of Christ. Since pastor and believers are all parts of the body of Christ, and definitely all parts of the body depends on each other to function effectively according to the will of God. Since Christ has pastors and believers as a part of the body, so eventually the pastor and believers are depending on each other to function effectively.

RP01 put an emphasis on the trust among individuals for effective function of multiple roles of leaders and believers. "Trust among individuals increase interdependence relationship."

Second, in the data, the research participants counted the roles of the believers: using of gifts, common goal and leadership of layperson. It is important not only for a leaders' multiple roles but also the roles of believers in order to improve the interdependent relationship among individuals in the house church. RP26 described one of the believers' roles that they can use their gifts and influence to support each other in order to reach their common goal. "Interdependent is relational, where everyone uses their gifts and influences to support each other and work towards common goal."(RP26) "Few believers who mature equally handle all of the people" (RP03).

Third, according to the data, the research participants counted the spiritual dimension of interdependent relationship as: Spiritual relationship and growth, spiritual leadership and mentoring, and spiritual care and concern. The multiple roles of several leaders and the individual role of the believers improve the interdependent relationship in the house church. There is a close relation between the house church pastor and the believers' spiritual dimension.

RP34 responded that the word of God is the main factor to maintain and form an interdependent relationship in the house church. "The word of God is the key element which will help us to be in interdependent relationship" (RP34).

RP03 also described that he can grasp spiritual the status of the believers through interdependent relationship between the pastor and the believers. "We have liberty to know each other personally. As you interact, you know their social status, their spiritual growth."

As RP06's expression, "Leader is the spiritual head", he emphasized the spiritual leadership in the relationship between the pastor and the believers. RP31 also stated spiritual leadership and mentoring as a promoting factor for an interdependent relationship in the house church. According to him, these two factors take important roles for the believer to have the sense of belongingness. "Spiritual leadership and mentoring are the key contents of our relationship. People have the sense of belongingness when they come to our house church. This promotes our relationship with others." RP13 also expressed that mentorship is a promoting factor for interdependent relationship. "The relationship is developed through a regular mentorship and through fellowship groups. These relationships are ways we can build the church" (RP13).

Furthermore, spiritual care and concern is a promoting factor for interdependent relationship in the house church. RP06, RP15 and RP26 portrayed care and concern as promoting factors for an interdependent relationship.

RP06,

> The factor that promoting interdependent relationship is in the matter of caring and being an extended family member....when people are sick, we give them the best care and concern. Death is another important factor, which gives the strong sense of interdependent relationship. When some believers die, we are with their family

RP15 described that "Spiritual needs are given, health awareness, life style counseling, and family counseling" as factors for promoting interdependent relationship. RP26 also expressed promoting factor for interdependent relationship. He says, "Bond, friendship, care for each other and affinity is often the starting point."

Proposal for House Church Ministry Model that Promotes an Interdependent Relationship

Proposal for a house church ministry model that promotes an interdependent relationship between pastor and the believers (RP01,RP03, RP19, RP25, RP30) centered around two types as follows: Suggestion for Self-support church model and Team ministry model.

First, RP03 expressed that a house church should be a self-supporting church. He stated that economic independence of the church and to support pastors (leaders) is an important part of a self-supporting church.

> We teach them to bring their tithe and offering to support the church and leader. Not only for money but also in kind. Once we receive the

> kinds, it is kind of blessing to the pastor. Since we have many house churches, there is central fund from the house churches for supporting the leaders. As they grow, the house church established as self-sufficient church. Then they can support to the leader of the house church.

Self-support church and supporting leaders is closely connected to the interdependent relationship between the pastor and the believers. In order to become a self-supporting house church, it is essential for pastor (leaders) to carry out their roles equally. This view is also expressed by RP01, RP19, RP25, RP30 who propose a team ministry model.

Second, in the data, research participants supported a team ministry model for house church ministry. The team ministry model stresses the role and function of the believers as a voluntary community and its interdependent relationship between the pastor and the believers. RP01 stated the leader and believers are essentially in equal positions. "… Leader or elder is a member of congregation… Several leaders take in charge of multiple roles in the house church." RP30 also stated the pastor and the believer minster as a team. "The pastor and the congregation they work together and they cannot work independently they have to have an interdependent relationship as one body." RP19 described church as a voluntary community that make decisions as group not by the leader alone. "My leadership qualities help them to take decisions. I don't ask for tithes or money since it is a voluntary fellowship, people love to come for this fellowship." RP25 portrayed the role and function of the believers in the house church ministry.

> The believers function together in the house church. One of thing in the church fellowship every Sunday all believer need to take a role. Open prayer will be done by one believer and distribution of the Lord's Supper element will be given by other people, worship is done by other believers. Sharing is done by other believers and all of activities that we have we gather for the church. Every almost believers have function and contribute to the ministry of the church (RP25).

## Problem-Solving of House Church

Problem-solving of house church promotes an interdependent relationship between pastor and believers (RP03, RP07, and RP19).

First, research participants expressed how leadership acts to solve the problem in the house church. "When they face some kinds of hostile situation at home; they come and share with us first" (RP03), "In times of hardship, the leader is the first one to be contacted. And it is the leader that gathers the believers to respond to the situation" (RP07).

Next, research participants described how leadership helps the believer make a decision by themselves in the house church. RP03 stated that the believers are looking for the leader to solve the problem through counseling. "They look at for more of counsels, how they get the solution from the problem." This counseling is a way to solve the problem of the believers. RP19 also depicted how he helps believers to solve their problem by themselves. "My leadership qualities help them to take decisions."

### *Father and Children*

"The best way to describe the interdependent relationship between the pastor (leader) and congregation is that of Father and Children." (RP02). Twenty-six and one half percentage (26.5%) of research participants understood the relationship between pastor and believers in the house churches as father and children (RP02, RP12, RP14, RP16, RP17, RP18, RP20, RP21, RP32).

> "Pastor is spiritual father" (RP14), "We follow - One family Concept. I am their Father."(RP16); "Spiritual Father" (RP17), "As a spiritual father or Pastor" (RP18); "Since I am above 60, it is a Father and Child relationship that maintains our house church; People know about my life, therefore, it brings and promote interdependence relationship among the congregations" (RP21). "People accept me as their spiritual father" (RP32).

Only RP12 expressed their relationship as parents and children, all the rest expressed it as father and children. Thus, research participants understood father and children as an expression of the interdependent relationship between pastor and believers in the house churches.

However, we need to heed the question: What are the main factors that promote these interdependent relationships between the pastor and believers? The main factors that promote an interdependent relationship between pastors and believers by research participants who expressed their relationship as father and children are categorized by three factors: servant leadership, decision making authority, and life sharing.

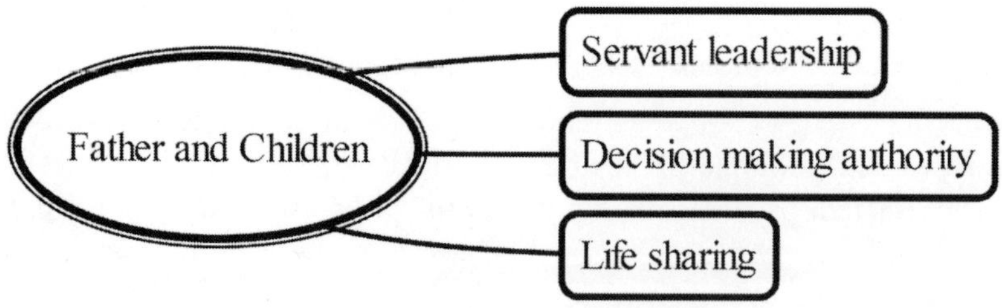


**Figure 5.** Father and Children

Servant Leadership Relationship

Servant leadership relationship promotes interdependent relationship. How servant leadership promotes an interdependent relationship between pastor and believers is categorized by three sub-factors. Research participants understood that these three sub-factors were: providing each other's needs, leadership emerging in the interdependent relationship, and intimated and close personal relationship.

First, research participants set forth their ideas that providing for each other's spiritual and physical needs is a factor promoting an interdependent relationship: "Both (the pastor and the believers) need each other. Father is need of affection in return of the care he takes of children. Children need father to nurture them holistically. Pastor provides spiritual truth to his believers of day life situations" (RP02); "We take care of people spiritually when they are in needs" (RP32). Furthermore, participants described not only the relationship between pastor and believers who provide for each other's needs, but also the relationship among the believers who provide other's needs in the house church. "They depend upon each other because each provides something the other needs" (RP12), "Sick people are taken care" (RP17). Meanwhile, even though RP11 did not make use of the expression 'father and children', his statement clearly sets forth his idea that the pastor leads the believers to provide for each other's needs in the house church: "During the week, we have prayer meeting for one another so that we can have not only fellowship but also we can explain each one of problems, so we can communicate each other. Sometime we help each other financially. We are usually praying for each other in the house" (RP11).

Second, participants who understood the relationship between pastor and believers as 'father and children' depicted leadership as a promoting factor of an interdependent relationship. In light of this understanding, leadership emerges from the interdependent relationship as they depend on each other as well as lead each other. RP12 and RP02 portrayed this. "They depend upon each other because each provides something the other needs" (RP12). "They (pastor and believers) lead themselves and each other" (RP02). Thus, the pastor and the believers both depend on each other as well as leading each other.

Third, research participants who understood the relationship between pastor and believers as 'father and children' described intimate and close personal relationships as a promoting factor of interdependent relationship. RP12: "An interdependent relationship is a close personal relationship between two people, who live together. In church, pastor and congregation must have intimate relationship."

While RP22 did not use the expression 'father and children', his statement clearly set forth the relationship between pastor and the believers as very close, an intimate personal relationship, like family.

> You can build the relationship between the pastor and the congregation. You just have handful of people, you know each of names, and you knows names of the children. The house church is like family structure. So, that base bond between the pastor and the church members. the role of the house church pastor in India is more

> intimated relationship. For example, if somebody is sick, I went to them, I attend them; I spend time with them. That is great bond that developed between the house church pastor and the congregation. But in the house church, we know the children, we know their parents, we know their family financial problem go through, we know if there are other issues, so that's greater communication that is built in the house church between the pastor and other congregation's families.

### Decision Making Authority

Decision making authority promotes interdependent relationship. How does decision making promote an interdependent relationship between pastor and believers? It categorized by three sub-factors as follows which research participants understood as: Pastor as decision maker, Attitude for problem-solution, decision making authority as a serving tool.

First, research participants who understood the relationship between pastor and believers as 'father and children' expressed problem-solving as a promoting factor of interdependent relationship. RP14 said, "Problem solving attitude promotes the relationship." RP17 described that "Pastor is concerned about to pray for them in their problems." RP18 said, "I care for them as I help in their trouble." Thus, a problem-solving attitude with care and concern toward the believers in the house church promote an interdependent relationship between the pastor and the believers.

Second, research participants (RP16 and RP29), who also understood the relationship between pastor and believers as 'father and children', depicted the pastor as a decision maker that as a promoting factor of an interdependent relationship.

RP16 said, "I am their Father, it is all depend upon my decision." His statement shows us the pastor has the significant decision making. It seems that the pastor who has decision making ability directly connects to the believers' problem solution. Furthermore, even though RP29 did not use of expression 'father and children,' his statement clearly set forth his idea that the pastor has decision making in the relationship between pastor and the believers.

> They are dependent on Pastor in various ways as they are illiterate; therefore, they are completely dependent on Pastor for their spiritual growth. They follow the oral tradition and therefore, what the pastor says is final verdict for them. Even for other things like decision making in the family also consulted with the Pastor because he is considered as person with Divine knowledge etc.

Third, participants considered decision making as a serving tool to a promoting factor of interdependent relationship. As RP17's statement, "For all major decisions, I help the members", the decision-making authority of the pastor is for helping and serving the believers.

Research participants portrayed that the relationship between the pastor and believers is not a relationship of "hegemony and dependence" but of "practicing decision-making authority for serving, helping and problem solving." In other words, the pastor has decision-making authority for problem-solving to serve the believers.

Life sharing

Life sharing also promotes an interdependent relationship. Knowing each other's life promotes an interdependent relationship between pastor and believers. Research participants categorized such life sharing by three sub-factors: love, concern and care. These three sub-factors promote an interdependent relationship between the pastor and the believers.

Research participants noted that the pastor should understand the believers' desires for their life. According to RP16, the believers' desire for loving each other promotes an interdependent relationship. "The love we show them is marvelous. People long for love outside the society, but we care for them like Jesus. It promotes our relationship in the house church." RP21 expressed that love is the core of an interdependent relationship. "Sharing the love, we show the love to members who comes to our doorstep. Love is the key content of interdependence relationship which unites and builds together." RP17 commented that love between the pastor and believers lead them to pray for each other's problems with concern. This concern continues in caring for other. "Love between Pastor and believers. Pastor is concerned about to pray for them in their problems. Sick people are taken care" (RP17). Reversely, the believers should know pastor's life. According to RP21, "People know about my life, therefore, this brings and promotes interdependence relationship among the congregations." RP20 also stated "True love and discipline" is a promoting factor for an interdependent relationship.

## *Friend*

Research showed that 8.8% of the participants understood the relationship between the pastor and believers in house churches as that of friends (RP04, RP05, and RP10). RP04 said, "The relationship between Pastor and the believers are friend types of interdependent relationship." RP10 also illustrated that the leader (pastor) is the one who builds friendships in the house church. "Leader is person who makes friendship with the believers with interacting individually and visits their house." Although RP05 did not mention the word 'friend', he illustrated the relationship between them as a close intimate relationship like friends.

> When we talk about interaction as a whole in spiritual, social and whatever, access to the leader and pastor is easy in the house church… it becomes easy to open up to access to the pastor to ask some very

personal questions. It also becomes for the pastor and leader to address them at very personal level… now that we become too closer one another" (RP05).

The main factors that promote an interdependent relationship between pastor and believers are categorized by two factors as below in the diagram. The research participants who expressed their relationship as like a friend, understood the main factors as: the Pastor's Right Attitude for the Relationship with Accountability and Adoptability, and Easiness.

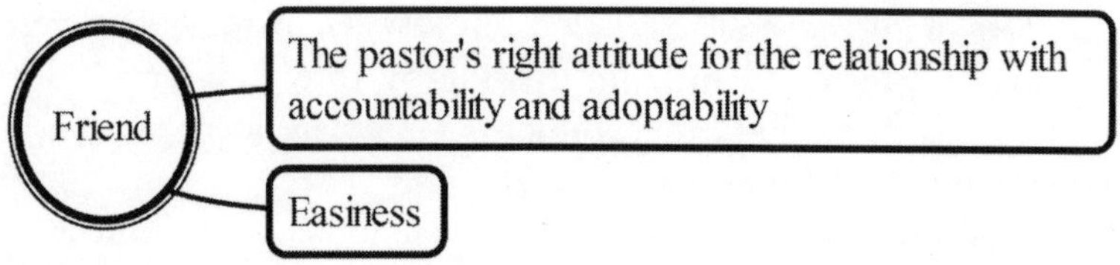


**Figure 6.** Friend

The Pastor's Right Attitude for the Relationship

It was found that research participants (RP04, RP10) believed that the pastor's right attitude (influence of pastor's life style and responsibility) promoted an interdependent relationship between pastor and believers.

RP04 emphasized that the importance of leader's life style is the main content of a relationship. "My ethical life and simple lifestyle, respecting others, and godly nature are contents of the relationship." RP10 put an emphasis on the pastor's responsibility. "Pastor has more responsibility to the believers…" Especially, RP10 expressed that the matter of what the pastor should know for the believers is accountability and adoptability.

> The person who starts the house church should know about accountability and adoptability. Leader need to make a climate for the congregation to adopt their house church. Most people are not educated, the leader need to adjust to them according to culture, language. The leader needs to adopt people's culture. The leader needs to learn people's language, the leader need to listen their needs… Pastor has more responsibility to the believers.

In summary, the intimate relationship between the pastor and believers is deepened when the pastor's life style becomes an example for the believers and when they have responsibility toward the believers.

Easiness

Easiness promotes interdependent relationship. In the data, RP05 and RP10 noted that easiness of access to the pastor, easiness of interaction, and easiness of the discipleship process promoted an interdependent relationship between pastor and believers.

First of all, RP05 expressed that the pastor who has a relationship with the believers like that of a friend has easy access to the believers. "..., access to the leader and pastor is easy in the house church. It is because setting is small and informal… it becomes easy to open up to access to the pastor...." Second, he stated the pastor who has a relationship with believers like a friend also has easiness of interaction with the believers. "When we talk about interaction as a whole in spiritual, social and whatever … We can interact with the believer closer. Let me talk about spiritual, it becomes easy … to ask some very personal questions. It also becomes for the pastor and leader to address them at very personal level." Third, he described the discipleship process is easy in the relationship of friend. "In fact, discipling process becomes very easy. Along with that course, now that we become too closer one another."

In the data, it was found that house visitations are examples of the ease of access to the pastor, easiness of interaction and of the discipleship process. RP05 and RP10 depicted this as follows.

> My house church is that basically new Christians, new believers usually come and asking question but sharing their spiritual experiences.... Main thing is that they come asking about their spiritual life and how to be now related to the world outside, the place that where they come from as they are Christian. It is basically right now it is about their spiritual growth. They are coming for asking about their spiritual growth and family matters. Basically they know how to related and respond as Christian (RP 5). The leader visits the house of the people two to three times a week, then asks them for prayer request, find what happen in the people's life. It makes leader and believer more closely. They are sharing their information about their family. As the leader visit the believer's house and people house, they are closer (RP 10).

Indeed, believer's house visitation by the pastor is an easy method to access to the believers. This leads the pastor and believers to interact. Through this, the discipleship process is going on naturally.

### *Spiritual Caregiver*

The date demonstrated 17.7% of the participants understood the relationship between pastor and believers as spiritual caregivers (RP08, RP09, RP23, RP24, RP27, and RP28).

According to RP08 and RP09, the believers recognize their pastor as a spiritual caregiver. "Believers look up to the pastor as the spiritual caregiver."(RP08). "They (the pastor and the believers) belong to the same social and economic strata. However, they look up to the pastor as the spiritual care-giver" (RP09).

Although RP23 and RP28 did not mention the word 'caregiver' directly, their expressions revealed that they understand their pastor as a spiritual caregiver. "Overall, people recognize me as pastor as I am shepherding them" (RP23). "Most of the time pastor is considered as doctor for them whether they should get healed by his prayer or he should lead them the doctor" (RP28). Thus, RP23 stated that the believer recognized their pastor who is shepherding and RP28 portrayed the pastor as a doctor who prays for a believer's healing.

RP24, RP27 and RP29 emphasized the roles of the pastor regarding spiritual care. Pastors are to care for all individuals, find the members' needs, and consult with the believers' about their spiritual condition. "Leader is care for all individuals in the house church" (RP24), "Pastor and leaders are sitting in member's house to talk to find member's needs. Pastor is to call this problem to the church/ congregation" (RP27). "Even for other things like decision making in the family also consulted with the Pastor because he is considered as person with Divine knowledge etc." (RP29).

In the data, research participants stated that spiritual care promotes an interdependent relationship between the pastor and believers. Research participants understood three sub-factors to promote an interdependent relationship between the pastor and believers: Managing crisis, fulfilling the expectation, and dependent relationship (see diagram).

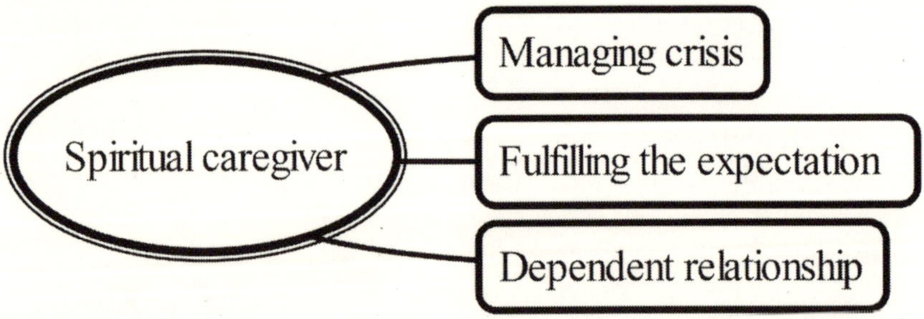


**Figure** 7. Spiritual caregiver

First, managing crisis promotes an interdependent relationship between the pastor and believers in the house church. RP08 and RP09 understood managing for crisis of physical health and financial crisis promoted an interdependent relationship between the pastor and the believers. They also see that interdependent relationship in the house church is improved through managing crisis. Especially, managing crisis of physical health or a financial crisis leads to an improved interdependent relationship.

Second, fulfilling the expectation also promotes an interdependent relationship between pastor and believers. RP23 and RP24 understood that an interdependent relationship between the pastor and believers promotes expectation and satisfaction for the pastor, and knowing and dealing for the believers' concern and problems.

RP23 said an interdependent relationship improves when the pastor fulfills the believers' expectation: "People come with expectation. They are satisfied with my answers. That develops as good relationship." RP24 saw an interdependent relationship improving when the pastor recognizes and deals with believers' concerns and problems:

> As leader you have to change to make relationship very strong with the members. By teaching the word, showing love and care, knowing their problems and praying for them daily, knowing their concerns, being with the members in very important aspect. At the same time, you(pastor) get same kind of response from the other side (congregation) to build the Good house fellowship center or house church (RP24).

Third, an initial dependence relationship promotes an interdependent relationship between pastor and believers. Research participants (RP27, RP28, and RP29) understood that the problems of spiritual and physical dimension, and dependence of uneducated migrants who move to the city promote interdependent relationship between the pastor and the believers.

RP27 expressed it this way:

> Interacting with them in spiritual aspect promote interdependent relationship. First, giving much time for them to speak (physical problem they will say - physical and emotional aspect). What are the problems they are facing their today life Giving them time to speak about it. Second, other contents of interdependence relationship are praying for them. (Spiritual aspect) Preaching theme and style is depending on their life style. Emotional problem - one common problem is that husband alcohol problem affect to the family. Wife comes to us to get some counsel. In this way I am interacting with them. Physical problem - physical sickness is one of motivation to bring them to the congregation. They come to us to get counsel and sometime we bring them to the hospital. We sometimes support money to them for treatment. We are gathering money from the congregation. After that, we (pastor and leader and some members) sometime gather their house to pray for healing.

The interaction above emerges when the believers start to see they can depend on the pastor. Furthermore, RP28 also recognized this interaction between the pastor and the believers. He spoke of interaction with uneducated migrants in urban. He said that an interdependent relationship between the pastor and believers started by the pastor's spiritual care to the believers:

Almost all the members of my house churches are uneducated and Pastor is all in all for them. He is like magic stick for them; they are fully dependent on pastor for advice even for small things. They are tribals and do not have basic knowledge of cities and their practices therefore, Pastor is the one who guides them teaches them and they all the time get surprised for the information they receive (RP28).

In this aspect, we can assume that an interdependent relationship in the house church is started when believers depend on their pastor.

We can see this analysis in RP29's statement. The believers who are urban migrants depend on the pastor in various ways, especially in spiritual aspects. Therefore, their final decision depends on what the pastor says. "They are dependent on Pastor in various ways as they are illiterate; therefore, they are completely dependent on Pastor for their spiritual growth. They follow the oral tradition and therefore, what the pastor says is final verdict for them" (RP29).

Benefits of Interdependent Relationships in the House Churches

Under research question 1, operational question 2 (protocol question 3) asked what were the benefits of an interdependent relationship between pastor and congregations. RP02 responded, "Yes, there are benefits of interdependent relationship between pastor and congregation such as it allows them to strive for better progress in their behavior, attitude to be Christ like."

The researcher categorized the expressions as concepts of positive aspects when research participants counted the relationship between the pastors and the believers in the house churches. As a result, the contents that research participants expressed regarding the benefits of an interdependent relationship in the house church are categorized below.

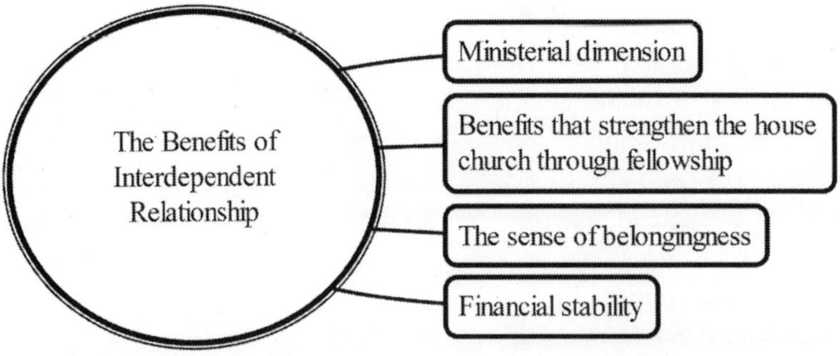


**Figure 8.** The Benefits of Interdependent Relationship

## *Ministerial Dimension*

When research participants expressed the benefits of an interdependent relationship, 35.3% (RP05, RP14, RP18, RP19, RP20, RP23, RP24, RP25, RP30, RP31, RP32, RP34) expressed benefits of an interdependent relationships in ministerial aspects: recognizing the believers as partners, sharing ministry with the believers, and expanding ministerial network with other house churches.

### Recognizing Believers as Partners

There is a benefit in recognizing believers as partners. RP20 recognized the relationship between the pastor and the believers as a partner relationship. "God's work will go in a smoother way. There is a mutual understanding between both the pastors and people. No one is to dominate others." RP25 also described that an interdependent relationship in the house church helps and gives understanding of partnership and sharing ministry with the believers. "it (interdependent relationship) is very beneficial for the pastor and the believers since the believers and the pastor do work together."

RP30 emphasized the teamwork between the pastor and believers for mission and church growth. He recognized the relationship between the pastor and believers as a partner relationship. "There would be a team work and can easily carry over the mission. The church can grow rapidly. The church can be effective." RP 34 also expressed the attitude for ministry of both the pastor and the believers, that "Congregation and pastor will be responsible for the growth of the church."

RP31 stated that the closer the relationship is between the pastor and believers makes for an effective and easy carrying out of ministry in the house church. This expression is that the believers are partners of the pastor. "1. Close relationship. This means we have relationship just like a Father and son in the family. This helps the sons (the believers) to carry the vision of the father. Naturally the father desire is fulfilled... 3. Willing to do anything. At one stage, when relationship is built, they are willing to anything the pastor asks."

RP24 expressed how the believers take care of the pastor. We can see this as the expression that the believer is the partner of the pastor. "Members show love and care towards leader with remembering the pastor in their daily prayers." For instance, RP05 who is in a bi-vocational pastor job, expressed how the believers help him. RP05 described that the pastor considers the believers as a partner because the pastor often requests his or her work for the believer to do. "In my case, the pastor still is working for bring food to his family. Sometimes, it is difficult to go to work because he is sick and he is out of work. I am asking the believers to go the place for doing work instead of me because I am engaging this particular place. Would you kindly go and do it for me?"

Sharing the Ministry with the Believers

There is a benefit to sharing the ministry with the believers. RP18 spoke of the ministerial participation of believers in the house church. "I don't disturb their (the believers) concerns for all my house church work." RP14 expressed the believers' ministry, "God's word is spread through locals (Christians) …." RP19 states that "Members do also carry and share the burden. It helps to develop the church too." RP34 pointed out that resources for ministry will come from within the church. For example, like RP32's expression, the believers provide their place (house) for worship. "Believers have a place to share openly for the worship" (RP32). This is how the believers participate in ministry of the house church.

Meanwhile, RP24 portrayed that he guided the believers to participate in the ministry through interdependent relationship. He says, "(Interdependent relationship help us to) recognizing (the believer's) talents and used for god's glory."

Furthermore, RP25 expressed the effectiveness (strongpoint) of sharing the ministry. First of all, the believers grow when they are involved in the ministry.

> Often the pastors are more growing than the believers because the pastors invest their life in the ministry. The reason why the believer is not grown is that they don't getting involve the ministry. As the believers also involve the ministry along with the pastor, the believers grow in spiritually and become mature because they are working for the kingdom of God.

Second, the pastors are not burned out when the believers participate in the ministry.

> When they do interdependent ministry, the pastor will not get burning. The pastor's state called the responsibility upon themselves, so physically they get stressed. Many pastors are suffering from pressure, burn out, tension, and anxiety and all those things because they are taking all the responsibility of ministry. And they are physically suffering. These kinds of matters lead the pastors do interdependent ministry with their believers. Because they are spend more time with the family, more time to spend spiritual retreat.

Third, an interdependent relationship is forming among the believers when they do ministry.

> When the pastors and believers work together, the interdependent relationship between the pastor and believer build the relationship between the believers and the believers. Because they are all engage doing ministry to one and another, socially the fellowship will come very strong. Therefore, they have spiritual, emotional, social and

physical benefits through the interdependent relationship between the pastor and the believers.

Besides, as RP23 mentioned, "members go further relationship and develop house churches in new villages," when the believers do ministry. This is one of the benefits of an interdependent relationship in the ministerial aspect. Throughout the conduct of the ministry, believers expand their relationships and help church grow.

### *Benefits that Strengthen the House Church through Fellowship*

In the data, it was found that 29.4% of the participants (RP03, RP04, RP08, RP09, RP17, RP22, RP24, RP27, RP28, RP30) depicted the benefits that strengthen community through fellowship: Forming direct fellowship with each other, the dimension of spiritual aspect that strengthens the community, and the positive influence of a strengthening the fellowship.

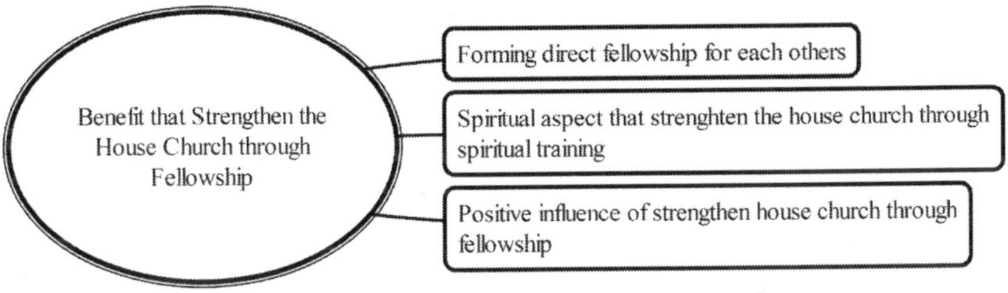


**Figure 9.** Benefit that strengthen the house church through fellowship

Forming direct fellowship for each other

RP03 expressed that the pastor can have a direct relationship with the believers since they understand the culture and language of the believers.

> With regard to culture, you understand the culture, once you understand culture and heart language; you are able to make worship relevant to their style of worship. You understand them better, spiritually, physically, you better known family matter, even you better know them emotionally. Relationship is direct; nobody is there between you and believers. You can be a master, and you can encourage them up to your level. Because you can direct teach them whatever you know the biblical principle.

RP08 and RP09 stated that an interdependent relationship in the house church form more easily and deeper relationship with each other without anyone's help. "The absence of intermediary opens the door for closer relationship."(RP08), "Easy/quick access to each other with no intermediary since house church is primarily with small gathering." (RP09).

RP27 described that the fellowship of house church believers in an independent relationships as direct and easy.

> House church is small group. Eight to ten or ten to twelve members. It means it has more room to know the people and talk (expression of direct relationship). They can interact easily. House church as a small group makes people not hesitate to come to church. The purpose of this house church is to promote people to fellowship.. Developing relationship very easily in house church.

RP22 noted that forming a relationship of a personal dimension is not difficult in the interdependent relationship of the house church.

> There is transparency between the pastor and the congregation. Relationship is personal level. This is built a small house church. You can have more time with them. You can have more activities. It is not an expensive thing. You have small group to have go out for picnic. Family they go outside. If just it is a group of thirty five (35) people, hire the bus which cost not much, but this is not happen with big church. Sunday we are going to have family Sunday. We are going out for the picnic. All the church members are going out. It is easily possible for the small church, but not in the big church. We are able to give them time and our presence. We are also able to understand them when they are going through some problems.

RP04 stated that expression of a direct relationship gives a better understanding for the community since the believers know each other's life. "We become one family. People (believers) will know the economic condition of the neighbors (other believers). It gives a better understanding towards our lively fellowship."

RP30 saw that an interdependent relationship between the pastor and believers is not formed by controlling power, but by an intimate relationship (direct relationship). This becomes the basis of trust between them. "There would be no chance for a pastor to misuse his powers and neither can the congregation dominate the pastor. There would be a fair understanding between the both. There would be transparency between them. The Pastor can know the individuals much more intimately (direct relationship). The congregation develops a trust on the Pastor."

RP24 expressed that an interdependent relationship makes believers grow in a fellowship of love together (direct relationship). The benefit of an interdependent relationship is that "Harmony among the members and showing love and care. Growing in fellowship with other believers."

Furthermore, as seen above, RP22 and RP30 depicted that transparency is one factor for a direct fellowship between the pastor and believers in an interdependent relationship. "There is transparency between the pastor and the congregation"(RP22). "There would be transparency between them" (RP30).

Spiritual Aspect that Strengthens the House Church through Spiritual Training

RP08 expressed that an interdependent relationship creates "Good fellowship in the house church to be glorified God's name." RP24 noted that the benefit of an interdependent relationship is that the believers "learn to mediate the word and grow in the Lord, advance in the faith and learn new things about God." These factors strengthen the house church. RP22 stated that active interaction in the house church leads believers to discipleship training.

> We can disciple them which is a spiritual part. We have small group bible study where a lot of interaction is going on. They come to know knowledge of the bible, and they come to know knowledge of Jesus Christ. They are able to understand, they are able to accept. That is transformation of their lives.

RP27 put an emphasis on the direct fellowship between the pastor and believers that makes spiritual training easy for them. "Pastor and leader can teach them more effectively train them equip them what the bible said. They can understand it easily."

RP28 reported that trusting the pastor is a direct factor that guides believers in spiritual training. "Because of great faith in their pastor, they do not go astray by others influence since pastor is their guide and advisor. It helps pastor to give them enough moral and spiritual training and they do humbly accept everything pastor says. It is easy to equip them."

Positive Influence of the house church that strengthen through fellowship

Participants RP22 and RP10 expressed that a positive influence of the house church is the strengthening of fellowship as a benefit of an interdependent relationship. Thus, there are positive influences that help to strengthen community through fellowship. One influence is in social issues, others influences provide for the needs of pastor's family and believers' needs.

RP22 described that strengthened community through fellowship give a positive influence to social issues like alcohol addiction.

> (Interdependent relationship affects social issues). For example, as a pastor, I can personally support to the alcohol addiction people. For almost several years, I have been telling one person who addicted the alcohol. I try to work and help him. I saw him in the church, he came to the church, after I spend so much time encouraging him, trying to push him, he looks guilty, people knows him who is in alcoholic. He thought church member will not accept him. I said no no, it takes so many months. He came to my church. I build them up personally.

RP22 continuously stated that the house church strengthens the fellowship to provide the needs of pastor's family and of believers' needs. RP10 also expressed that an interdependent relationship strengthens fellowship and influences members to provide for each other's needs.

> Because of the bond, the pastor has with the families of the church members, it is same thing you see reciprocate. When our family goes through some kinds of struggle, we have our church members, who stand for us to spend timing for prayer. They know our personal problem, they know our needs. They have been trying to invest their lives, whether it is prayer support and whether it is some other kinds of support. We always have seen that church member's response back. They have been seen us, they have been with us. For example, my daughter admitted in the hospital, my house church cell group members, they have fasting prayer in the house, even without anybody telling them. I did not asking them go and do fasting prayer. They treat my daughter as their daughter. That's kinds of bond build the house church.

RP10, "Pastor support and encourage them. Believers try to help the pastor's family with some food and finance."

### *The Sense of Belongingness*

RP30 pointed to the sense of belongingness as a benefit of an interdependent relationship in the house church. "People have the sense of belongingness when they come to our house church." According to the data, 26.5% of the participants (RP06, RP07, RP10, RP11, RP12, RP13, RP26, RP29, RP33) portrayed the sense of belongingness as a benefit of an interdependent relationship in the house church: the sense of security, protection of ministry and the sense of community.

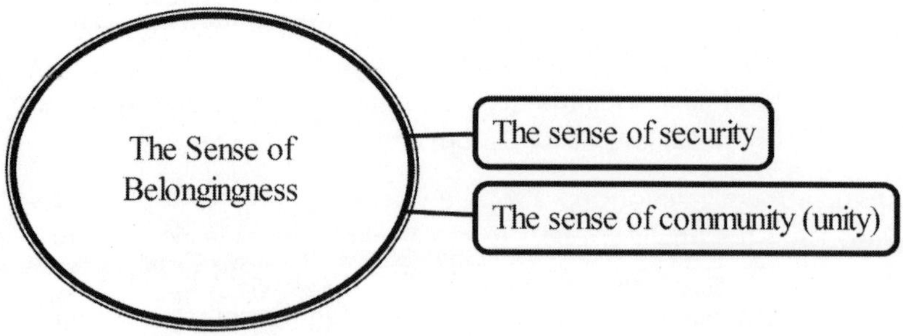


**Figure 10.** The Sense of Belongingness

First, participants RP06, RP07 and RP12 expressed the sense of security as a benefit of an interdependent relationship in the house church. "The sense of security is emotion when the believer becomes a member of house church community" (RP06). In the house church, "The sense of being a part of the same family is experienced. No one is left alone" (RP07). RP12 also stated that "There are lot of benefits in interdependent relationship between pastor and congregation, but I would like to mention mainly four benefits. The first benefit is... The second benefit is, it makes church in stability. The third benefit is... The fourth benefit is…"

In addition, RP10 said, "When the pastor preaches the gospel in the street of the local area, some people attacked us; the believers lived in that place advocate the pastor and protect the pastor from the opponents like the Hindu people. The house church believers stand with their pastor." Indeed, the sense of security makes it possible for the house church to overcome the persecution against evangelism.

Second, participants noted the sense of community and unity among the believers as a benefit of an interdependent relationship in the house church. "I wish all the believer come and take care of each other, then make good relationship with the believers; they are also cooperating with each other. I used to pray in this way in order to make them in unity" (RP11). Especially RP26 understood a sense of community as commonness, moral support and sharing. RP33 stated that "It strengthens the moral support; it helps one another in proper counseling. It also helps someone to grow holistically." RP29 describes the benefits of interdependent relationship as "There is real sense for family bond where mutual understanding plays important role (in the house church)"

RP12 also portrayed the interdependent relationship bringing unity to the house church. "There are lot of benefits in interdependent relationship between pastor and congregation, but I would like to mention mainly four benefits. The first benefit is... The second benefit is.... The third benefit is… The fourth benefit is, it brings unity, and unity brings strength." RP13 noted that an interdependent relationship "is developed through a regular mentorship and through fellowship groups. These relationships are ways we can build the church." In other words, an interdependent relationship in the house church brings unity between pastor (leader) and the believers.

### *Financial Stability*

According to data, 8.8% of participants (RP01, RP21, RP24) expressed financial stability as a benefit of an interdependent relationship in the house church. RP24 explained, "Financial support from the members (ex: offering, tithes)" as a benefit. This means that the house church can support herself financially.

## 2. Interdependent Relationship and Evangelism in the House Churches

This section deals with the data regarding how an interdependent relationship between the pastor and congregation influences the house church members to reach migrants and locals in order to evangelize.

Under research question 1, operational question 3 was, in what way do the roles of an interdependent relationship influence people in the house church to reach migrants and locals to evangelize and catechize? In order to respond to this question, I categorized the expressions of concepts that participants said an interdependent relationship in the house church influenced evangelism positively. As seen in the diagram, three nodes (Economic independence and three-self principle, Life testimony, and Active evangelism of the believers) were categorized under the theme, Interdependent relationship and Evangelism.

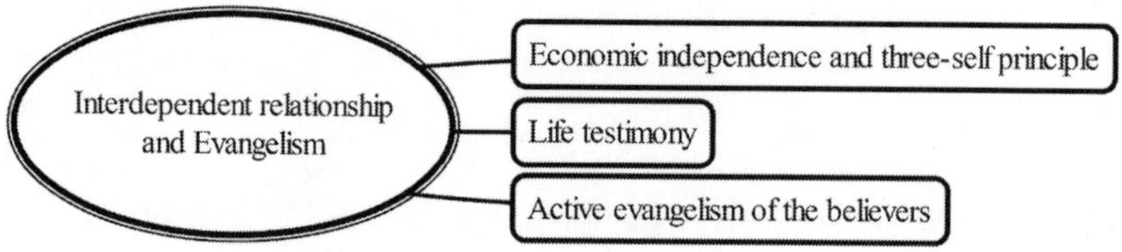


**Figure 11.** Interdependent relationship and Evangelism

Economic Independence and Three-self Principle

It was found that 8.8% of the research participants (RP01, RP04, and RP12) expressed economic independence and the three-self principle correlated to evangelism. As PR01 notes,

> Interdependence relationship connects to the 'three-self' principle. Individuals in the house church can help each other and depend on others in the economic and physiological independent position. This encourages members of house church to approach to the migrants or locals with self-confidence.

PR04 says that economic self-support of the pastor motivates the believers to evangelism. "People stand with me because they know who I am. They are aware that I don't get any financial support from anyone. Since I don't burden them with finance, they are motivated to follow Christ." PR12 declared that evangelism is possible through the indigenous church because it is established by the Three-self principle.

> When we look at the New Testament, we see that independent, indigenous churches were consistently planted by missionaries. It can be safely said that the New Testament Church and indigenous church are one-and-the same. The concept of an established church being financed, governed, supported, or in any way dependent upon another church, the result of the indigenous church-planting labors of the apostle Paul and others was the propagation of the gospel throughout the entire Roman Empire in less than 20 years. If we truly want to follow the NT as closely as possible and see the gospel powerfully

> propagated to the ends of the earth, we must be committed to the planting and establishment of house churches.

Life testimony

It was found that 26.5% of the research participants (RP06, RP07, RP08, RP20, RP23, RP24, RP27, RP29, RP31) expressed that life testimony correlated to evangelism.

First, the image of an interdependent relationship in the house church becomes a testimony for evangelism. RP06, PR07, and PR08 expressed that "The interdependent relationship, sharing of love and care, itself becomes a testimony."(RP06), "The interdependent relationship itself stands as a testimony" (RP07 and RP08). But, since RP06, RP07 and RP08 are house church pastors in the same area, there is a great possibility that they may have similar ideas on this matter or they may have discussed this matter.

Second, the transformation of the believers' life in an interdependent relationship becomes a testimony that influences other's life to change. RP23 stated this as "The change what happened in their life, one man's change in a village brings a change for whole village."

Thus, the believers evangelized other people through the testimony of their life experience and change. RP29 also depicted this:

> Congregation members are illiterate and therefore not really able to communicate the gospel as the need to be, but they have their own way of explaining the Christian faith to their neighbor or migrants, they talk about their own experience like healing, divine providence, Demon possession and these are the common needs of locals, therefore, get attracted to the Leader of this Christian people that is Pastor.

Meanwhile, an interdependent relationship influences believers to approach local people. The believers' testimony, their life change, and their good life style as results of an interdependent relationship become a way of evangelism. According to RP24,

> Yes, interdependence relationship between the pastor and the congregation influence the house church members to reach localities. First, Members testimonies influence a lot in the locality and there is scope of evangelism in the area to preach the good news. Change of life of members will have greater impact on society. Good Life style of members helps us to reach the gospel to the unbelievers.

As such, participants (RP27 and RP30) noted that the believers' life testimony of their faith in the interdependent relationship leads to evangelism. "They (the believers) would certainly reflect Christ through their lives. This includes personal life and as Church. When the Pastor and the congregation have a good interdependent relationship they would stand as a living testimony to many people in influencing them" (RP30).

> House church helps the member to reach the local people. e.g. one lady come to house church because of her physical sickness, when we pray for her, she feel this house church help me a lot to develop her physical stand. Automatically she go and share the message to next lady who are in sick, and said come to the house church. This is a way of evangelism of local people in our area. One the lady who are in sick is cure in the house church, because of this house church is good for me, because they talking to me, helping me, they are praying for me, if one lay has relation that, automatically, the lady go and tell to other lady and other people, to come to the house church (RP27).

Third, the role of the pastor is to encourage and lead believers to live as witnesses. RP20 expressed that the pastor encourages believers to witness for evangelism and to live as role model of life. "In urban set up, it is difficult to send people exclusively for evangelism as a few members only cooperate. I encourage to be witness in marketing places and to be a role model to their neighbors." RP31 portrayed that the believer sees evangelism as taking the pastor's life as their life model. "People watch the life of the pastor. My simplicity, role model life, and disciplined life are matters for the congregations. Once people accept the pastor as role model and then they are willing to listen and submit to the vision of the pastors. This is also depending upon how and what do we teach about mission."

Active Evangelism of the Believers

Research showed that 64.7% of research participants (RP03, RP07, RP09, RP10, RP11, RP13, RP14, RP15, RP16, RP17, RP19, RP21, RP22, RP25, RP26, RP27, RP28, RP32, RP33, and RP34) noted active evangelism of believers.

### *Interdependent relationship influence to the believers to do evangelism voluntarily*

An interdependent relationship in the house church shows example of the early church mission and activities like sharing the gospel are voluntary. "We show the 1st century model of mission through our house church. Since it is biblical, members bring others and share gospel. It is all voluntary" (RP16). RP03 also expressed that believers share the gospel to family and friend voluntarily:

> We share the gospel of grace. People are hungry. People need someone who can understand. God understand their needs. God is to be purpose God. When they receive the grace from God, they excite to share the gospel to their family members and friends. Ultimately/ automatically, they are also seeking interest to know about God, their family member, friends share with them. Through them we get the

> other people into worship service. Interaction during the worship, not only after the worship, we make it very informal. When we share the word, during the sharing time, anyone can ask the question. They can stop the person who sharing to clarify their doubts. After sharing there is also time to discuss about the word. The person is not left just listening there to go.

Such active evangelism of the believers begins with the attitude of their heart. RP28 described that the believers' attitude is well equipped for evangelism in the interdependent relationship. "They are not afraid in sharing their testimonies or do not feel shy in telling what their pastor has told them to do. They do suggest people in need to come to their pastor and he would pray for them as they had already experience the power of prayer."

### *Interdependent relationship motivates believers to do evangelism*

RP14 expressed that an interdependent relationship provides believers to have "passion to reach people from their heart" for evangelism and to "follow the Great commission." RP32 stated the interdependent relationship motivates believers for evangelism. "The openness in mind and spirit are the motivation for the believers to evangelism. They own the mission. They challenge others to come and participate in the church." RP33 depicted that an interdependent relationship influences believers to bring people to the house church through evangelism. "People come with needs to the church, and when they are taken care and helped, they share with others to come to church. Once love is received from church, they are able to bring others who are in need."

### *Interdependent relationship penetrates local society for evangelism*

Participants see that an interdependent relationship penetrates the local society (caste, Hindu people). As an example, RP11 stated that an interdependent relationship in the house church gives a positive influence to evangelism for the Hindu neighbor and the believers' spiritual growth.

> Spiritually we have good relationship with the believers. They are growing in Christ not only growing but also expanding their relationship to the Hindu neighborhood. They sometimes invite their Hindu neighbor into their house. My house church believers are most from Hindu background. First of all, we are going to go door to door. When we can share the gospel to them, they open their door to us; they invite us to their house. Some are received; some are not receiving the gospel (RP11).
>
> As another example, RP10 saw that an interdependent relationship in the house church leads believers to approach low caste people because it overcomes the caste system.

> We are not showing we are higher than the people who are in low caste and class. We are adopting the situation of the people; we are not revealing the difference from the people in the low caste and class. We are visiting their house, and we have to go inside, enter their house and stay there, whatever they give, like some water and some snack to us, we need to accept that one, we are supposed to reject that, once we reject their hospitality, they feel bad. Since we are low caste people, these people and pastor are not willing to take them. If one do not want it, he or she should kindly say and explain why he cannot accept it so that they can understand. Water, tea, or coffee whatever they give, once the pastor receive it, they will honor the pastor because of accepting it. For example, since I am from high caste, educated person, once I visited to the house, the house owner gave some kinds of fruit on the clay plate. I prayed for it and eat. They were so happy and they inform other people about me, through this people, I can approach to many people to preach. It was in 2006.

RP09 expressed that an interdependent relationship gives opportunity for evangelism to local people by showing itself to the local society. "Since the house church depends on each other already, the locals notices that and help is extended whenever opportunity arises." As an example, RP13 described this as "Our way of reaching to others for evangelism is through fishing pools, where I meet common friends with some creative abilities. So we can meet together, for example, at running groups or at tea meeting."

### *Interdependent relationship reveals the role of the pastor for evangelism*

RP34 emphasized the role of the pastor for evangelism. "When the whole body of the Church feels responsible then we can reach the people. Pastor's role is crucial here, he/she need to lead congregation to evangelize." RP15 put an emphasis on the factors (such as friendly relationship, transparent leadership and trust) of an interdependent relationship in the house church influence to the evangelism. Thus, relationship and leadership based on trust is connected to the pastor's important role and believer's evangelistic activities the interdependent relationship. According to RP07,

> Pastor encourage people to bring other people to the house church. Pastor is not directly going to the society. Going through the member in a congregation to the society. The Pastor encourage that Evangelism is conducted through house church members. Pastor often visit members' house in the village. People in the village recognize this. They thought the pastor who hold higher education degree and higher caste than their visit to their neighbors. People recognize this house

> church member differently. In this way, people in the village consider and evaluate this pastor's visiting to the member as valuable matter.

Meanwhile, RP25 expressed that the pastor and the believer work together for evangelism in the interdependent relationship because it is a more effective and strategic way for evangelism

> The pastor and the believers work ministry together is great benefit to society and unbelievers because they preaching the gospel together. Most people think evangelism is responsibility of the pastors because he is full time worker for the ministry. People think he supposes to go out and preaching the gospel. He has a responsibility for growth of the church. For example, in our house church, twice in a month, we all do local church evangelism to the city. As I am a pastor go along with the believers. Evangelism together is more effectively and strategically.

Research participants (RP17, RP19, RP21, RP22, and RP26) depicted how they lead believers to participate on evangelism. RP17 stated that missional preaching by the pastor leads believers to evangelism. "My preaching on Great commission influences the members, God's word inspires." RP19 says that the pastor requests believers do evangelism. "Locals receive blessings of God from me. I ask them to share with others. And then a few members are added. This is going on by extending the kingdom of God." RP21 says that the pastor stressed the needs of evangelism in the interdependent relationship, and the believers understand evangelism in the spiritual meaning. "We emphasize the need of evangelism to their neighborhood. Members do not expect anything rather they do this as their spiritual duty." RP22 stated that the pastor motivates believers in the independent relationship, and to invite their neighbor to the house church.

> I try to motivate our church members to follow the Master's footstep, also move forward to share the gospel. We've been trying to motivate members as specially being salt and light of the world to influence people around us. We try to attract the people with Jesus' life style. In the present scenario, we cannot go and have open meeting in India. So, what we are doing is trying to increase church members now you know friend, make friendship that is friendship evangelism, life style evangelism that influence people through life. You bring them for some programs. As house church, how to evangelism? It is try to motivate our church members through the Bible study. During Christmas I bring my church member to the Jail to give some present to the prisoners and share the gospel to them. The most of our believers in our house church is from Telgu, other are from Orissa, and other rural area.

RP 26 pointed out that the pastor prioritizes evangelism to the believers.

It is through persuading the members of the priority of reaching people for Christ. Reminding them of God's goodness in their lives (salvation and changed lives) and share it with their community. In a fatalistic worldview, the interdependence becomes an example of helping someone in need (counterculture). Believers take this example and share it with their community.

## 3. Interdependent Relationship and the Practical Meaning of House Church

This section deals with data regarding what the practical meaning of the house church is in light of the interdependent relationship between the pastor and congregation. Under the research question 1, operational question 2 was, what are the results of the leadership and of an interdependent relationship in the house church? Under this operational question 2, protocol question 5 was, what is the practical meaning of house church in light of the interdependent relationship between the pastor and congregation? I categorized the expressions that participants offered about the practical meaning of house church. As a result, the contents that research participants expressed regarding the practical meaning of house church categorized are below. As seen in the diagram, three nodes (worship community, ecclesiological understanding for house church, and mission strategy) are elements of understanding of interdependent relationship and the practical meaning of house church.

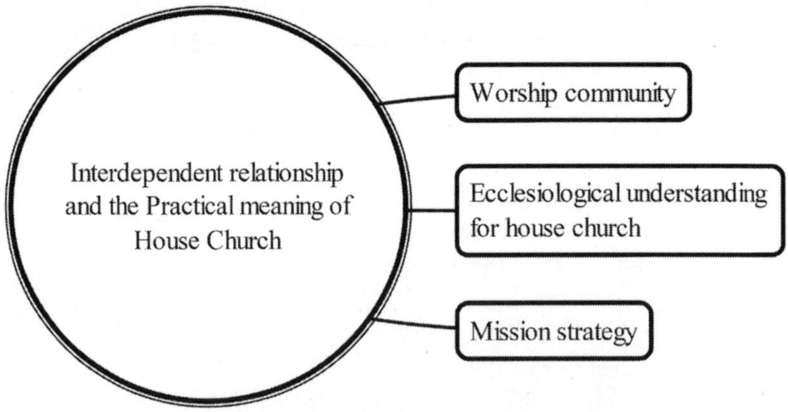


**Figure 12.** Interdependent relationship and the Practical meaning of House Church

Worship community

The data demonstrated 14.7% of the research participants (RP04, RP16, RP17, RP22 and RP23) expressed worship community as a practical meaning of house church.

First of all, the participants emphasized worship itself about the practical meaning of house church. RP04 described that "House church is a practice and life of worship God together" as a practical meaning of the house church in the interdependent relationship. RP17 also stated that the practical meaning of house church as "according to my opinion, house church is a place where people can worship and have true fellowship."

> RP22 also considered the house church as worship center of God's family.
>
> House is used for the worship center more than that just like house having family. Living together, more like small family whom meet together every week different times, though they have formal time for worship. House church is more kinds of, you seeing the bond and deepens families in the house church. Usually the bond in the family is like me, daughter and wife. But in the house church, you have different family having the bond together. That's the practice part of the meaning of the house church. House is the worship center.

Second, the participants understand the practical meaning of house church as the first process to build a worship community. RP16 stated "House church is the first stage of making people to become a worshipping community. It is like win - win situation. People want good care through house churches, I as pastor care for those genuinely." RP23 understood it as a process and a tool for growth of a house church ministry. "To grow ministry, it (house church) is a useful tool. As John 4th chapter, we can worship anywhere. This is the biblical concept we follow in house church."

Ecclesiological Understanding for House Church

RP05 emphasized the essential understanding of church when he expressed the meaning of a house church. "Church is not located in one particular place, we are the church. We need to go back to the understanding of her again."

According to data, 58.8% of the research participants (RP02, RP03, RP05, RP07, RP10, RP11, RP14, RP15, RP18, RP20, RP24, RP25, RP26, RP29, RP30, RP31, RP32, RP34) expressed their ecclesiological understanding of house church as its practical meaning: Small group of believers (small church), The primitive early church, Understanding of emotional dimension, and Understanding of functional dimension.

### ***Small group of believers (Small Church)***

Participants expressed their understanding of the practical meaning of house church as a small group of believers (small church). RP33 depicted it as a "Small group of families coming together or I can call house church as 'semi-closed group"

RP03 and RP30 saw it as a small group of believers. RP03: "I will just call it as a small group of believers who are liberty to ask any questions and liberty to seek any kinds of help, liberty to connect with you, because they know it is a personal relationship not as a member, but as a member of family." RP30 also expressed it as a small group, "House church is a small group concept where a tiny group of people gather together exchange their thoughts, experiences, and fellowship."

RP32 and RP31 portrayed it as small group of family. "It is just sharing. It is a group of family coming together" (RP32). RP31 explained it with more detail, saying, "Sharing the same mind of Christ while practicing the attitude of belongingness. More families come together and become a one family."

Especially, RP25 described it as small church and he focuses on the essence of church.

> I prefer using the word small church rather than the house church. Because the church is not a building, it is not confine a place. House churches are trying to multiply the house more than the church. Rather before using the word family church or small church rather than the house church, focus is not the place, the function of the New Testament, and church is small, people gather in small group, in small hall and house. House church and small group church is more like family. Pastor has relationship with the believer and believer has relationship with their pastor, and their relationship will be quality relationship. I see house church and small church provide very good platform that the pastors and believers know each other, they relationship together, serve Lord together.

### *The Primitive Early Church*

Research participants expressed their understanding of the practical meaning of a house church as like a primitive early church. RP11:

> In the book of Acts, we can see how house church had started. The primitive church was not gathering in the place like today. Acts 2:41-42, people were gathering in the house, breaking the bread, having fellowship as house gathering. Build communication between the believer and the servant of God.

RP14 said, "*Following early apostle period* to break the bread in house and to enjoy godly fellowship." RP31 also expressed it as saying "A place to share our feeling and burdens according to the early Church model."

RP28, RP29 and RP30 explained it as the biblical pattern from the early church. RP28 stated it as the biblical pattern of New Testament,

> As per my knowledge is concern I see here the biblical pattern of New Testament as majority churches in New Testament were House Churches, and there was warmth of house, the bond of family and it

> was functioning as unit or family, caring for each other, helping one another, forgiving one another and there was a sense of belongingness. This is what we are experiencing in our house Churches (RP28).

RP29 also expressed that "It is real pattern of first century church and house church fits into the category of first church of Acts chapter 2:42-47." RP30 also stated it a classic example of the early church that had accountability for believers and overcame difficult times. "A classic example would the early church in the book of Acts where they gathered together in a house and had fellowship. This type of fellowship makes people to be accountable to each other and help each other in time of trouble as the believers in the early church did."

### *The Understanding of Emotional Dimension*

Participants understood the practical meaning of a house church in the interdependent relationship as from the emotional dimension.

RP02: "It is the visible reflection of God's love for His people." RP32 also said, "(In the house church), they (believers) are touched by the word of God seeing our genuine love for them." RP24 described it as "harmony among the members and showing love and care." RP34 commented it as the meeting that feels love and care for each other. "It's a gathering with a few groups of believers to have fellowship together. By gathering in houses, members of the church will feel cared and loved. House church gatherings will be regular." RP18 also depicted house church as "a place where sharing the joys and sorrows with the headship of Christ."

RP20 portiaryed it as "a place to share our feeling and burdens according to the early Church model." RP09 expressed it as "a place/unit that fosters close relationships and being there to be the extensions of the body of Jesus Christ." Especially, RP09 emphasized both emotional and functional dimensions for the practical meaning of the house church.

### *The Understanding of Functional Dimension*

Participants understood their practical meaning of a house church as one in the functional dimension. RP28 expressed that the meaning of house church is unity and cooperation. "Practical meaning of house Church in One Body and Christ is the head of that body and there is unity and cooperation in the organs of the body." RP03 stated that it is helping the believers' needs. "The house church is a like how we feel about our brother and sister in need seeking help. In a similar way, we understand people in need connecting with us. We seek their help and need." This can be a functional dimension of a house church in the interdependent relationship. RP26 described it as a functional dimension, saying, "House church in light of interdependent relationship is that the pastor (leader) in most of the sense shares and identifies him with the believers. It becomes like a family in sharing, encouraging and more engaging in each other's family in their day-today life." RP07 also depicted the house church as "a place where to grow up as a member of the same family with God as the father." As RP24 said, "In the house church, we learn and mediate the word and grow in the lord. Learn new things about God. Growing in fellowship with other believers." He expressed the functional dimension of house church as its practical meaning. Thus, when participants expressed the practical meaning of the house church in the functional aspect, house church is the place where believers' needs are met and helps them to grow as God's family.

Mission Strategy

Data shows that 26.5% of the participants (RP01, RP06, RP08, RP09, RP12, RP13, RP19, RP21, and RP27) expressed mission strategy as practical meaning of house church: House church of three-self principle, House church as preparation place for mission and its expansion, and House church as local church that is fitting for the local needs.

First, research participants expressed their understanding of the practical meaning of house church in the interdependent relationship as house church of the three-self principle. RP01 stated it in the strategic aspect. He asserts that the three-self principle is needed for the house church in order for it to play her role. "Therefore, the three-self principle needs to be applied in the house church to take its role wholly. So, the practical meaning of the house church is a church applied by the three-self principle."

> RP02 also wrote that the practical meaning of house church is a three-self church
>
> In my opinion, the practical meaning of the house church is, it must be established with three principles in mind: (1) Self-support: Paul himself set an example concerning self-support he never asked for financial support from churches for himself. (2) Self-governance: Paul appointed elders in every church that he had planted (Acts 12:23). (3) Self-witness: Paul asked the churches that he planted to be self-witnessing in planting house churches.

Second, participants understood the practical meaning of the house church as a preparing place for mission and its expansion. RP06 expressed that a house church is the church accomplishing its missional goal, "(The practical meaning of the house church is) to nurture and equip believers to fulfill the Great Command." RP09 also commented it as the preparation place for the church's mission and expansion. "(house church is) a place/unit that fosters close relationship and being there to be the extension of the body of Jesus Christ." RP19 emphasized the meaning of extension as expressing "house church is a quick way to extend God's kingdom and grow together."

Meanwhile, RP21 described how the house churches attracting the neighbors. In this sense, attraction is another expression of extension: "Acts 2 talks about the early Church believers who broke the bread in their houses. So, it is a model to influence the migrants. When we pray, the neighbors are attracted, so they come home. We show love, so it goes on" (RP21).

Third, participants understood the practical meaning of a house church as a local church that is fitting for the local's need. RP08: "(the practical meaning of the house church is) extension of an established church to meet the local needs."

> RP27 portrayed the house church as a church to approach the local people.
>
> House church is a feather church. It means that house church is to educate local people to attend the main church without any hesitation. Though their social status is low status, they are in the equal status of the church called house church. So, they feel not much different with the main church. The house church means we are going into our own place. Renting in own house and gathering those people there, we make them to feel we are one among them. Not we are different. We are part of the people. We make them to realize they are also part of the main church. In this point, I start the house church. In India context, the members of the main church are in high social status, wealthy, educated people. Low caste people feel some insecure, or what shall I want to go? If I go to there, are they respecting me? This is their question. Can they recognize me? Although, the pastor encourages people of the main church to talk each another, people stick one another only according to their status. I observed the colony people (low caste) also feel how can go to the main church. Though low caste people want to come to the church, though they want to share to the pastor, though they want to about Jesus, those social statuses divide them. The house church help them this problem. The house church bring them into one pot, and encourage them, when the members of house church become familiar with the main church, we bring them the main church for baptize. We practice this process for last 6 years in the house church. It is good strategy to reach to the low status people.

RP13 used the example of how the house church approaches local people in practice. "Our way of reaching to the people is, for example, through fishing pools, where I meet common friends with same creative abilities, so we can meet together with running groups or meeting for a drink."

## 4. Application of Theoretical Premise for Research Question 1

The first finding from research question 1 can be applied to the theoretical premise of David W. Johnson: *How do individuals interact to create outcome?* Outcomes from question 1 are the factors that promote an interdependent relationship between the pastor and believers in the house church

In my study, two theories in Johnson's social interdependent theory can be employed. First, promotive interaction may be defined as individuals encouraging and facilitating each other's efforts to complete tasks, to achieve, or produce in order to reach the group's goals. It consists of mutual help and assistance, exchange of needed resources, effective communication, mutual influence, trust, and constructive management of conflict. Second, positive interdependence creates forces for responsibility that increase members' feelings of responsibility and accountability. It is founded that Johnson's two theories is in the finding of research question one as follows.

**Table 3.** Johnson's Theories in the Finding of Research Question One

| Relationship between the pastor and the believers (Individual's interaction) | Factors that promote interdependent relationship in the house church (Factors= Outcome) |
|---|---|
| Father and children | Servant leadership (promotive interaction)<br>Decision making authority (positive interdependence)<br>Life sharing (promotive interaction) |
| Leader and followers | Interdependent relationship model (positive interdependence)<br>Proposal of house church ministry model (promotive interaction)<br>Problem-solving of house church (promotive interaction) |
| Relationship like Friend | The pastor's right attitude for the relationship with accountability and adoptability (positive interdependence)<br>Easiness (promotive interaction) |
| Pastor as spiritual caregiver | Managing crisis (positive interdependence)<br>Fulfilling the expectation (promotive interaction)<br>Dependent relationship (promotive interaction) |

According to Johnson, positive interdependence results in promotive interaction. Therefore, outcome (positive interdependence) results in other outcomes (promotive interaction). In other words, 'decision making authority' (positive interdependence) results in 'servant leadership' (promotive interaction) and 'life sharing' (promotive interaction). 'Interdependent relationship model' (positive interdependence) results in 'proposal of house church ministry model (promotive interaction) and problem-solving of the house church' (promotive interaction). 'The pastor's right attitude for the relationship with accountability and adoptability' (positive interdependence) results in 'easiness' (promotive interaction). 'Managing crisis' (positive interdependence) results in 'fulfilling the expectation' (promotive interaction) and 'dependent relationship' (promotive interaction).

The second finding from research question 1 can be applied to the theoretical premise of David W. Johnson: Positive goal interdependence is sufficient to generate higher achievement and productivity than is engendered by individualistic efforts. Positive interdependence motivates individuals to try harder. The benefit of interdependent relationship in the house church is the achievement that is influenced by others' behavior. The following diagram describes the contents of the achievement of the influenced by others' behavior (between the pastor and the believers) in the house church.

**Table 4.** The Contents of the Achievement of Those Influenced by Others' Behavior (between the pastor and the believers) in the House Church

| The benefits | The achievement influenced by others' behaviors |
|---|---|
| Ministerial dimension | Recognizing believers as partners<br>Sharing the ministry with the believers |
| Strengthen the house church through fellowship | Trust each other |
| The sense of belongingness | Security and unity |
| Financial stability | Financial support |

The third finding from research question 1 can be applied from another theoretical premise of Johnson: self-interest becomes expanded to mutual interest through other people's actions. The diagram below shows that evangelism in the house church is motivated and started from the believers' self-interest.

**Table 5.** Evangelism and Believers' Self-interest

| **Self-interest** | **Mutual interest** |
|---|---|
| Economic independence and three-self principle | Evangelism |
| Life testimony | |
| Active evangelism voluntarily | |

From the data, the fourth finding from research question 1 is to define the practical meaning of the house church through the understanding of interdependent relationship. The house church is a worship community. House church can be understood in the various ecclesiological stances. Such a church itself is a mission agency as well as a mission strategy of *missio Dei.*

Chapter 6

# Research Finding 2: House Church Model

This section deals with data regarding what is the proper model to influence the house church to evangelize and catechize migrants and locals in the city.

## 1. The House Church Image (Model): Before Starting Church Planting

Under the research question 2, operational question 1 was, what was your idea about a model for a house church that influence the house church to evangelize and catechize migrants and locals in the city? In order to respond to these questions, I categorized the expressions as concepts that research participants thought were house church models before started church planting. As seen in the diagram below, six nodes were categorized under the theme, The House Church Image (Model): before starting church planting, Self-Supporting House Church Model, House church as Alternative Model for Traditional Church, Dependence Model (to the Pastor's Ability), and Church Planting Mission Model, Perspective for the church, and the motivation and methods for house church planting.

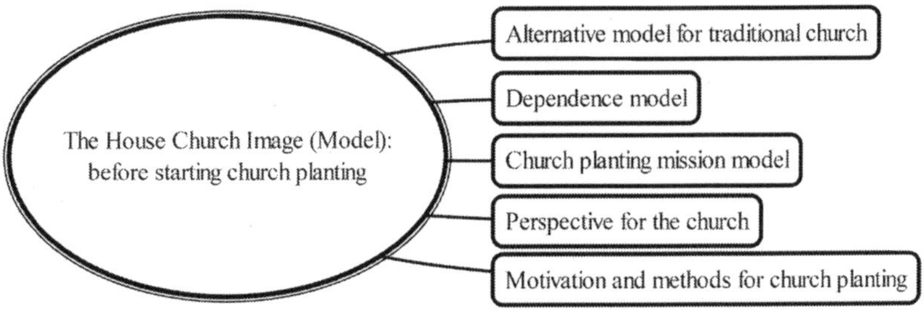


**Figure 13.** The House Church Image (Model): before starting church planting

### House Church as an Alternative Model for a Traditional Church

Research participants RP21, RP28, and RP32 understood the house church as an alternative model for a traditional church. RP28 expressed his failure in a previous church planting that was started with the concept of the western tradition church. Therefore, he thought of the house church planting as an alternative model for his traditional church.

> I had a western traditional idea of Church, where most of the educated people gather and maintain their dress code, manners and system. They are time bound weekly based people, with that Idea I started evangelism to win the people for Christ and add them to these traditional churches trying to fit them in new culture in which I utterly failed, therefore, decided to follow my own tradition or tried to adopt the people friendly system and people drove me to their houses and it started working well and then discovered that it is biblical pattern of the first century churches (RP28).

RP21 and RP32 thought the house church could overcome the weakness of traditional mainline churches: "While traditional churches are not giving the full support and care to the members, I thought I can give the best care by starting a small group i.e. house church" (RP21). "Earlier my idea of house church was to create deeper relationship with each other's, because mainline church did not give this" (RP32).

### Dependence Model (to the Pastor's Ability)

Research participants (RP02, RP05, RP31 and RP33) expressed that they thought of a house church as depending on the pastor's ability and leadership. RP31 stated that "Moreover, at first I tried alone, later all house church members work together towards my vision of building God's kingdom in the world." RP33 also recalled that "If I preach well, many people will come to church - that is what I thought. But later, it was not so. It was much more than that." RP02 and RP05 expressed a dependence model of the church due to the pastor's leadership.

> (House church is) a place where each person comes and pray, praise God. It leads by a pastor. I thought that I have to lead people in some direction. I thought that the congregation depended on pastor and not the pastor dependent on people (RP02). "I was thinking I can work by myself and give more influence to others. I thought I can lead all the church members since the house church is small. But, I have changed my heart that the church should build together with the believers. I was thinking about so much interdependence (RP05).

RP05 stated, however, that his idea changed after he did church planting of his house church,

> Fellowshipping with them and encouraging them, but as we went on I found I also depend on them to be encouraged spiritually, to be motivated physically to carry on. This is a change what I saw. In other words, I have changed my previous understanding of the leadership after I planted my house church.

Most other participants also changed their ideas after they did church planting.

## Church Planting Mission Model

Research participants expressed that there can be various house church planting mission models: house church as the process toward a large scale church, house church as initial mode of church planting, and as an approaching model to the neighbor and local society.

First, research participants, RP03, RP04, RP14 and RP30 described the house church planting mission model as a process toward a large scale church. Research participants want to move to a larger scale church after they start the house church. RP30 stated that "We wanted to begin the Sunday worship in our house and switch to a mega church as the time passes by. That was the plan initially. But there are some constrains in terms of place in the urban areas as it is very difficult to find a place to have an exclusive structural church." RP04 also set forth his idea that "I wanted to start with a small community. My idea was to start from small then move to big building." RP14 set forth his initial idea of house church as "Previously, I was an assistant Pastor which helped to sense about house church in a certain level. But the reality is always different. Yes. I wanted to move to bigger church buildings. But God did not allow moving out as I had to care for the existing people." RP03 said, "Once I started church, I look forward big place first, there many people come and church will grow." Thus, the reason why participants considered the house church as the process toward a large scale church is because they had plans for church growth at the first stage of church planting.

Second, research participants, RP12, RP13, RP18, RP23, and RP27 expressed that house church is an initial mode of church planting. RP12 and RP13 stated that house church is the first step for a church planting ministry. "Before I planted house church I was thinking that, house church would be the first step to start church planting ministry and if I success in the house church then only I could go for next step and I planned to established small rented house church in a village"(RP12). "It (house church) is an established church, though we started as a bible study in a house first. The primary mode of ministry is through the house church" (RP13).

RP23, PR27, and RP18 expressed their view that house church planting is a unique initial mode for approaching a specific area: "House church was an entrance to enter a place/area/town/village for further ministry" (RP23). "Before

I started the house church, there were only two members from two families in the particular locality. Before start, I only talk to these two members, since no one talked to me in this particular locality. No one wants to me to make relationship" (RP27). In this type of environment, a house church was a natural mode for RP27 in the beginning of church planting. RP18 also stated that the house church is an initial mode for church planting in the rural area. "I was planting churches in some other areas. House church, I thought, it is to start with especially in rural areas. It is a small scale type who cannot afford for bigger buildings."

Third, three research participants, RP06, RP24, and RP34 depicted that a house church was an approaching model to the neighbor and local society for church planting. RP06 stated that he was thinking house church as a church approach to the neighbor with passion. "It (house church) was started with the desire to reach my neighbor since it is difficult to invite non-Christian to attend church." RP24 also said, "Only idea is to preach good news to the society to save more souls to extend the kingdom of God. Because many wandering, peaceless, hopeless, restless." When RP34 expressed the house church as an approach model, he put an emphasis on both evangelism and social activities of the house church. "The idea was to plant a church and do more evangelism in the selected area. And also to do many social activities so that people may know that church is being planted for the welfare of society. The primary idea was to gather in believer's house" (RP34).

Perspective for the Church: House church as People, not Building

Four research participants (RP16, RP20, RP22, and RP25) expressed their perspective for the house church before planting a house church. It was that a house church is not a building, but people. Research participants described how they focused on the people.

RP20 set forth his concern for the people's need for church planting. "I had thought of doing some mission by some means. I was nervous that how I am going to answer the spiritual thirst of people." RP25 also shared his idea about what is important (people, not program and place) for the house church before starting church planting.

> There are different opinions for the house church. Not every person has same meaning and same function of the house church. My view about the function of the house church is that the most important thing is not the program and place, but it is coming into Christ. They themselves is the temple of God, not the place, the most important thing is they will see the church as a family, not a formal service (RP25).

RP16 and RP22 said they thought that house church ministry is to focus on only a few people. RP16 stated that "a few invited friends are allowed in house church. That was my idea about house church." RP22 expressed that "when we started, we did not think it develop to big group. We planned to strengthen few believers, just a couple of believers."

Motivation and Method for House Church Planting

Research participants expressed their motivation and method they had before planting the house church.

First, two participants (RP11 and RP18) expressed economic reasons for the motivation and method of house church planting. They stated that they wanted to start a house church because of the costs to build the church building. RP11:

> When we approached the people, we visited their house to have friendship, and then slowly we contact them by the phone, then we have fellowship. (For example) In Bangalore, it is difficult to build the church building. It is good to rent the house for the church. Cost of living is very much high.

RP18: "I was planting churches in some other areas. House church, I thought, it is to start with especially in rural areas. It is a small scale type who cannot afford for bigger buildings."

Second, five research participants (RP06, RP07, RP09, RP15, and RP29) expressed environmental reasons for the motivation and methods of house church planting.

RP06 and RP07 stated their motivation was the reason why they wanted to start the house church. RP06: "It (house church) was started with the desire to reach my neighbor since it is difficult to invite non-Christian to attend church" (RP06). RP07: "it (house church) was started at the house of a new convert since they weren't open to attending church. It was with a purpose to give an alternate place to worship."

RP09, RP15 and RP29 also explained the environmental motivation for church planting. RP09 expressed "When I start the house church, my plan was to disciple the new convert in their home since they live far from the church." RP15 and RP29 expressed the political environment that he explains why he wanted to start house church.

> RP15: "Reach the people, worship in the house because of the Indian political secenio. Mega church cannot meet the need of rural areas to begin with. Therefore, we should with house church in rural area. People come to house church, just like visiting others because of our conservative culture." RP29: "I was going to visit different houses to preach the gospel but had idea of taking them to a Church building where they will worship the Lord but then I realized that people were not willing to come to a place called church because of fear of their locality, they would urge saying that why can't you come to our house,

> our house is always open for you, and so this is how started the church in house which was very well attended."

Third, four research participants (RP08, RP10, RP11 and RP26) expressed fellowship as a means for the house church planting. RP08: "It (house church) was initially meant for fellowship." RP10 described the house church as a means for intimacy among the people:

> House church where are intimacy, many Mainline church has not much intimacy between congregations. There are many services in the Sunday, but they don't know who are coming, who are not coming. But house church has more intimacy, personal intimacy what Jesus did personal interaction at Bethany. Big church, mainline church they don't have intimacy. I prefer the house church because of intimacy. In the house church, the pastor and believers they are closer (RP10).

Meanwhile, RP11 and RP26 depicted their motivation to start a house church was because the fellowship had already formed. "When we approached the people, we visited their house to have friendship, and then slowly we contact them by the phone, then we have fellowship" (RP11). "Had no thought of house church such as rather it started for prayer at house (prayer cell). Functionally, yes, it is a house church" (RP26).

Finally, RP02 saw the model for house church as an independent self-supporting church. Although he alone mentions it, it is meaningful. He explained an independent self-support church through his own theological belief and ministerial experience in another house church. RP01 stated that his self-support house church applied a three-self principle. "I was in C&MA. I was asking my denomination to plant the house church that applied by the 'three - self' principle. But they did not allow it. So, I left from the denomination and I had plan to plant the house church that applied by the tree-self principle."

## 2. The House Church Images (Models) that Emerged after Church Planting Started

Under research question 2, protocol question 2 was as follows: "After you planted your house church, did you change your idea about a house church? If yes, what made you change your idea about a house church?" These questions were intended to examine how the research participants possibly changed their view of the image of the house church. In order to answer to these questions, I categorized the models that participants employed after starting the church planting. As seen in the diagram below six nodes were categorized under the theme, The House church image (model) that emerged after starting church planting: House church as Three-self indigenous church, increase of interdependent relationship and cooperation, comparison with other churches, missional church (house church as mission strategic church), house church that is people-oriented, and need for a building.

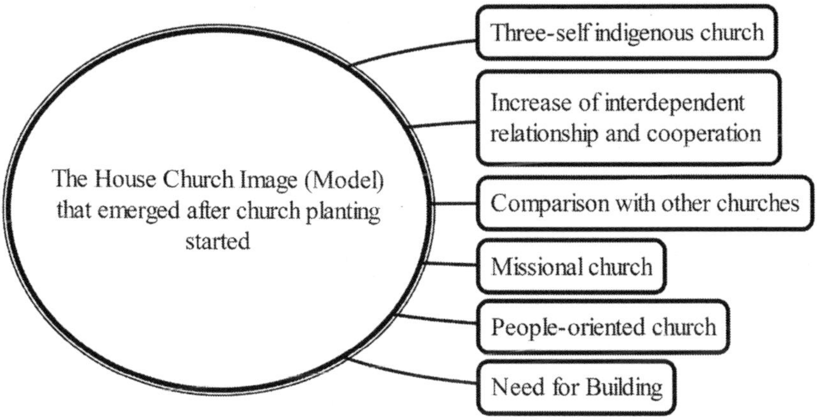


**Figure 14.** The House Church Image (Model) that emerged after the church planting started

House Church as Three-self Indigenous Church

Research participants (RP01, RP 26) considered the three-self principle and indigenous church as a house church model after they started church planting. RP01 expressed the house church model that emphasized the teaching of biblical doctrine with three-self principles after he started house church. "Although practical management of the house church is by three-self principle, I realize the importance of teaching doctrine in the house church. In this meaning, I want to define the house church as a church that taught by the biblical doctrine with three-self principle." RP26 stated his plan for a house church was an indigenous church. "The plan was that later this group would grow and take it to the next level of establishing an indigenous church."

Increase of an Interdependent Relationship and Ministerial Cooperation

Seven research participants (RP02, RP03, RP04, RP05, RP13, RP19, RP31) explained their image of a house church was now a church built by the improvement of an interdependent relationship and cooperation.

RP02 and RP05 stated how they had changed for house church image from their previous thoughts after they planted the church. RP02: "I thought that the congregation depended on pastor and not the pastor dependent on people. But, I have changed my idea about the house church. It is because the interdependent relationship between the pastor and the congregation."

RP05:

> I have changed my heart that the church should build together with the believers. I was thinking about so much interdependence. Fellowshipping with them and encouraging them, but as we went on I found I also depend on them to be encouraged spiritually, to be

> motivated physically to carry on. This is a change what I saw. In other words, I have changed my previous understanding of the leadership after I planted my house church.

RP13 described that the growth of a house church demanded ministerial cooperation of believers. "Before we met as a smaller group, but now as the church has grown we have many more challenges like Sundays school, worship team, usher team. etc."

RP31 depicted the ministerial cooperation between the pastor and the believer toward mission. "I began to think of the Church in an established manner. Moreover, at first I tried alone, later all house church members work together towards my vision of building God's kingdom in the world." As an example of ministerial cooperation between the pastor and believers toward mission, RP27 portrayed how believers cooperate in the ministry for evangelism and how an interdependent relationship between them impacted the ministry and mission.

> After I started the house church with these two members, they bring their family members, now twenty to twenty five members come to the church. So, house church impact that. After I started the house church, little by little, people start come to the church, I talked to them, I understand them, they also understand me.

When RP03 set forth his changed idea of his house church, he stated the importance of spiritual cooperation with the believers in the house church: RP03,

> Once I started church, I look forward big place first, there many people come and church will grow. It is not always like that. You got few people in hand, you still know worship together, socially you have prayer partner in a small fellowship, it is not that you be a leader and pastor always giving but you are also receiving. So, you find your partner in a group. Sometimes he comes to you on a regular basis, to prayer for the concerns of team members.

Also, RP19 expressed the necessity of physical cooperation of the believers in the house church. "Since people did not cooperate with certain rules in the house, I thought of moving to separate hall. People break a few things, and damage the plants made me to think in this way."

### Comparison with Other Churches

When four research participants (RP06, RP10, RP11, RP30) explained their image of a house church after they started church planting, they compared their churches with traditional churches. RP06 expressed the comparison between house church and traditional church as equal. "Now I consider the house church as at par with the traditional understanding of church. The understanding came gradually. House church is also capable of providing all that a traditional church can. In fact, a house church can do the same with panache."

RP20 and RP10 portrayed their satisfaction for a house church where comparing the house church to traditional church: RP20, "We are satisfied with the house church model although slowly people are moving towards traditional church building." RP10:

> I think the house church is better than mainline churches. More intimacy and relationship is in the house church. I know everyone's name, I know their family. I know individual's problem. I know what are they stressed. Big church does not know the person, problem. In house church, I am closer to them, they closer to me. Pastor and believers has closer relationship.

RP11 and RP30 compared the efficiency of a house church with a traditional church. RP11 expressed the economic efficiency of house church. "In Bangalore, it is difficult to build the church building. It is good to rent the house for the church. Cost of living is very much high." RP30 stated the mobility of a house church. RP30 wrote:

> As the ministry was growing we understood House Church concept is more effective than a mega church. It can spread more swiftly than of a mega church. We felt in a house church the relationships are stronger, intimate and has a feeling of a family or of one body. A small group can easily carry over the vision and the mission of the church. It would be little easy to bring everyone on the same page compared to a structural church or a mega Church

### Missional Church: House Church as Missional Church

When six research participants (RP07, RP08, RP12, RP16, RP23 and RP24) explained their image of house church after they started church planting, they expressed that a house church is mission strategic church. RP07 expressed the centripetal mission aspect of a house church for mission. "The initial idea was changed as more people were given easy access to a place of worship."

Meanwhile, RP08, RP24 and RP34 depicted the centrifugal mission aspect of a house church for mission: RP08 noted the house church as an evangelism tool for reaching local people. "Now it (house church) has turned to be tools of evangelism as well. It (house church) has also become a platform to bind the believers together. The initial idea was changed as the Lord opened opportunity to reach out to the people of the locality."

RP24 also expressed that the idea of a house church to reach (missional) people and society in order to share the gospel:

> Only idea is to preach good news to the society to save more souls to extend the kingdom of God. Because many wandering, peace less, hope less, restless. And I would like to establish powerful house church which lead by the spirit of God in every aspect and circumstances we face in our daily life. And set by house church example for others in the society.

RP34 set forth his idea about the centrifugal mission aspect of the house church. "Like we should not stick one house for gathering, within selected area we need to gather in different houses. Through changing of places we can reach many people. After the church is grown we can stick to one particular place."

RP12 and RP23 described they did not change their image of a house church. They depicted that a house church is the first step for church planting and a tool for reaching out to the local area. RP12, "Before I planted house church I was thinking that, house church would be the first step to start church planting ministry and if I success it in the house church then only I could go for next step and I planned to established small rented house church in a village." RP23, "House church was an entrance to enter a place (area/town /village) for further ministry."

### House Church is People-Oriented Church

When research participants, RP03, RP09, RP14, RP19, RP22, RP25, RP28, RP32, and RP33 explained their image of a house church after they started church planting, they expressed that "house church focus on the importance of people need." RP03,

> My idea started with this, this place must gate to not only to the need of people who come to the pressures but also this place should be training ground for the mature believers to get their strength for the ministry. It is like training program every week, weekly fellowship, bible study on Friday, they have prayer meeting on Monday, sometimes Tuesday, sometimes Wednesday, sometimes morning, sometimes evening. We don't give importance to the time and place. We don't give importance to the time and place. But we give importance of the people's need. You feel that these kinds of familiarity with people would help them grow and help them from their weaknesses. This idea I thought when I started the house church.

RP03 also described that believers need to practice their faith through activities in the house church. Therefore, house church becomes a place where the believers practice their faith through participating in church activities. "Later, I realized house church also demands more activities in Church. People would like to exercise their faith in different ways."

Research participants described the importance of people's context and believers' perspective for planting a house church and of shifting their house church to another building. As RP28 stated, house church is more people oriented. "I had to change my idea of house church. The idea of house church is changed just because of the situation of the people. I came to conclusion that house church is more people friendly and well accepted people to attend them to the church."

RP09 stated the reason why he started a house church in the people's context. "When I start the house church, my plan was to disciple the new convert in their home since they live far from the church." He started a new house church for new converts' family and relatives because new believers could not come to the present house church.

RP14 thought of house church as a process moving toward a large scale church building, but now he expressed that caring for the believers in the house church is much more important than previously thought. "I wanted to move to bigger church buildings. But God did not allow moving out as I had to care for the existing people."

RP 29 expressed that a house church is established by considering people's context.

> I was going to different houses to preach the gospel but had idea of taking them to a Church building where they will worship the lord but then I realized that people were not willing to come to a place called church because of fear of their locality, they would urge saying that why can't you come to our house our house is always open for you, and so this is how started the church in house which was very well attended.

RP19 and RP22 explained the reason why they shifted their house church to another building was due to the believer's stance. Although RP19 saw the conflict between house owner and the believers, he moved to a hall for worship to be free from conflict. "House owner will lose peace. It may hurt people when we say some rules. Since people did not cooperate with certain rules, I thought of moving to separate hall. People break a few things, and damage the plants made me to think in this way."

RP22 stated they will move to another place because the space is not sufficient to accommodate all believers.

> Now we are going to place other than that place because the place now we have that house church is not able to accommodate all the members. We have members sitting outside of the house church (people's context). Now we plan to shift from that place to another some other rented place where we can run the house church.

RP25 saw the function of a house church is people-oriented, not event-oriented. "My view about the function of the house church is that the most important thing is not the program and place, but it is coming into Christ. They themselves is the temple of God, not the place, the most important thing is they will see the church as a family." RP33 also argued that the function of a house church needs to be concerned about people's stance. "House church need means not just preaching alone. It is much more than that care, crisis management, frequent visitation etc."

RP32 also portrayed a house church oriented for believers is to have a good environment for believers to relate with each other: "Earlier my idea of house church was to create deeper relationship with each other, because mainline church did not give this. There people just come and go. I wanted the same deeper relationship to continue."

### Need for a Building

While some house churches (RP19, RP22) moved to a church building because of the believer's needs, six other research participants (RP15, RP16, RP17, RP18, RP20 and RP21) expressed the importance and needs for a church building because of certain reasons that follows.

First, RP15 portrayed that a house church needed to purchase land for constructing a church building like a traditional church. "We are here to develop people by making awareness to people, then people accept us leader. Once the work is developed, the local people will help to buy the land too. Later, people will be ashamed to go to Traditional church."

Second, RP16 described two hindrances or limitations of a house church: one is because of a Hindu cultural understanding; another is a conflict between the house owner and its neighbors. A house is not holy place in Hindu perspective, and a house has many hindrances to be used by church. These two reasons forced him to consider another alternative building for the church. "I found house church has its own limitations as it lacks sanctification. House has its own rules and regulations. I looked for alternatives." For the first reason, RP 21 said,

> there is no reverence to God in the house church in terms of building. A women about to worship the cross of my house church, later she realized that it was a home. So she left the place. Moreover, people look at the traditional church as holy, not the house churches. So, I began to think of bigger separate building for Church.

For the second reason, RP20 said, "I wanted to have own house for running house church as the owners and the neighbors made problem. After starting house church, I became bold. Not afraid of others."

Third, PR17 and RP18 also stated the needs of a church building or hall for church as the first stage of the model toward a large church. RP17, "We could survive only three years. Then we were in need of small hall or buildings.

I preferred that." RP18, "It is a prestige issue to move towards bigger church buildings."

## 3. The Present Image of House Church

Under research question 2, operational question 2 was as follows: After you planted your house church, now what is your idea about a model for a house church that influences to evangelize and catechize migrants or locals in your city? Protocol question 3 was, in what way can you describe your house church model in the present? What are the notable differences before and after a house church plant?

In order to analyze the responses to these questions, I categorized the responses according to participants' present image of their house church. As seen in the diagram below, five nodes were categorized under the theme, The present image of the house churches: From house church toward traditional church, Team ministry and entrustment, Evangelism, Model for Overcoming environment, and Worship place in House and Hall.

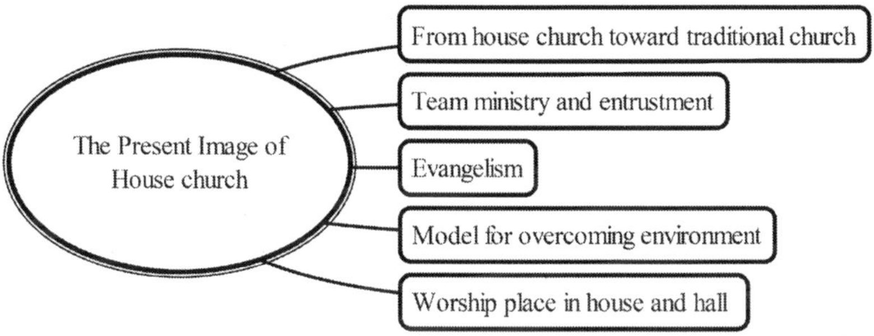


**Figure 15.**The Present Image of House Church

From House Church toward Traditional Church

Research participants, RP04, RP14, RP20, and RP21 expressed the present image of their house churches as 'from house church toward traditional church.'

RP 34 recalled that the essence of the church is not the building, but people. "Now after forming church building, non-Christians are considering the church building as holy place and coming with all respect. Earlier the same non-Christians watched us when we use to gather in house but they considered as the church as they don't have the idea about a church." RP20 expressed his satisfaction with the house church, but he also realized the people wanted to move to a church building for certain reasons. "We are satisfied with the house church model although slowly people are moving towards traditional church building." Like RP20, some other house churches are satisfied with their status; nevertheless, other participants expressed reasons why they need to move to a traditional church building.

Reason one (The Change of the Pastors' Idea): RP04 thought of house church in the beginning, but now his idea has changed to move to a church building.

"The mother church concept has come before moving to bigger building. I had to work hard then I originally thought of a house church." RP14 also stated why he wants to move to a church building. "In the initial stage this model is good. However, later, it should become a bigger church in order to provide support and care for people."

Reason two (The demand of the believers): RP21, RP16 and RP26 portrayed that believers demanded to move from the house to a building. RP21: "Jesus said, God is spirit, and those who worship Him must worship in spirit and truth (John 4:24). These generations do not fully believe in this as they expect for bigger buildings. In the beginning, people happily come to the house church, they think in different manners of moving to traditional building." RP16: "When we got new land, we asked a few house churches to move to new buildings. This is continuing. It is the way to grow." RP26: "Thought to integrate them with a main church but, now a member is ready to give his land if we want to build a church. This small group itself is becoming a church."

Reason three (Increase of house church believers): Although, RP22 did not express directly any need for a church building, he did remark on the increase of church members. "We are living by faith, we have vision, we want to build the kingdom of God, we have two churches, and we have seventy families here. We have thirty families in other cities." This vaguely alludes to the need of a church building in order to accommodate all the believers. As such, research participants described the need of large scale building for accommodating the believers.

RP18 said, "House church should not have more than seven families. When they reach this number, we should move to bigger buildings for better environment." RP17 and RP27 also expressed the need of a building because of the growth of the house church. RP17: "When need arises, when house church grows, break the house church into smaller groups or go for bigger buildings." RP27 said,

> I do not much change the idea about the house church, but, I have changed the field. Now small group become bigger group. Now we have more than thirty members. I can split it by two to two house churches. Now I plan to buy the land. I want to build the building for the small church for them. This building church is not for the Sunday worship. Now they can come to the

## Team Ministry and Entrustment

Research participants RP02, RP03, RP05, RP13, RP25, RP32, and RP33 illustrated the relationship between team ministry and entrustment when they stated the present image of their house church. RP25 and RP02 expressed the importance of team ministry among leaderships and entrustment, and ministry participation of believers. RP25: "Loving one another as a family of God is important, plural leadership is also important, body ministry, reaching others with the gospel. This is remarkable difference between the New Testament Church and traditional church." RP02:

> Relation with God and others reunited. Love for God and his church increased. Pastor and congregation relationship developed. Care, love and respect for God, His people. Actually at present I am leading a church congregation. The house church which I had started is now being led by some other leader pastor from the same house church.

Team ministry in the house church means the participation of all the believers for ministry. RP05 described the team ministry with believers and RP13 also stated the demand for team ministry in the house church. RP05:

> When I started I will be the one to do everything, but now I am sharing the responsibility. I picked someone to take responsibility of nurturing through the word of God. But I will also keep my responsibility to the believers of the house church. Participation of believer's house is more than before.

RP13 revealed the need for participation of the believers to the ministry: "We met as a smaller group before, but now as the church has grown we have many more challenges like Sundays school, worship team, usher team. etc."

Research participants (RP32, RP33, and RP03) noted that the house church model itself leads all the believers to participate in the ministry. RP32: "House church is to create deeper relationship with each other so that they own the mission and they involve ministry to challenge others to come and participate in the church." RP33: "House church is a very effective way of care and supports others. When they are taken care and helped, they share with others to come to church. Once love is received from church, they are able to bring others who are in need."

As RP03 mentions, the role of the pastor in the house church model is to encourage the believers so that they can be involved in the ministry as a team:

> You can encourage everybody for small group because you know their calling, you know their gifts, you understand the way their minister, you know how you see the opportunity coming in your way, to just grow as a family, team is growing, individuals are growing, not one pastor is growing, not his vision is growing, we just see for team growing, this group is for multiplying its group.

## Evangelism

Research participants RP06, RP07, RP08, RP09, RP10, RP15, and RP23 expressed their present house church model that related to evangelism. They discussed how their house church related to world mission, local evangelism, and family evangelism. Then they also explained the house church as a training place for evangelism and how they support other house church plants as their practice of evangelism. First of all, RP06 and RP15 stated the present house church model as a world mission agency. RP06: "It (house church) was meant only to reach-out the neighbor. Now, it has become a body of Christ in fulfilling the Great Command." RP15: "Modern world can be reached only by house church ...."

On the other hand, house church is not only a world mission model, but also a local evangelism model. RP23 stated the house church as an evangelism model for local area. "House church was an entrance to enter a place/area/town/ village for further ministry." That means a house church is planted for evangelizing the specific local area.

For the world mission and local evangelism, the evangelism of a house church always started from family, relatives, and neighbors. RP07: "It (house church) was meant only to be a place of fellowship. Now, we even reach-out to the neighbors." RP10: "Since we are having personal relationship with believers individually, this people inform this relationship to their relatives, when the pastor visit their house, other relatives happy because of the pastor visit their place. My house church is growing, expanded to different places."

Meanwhile, RP08 and RP09 stated the house church is a training center for evangelism. RP08: "It (house church) is a place to nurture and a center to commission believers in reaching out with the gospel of Jesus Christ." RP09: "It (house church) is a center to discipline and nurture the new converts. Now the converts are beginning to reach out."

RP01, who is pastoring two house churches, depicted how these two churches support the financial need for the church planting.

> We have two house churches now. Mumbai and Parutta. Mumbai house church support evangelists in other place (80% of financial support). Parutta house church also support evangelists worked in other area (20% of financial support). We recently plant the house church in specific area and conduct prayer meeting, bible teaching and worship. We apply three-self principle to the house church. Bible teachers from Canada teach the members of the house church. Self-support bible teachers came to the house church for teaching the bible to the house church members. My house church model is bible teaching house church.

### Model for Overcoming Environment

RP28 stated the vulnerable circumstance of the house church. "Persecution is increasing in India so much and especially in our area, church building is wasting of money and even getting targeted by the fanatic groups and becoming vulnerable to the attacks of anti-social elements." RP15, RP19, RP24, RP28, RP29, and RP31 expressed how their present house church model overcomes the various environments they faced. There are not only social and political circumstances that a house church needs to overcome, but also difficulties from other large scale churches. RP19 described that another large scale church wanted the house church to close, since that church treated the house church as their competitor. Therefore, only few believers are attending the house church, others are moving to that large scale church. "House church is a good model when people are mature, since there is another church nearby, wanted to stop our fellowship" (RP19).

RP31 criticized the reason why a house church could not overcome their environment. "Earlier people started house church because of the passion and vision for the Lord. But today, it is to have double income. I.e. to get income from Church too. People come for ministry without calling; therefore, they are not able to maintain their own testimony" (RP31). Research participants PR29 and RP24 expressed that the present house church is a model for overcoming circumstances.

RP29, "House church model is helping people friendly, non-threatening in Indian situation. People understand the need of Jesus in their lives but are afraid of society therefore; making them bold enough is important in the atmosphere of house." RP24,

> Only idea is to preach good news to the society to save more souls to extend the kingdom of God. Because of many wandering, peace less, hope less and restless, I would like to establish powerful house church which lead by the spirit of God in every aspect and circumstances we face in our daily life. And set by house church example for others in the society.

### Worship Place in House and Hall

Research participants RP11, RP12, and RP30 expressed how their present house church model relates to a place for worship, set up and an independent subsidiary church. Research participants portrayed their house church image as the worship place in a rented house or hall.

"When we approached the people, we visited their house to have friendship, and then slowly we contact them by the phone, then we have fellowship. In Bangalore, it is difficult to build the church building. It is good to rent the house for the church. Cost of living is very much high" (RP11). "My house church is rented average building, and the difference is, when I start house church, I just established in the believer's house and now it is in rented building"(RP12). "We have moved the worship from a house to a rented hall. We still consider it as a house church since it is located on the ground floor of a house. Not much difference we find since we planted the church. We used to sit on the floor and worship but now have chairs to sit" (RP30).

## 4. The Future Image of House Church

Under research question 2, operational question 3 was as follows: In your opinion, what is an ideal model for a house church that influences to evangelize and catechize migrants or locals in your city? Protocol question 4 was as follow: what is your future plan for your house church? What is your future model for house church? In order to analyze these questions, I categorized the expressions into four concept as seen in the diagram below: (1) Church planting and growth, (2) House church as a vital community, (3)Transition towards a traditional church, Missional church and church building, and (4) Missional church as the future image of a house church.

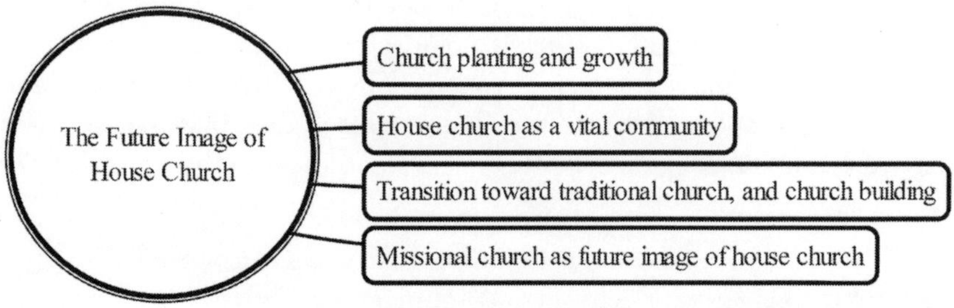


**Figure 16.** The Future Image of a House Church

Church Planting and Growth

Eighteen research participants (RP01, RP03, RP10, RP11, RP12, RP13, RP15, RP19, RP22, RP23, RP25, RP26, RP27, RP28, RP29, RP30, RP31, and RP32) expressed how their future house church model related to church planting and growth.

First, some research participants only focused on the church growth when they expressed their future house church. RP12, "My future plan is to enlarge every part of my house church, as well as my ministry." RP11, "I want to increase our fellowship by prayer, and bring them the God's word. It is most important to our lives. We will go to the doors and knocking the doors, and then we want to build the house gathering, house fellowship."

Second, some participants (RP03, RP13, RP22, and RP30) considered church planting as a natural process of church growth. They stated that they focus on the growth of the church, then they divide their church to plant another house church.

RP03 mentioned a clear goal for church growth of his house church with a vision for church planting.

> My future plan is more than 500 groups emerging out. Each group multiplies more than 2500 within 5 years. It is may be just ambitious target. But, I just believe in the Lord in five years that these emerging

> churches are going to make a different in our country. I believe that it is going to happen. It is not from my mental math, it is with the power of God, commitment, and people are going to the people who are in hunger and thirty. These groups will multiply. God will do something great for these groups. This emerging church is answer. We need to reach to the all India to fellowship the people. House church is the answer for it.

RP22 expressed to set up an independent subsidiary church when the house church grows.

> As the church grows, they need to separate, forming to small group, and again build up as a church again. I believe this pattern should work on. It is almost like cell group ministry like Korean full gospel church. It is one church with small group different area. Those small groups become small church. And that one grows, and then they are start small groups. In future, this strategy will apply to my house church ministry.

RP30 and RP13 also understood the numerical growth of house church as demanding its splitting to plant another house church. RP30: "We would like to limit each house church to 100 people and if it exceeds we would like to start another one in their respective areas. This would be for sure that we would conduct worship either hiring a small hall in the house or having it in one of the leader's house." RP13, "After the church has grown to 250 we divide and plant another church in a different part of the city. We plan to do the same in other places."

Third, some participants focused on the church planting itself more than church growth of their house church. RP01, "We pray for planting the house church continuously through the efforts of evangelists. Idea model for house church is a church applied three self-principles and taught by biblical teaching in sound doctrine." RP32, "Every community and area should have house church. I am not interested in mega buildings." RP27 expressed church planting in the village and city as his future house church model. "I believe the biblical model of the house church is ideal model in Acts. My future plan is plant the house church in other village in the center of the urban town. Urban town will be a center for reaching other small village. Through the house church, We can deliver the gospel from the village to village, individuals to individuals." RP28, "I want to focus on starting house churches only. I am encouraging believers of different locality to start worshipping the Lord in the houses where people will find easy to attend."

RP 23, RP 25, RP 29 and RP 26 described how to employ their house church model for church planting for the future model. RP23, "Monthly once, I would like to gather all in one place. Through them I want to start another church."

> RP25: For future model, I want to really plant more churches similar to we have seen in the Bible, so we want to plant more churches and raise more leaders and send more missionaries, and encourage believers to become more active ministry. Church planting means people think we need a building and we need a full time pastor and paid pastor. So, our desire to plant churches is not focus on the building, not focus on salary pastor, but focus on the people. Money is not issue for planting churches.

RP29, "House church planting is the model I would like to adapt and I am working towards the goal." RP26, "Future plan is to build a church that would be indigenous (Three self-principles) to start another prayer cell (house church) and eventually to form it as a church."

Furthermore, RP 19 and RP 34 expressed that they wanted to plant a house church where there is no church. RP19, "I want to focus planting house church where there are no Christians. That is my vision." RP34, "The future plan is to plant a church where there is no church. Now we have planted a church in the present locality."

House Church as a Vital Community

RP02 and RP05 expressed that house church as a community are providing people's need and gathering as a family community.

> RP05: Actually at present I am leading a church congregation. The house church which I had started is now being led by some other leader pastor from the same house church. I have not left the work of house church. I have a model of blood donation type for the house church. That is giving out or donates the blood and it will replace it in body within next 24 hours. Same way if a house church donates its love and place, it will be filled in next few days.

> RP02: House church closely need to community. Head of family which is the father is usually the priest. Father and mother take more responsibility in the house. Since father and mother as older, we look at them respectively and society where they confirm any one who older to us, we don't usually ask them questions and we don't questions what they states. We give them space respect. That's exactly like the priest that we see in the Old Testament. In the Old Testament, old people they were look up to. So we would like to see that kinds of model being followed at the future for the house church where the father will be given the responsibility as a leader pastor in spiritually. The house church when we just one family which is joint family may be one or two neighboring houses together where we looking at that model.

### Transition toward Traditional Church and Church Building

Research participants expressed how their future house church model related to a traditional church (RP04, RP16 and RP 17) and church building (RP14, RP18, RP20, RP21 and RP33). RP31 stated that a house church should be part of a tradition not simply be a model.

> My vision is to build a church surrounded on the word of God. Caste practice should be removed in the churches. Cornelius household's testimony made his church became viable; therefore, my model of the future church is sharing testimony and impacting people for God's kingdom. House church should become one of the traditions instead of simply a model.

This means that the house church model itself should settle down into a tradition.

Nevertheless, RP04 depicted that his house church is transiting to the traditional church. "Presently, our house church almost become like other traditional church. We bought a separate land, so believers are happy about the move." RP17 also stated, "Good to start with house church and then move to the traditional church pattern"

RP16 explained why they wanted to transition to the traditional church. "To become a regular church, present generation demands for this." In the view of a house church, to follow the traditional church pattern is to move to a large scale building. RP14 and RP33 expressed that their future plan for the house church is to move building. RP14, "I am thinking of bigger building soon for future house church." RP33, "Moving to bigger building is our future plan and future model too."

Participants RP21, RP18 and RP20 explained the reason why they need to move to large scale building: RP21, "To go for big building as people prefer." RP18, "Seriously praying for new land for Church buildings. The present house church is facing enormous problem from the neighbors" (RP18). RP20, "Have own house, so that the church is not troubled. Further, to think of huge building for church, which gives a satisfaction in people in terms of worship." Transitioning from a house church towards a traditional church seems to be justified by the reasons above.

### Missional Church as the Future Image of a House Church

Participates (PR06, RP07, RP08, RP09, and RP12) expressed their future house church model as a missional church. RP06 said, "It was meant only to reach-out the neighbor. Now, it has become a body of Christ in fulfilling the Great Command." RP07, "It was meant only to be a place of fellowship. Now, we even reach-out to the neighbors." RP08, "To become an outreach center." RP09, "It's a center to discipline and nurture the new converts. Now the converts are beginning to reach out." These participants recognized the house church as a missional church.

## 5. Application of Theoretical Premise for Research Question 2

Many scholars' (Christian A. Schwartz, Prosperly Bell Lyndoh, David L. Mattson) previous research work on house church planting theory have focused on leadership development for the next generation and laity by addition of new churches. Some scholars like Rad Zdero proposed his theoretical approach for the house church planting model. Other scholars' general church planting theories also can be employed for defining the house church planting model. Furthermore, I categorized the change of research participants' understandings of a house church model as time has gone on and put them into the form of a diagram as follows.

**Table 6.** House Church Model as Time has Gone

| **Before planting church** | **After planting church** | **Present** | **Future** |
|---|---|---|---|
| Alternative Model | Interdependent relationship and cooperation | Toward traditional church | Church planting and growth |
| Dependence Model | Comparison with traditional church | Evangelism | Hand over Leadership |
| Church Planting mission Model | Missional Church | Nurturing and training of the believers | Transition toward traditional church |
| Large scale building | People-oriented church | Place for the worship | Missional church |
| Church is person | Need for building | Independent subsidiary church | Church building |

The finding that the pastors expressed about the house church model from the research question 2 can be defined by some theoretical premises of the various scholars mentioned above.

According to Rad Zdero's theoretical premise, every setting should be considered as a potential area for a new house church. In the initial stage of house church planting, one must consider the place of worship. As we see it above, a building as well as a house have been one of the first considerations for planting a house church in the initial stage.

As we have seen in the literature review, Roland Allen considered church planting and growth (expansion) by addition of new churches. For this, some scholars like Prosperly Bell Lyngdoh emphasized the role of new believers to be part of it. Christian A. Schwartz also stressed the engagement of new believers to the church planting. Klaus Detlev Schulz argued to utilize already existing Christian communities and to incooperate individual believers for church planting. These ideas contribute to the mission (David L. Mattson). As we see in the diagram above, research participants had an idea of a church planting model that focuses on evangelism and growth.

In the literature review, Schulz proposed one theoretical consideration for church planting: Church planting efforts should focus on establishing communities that identify themselves (with their own theological identity). In order to identify a house church, as we see in the above diagram, research participants reveal their own ecclesiological idea about the church. For them, a house church is a person and people-oriented church. They focus on the nurturing and training of the believers so they can lead the house church for the next generation.

According to Thomas Schattauer's model for an urban church, the 'Inside out' model, reveals that worship signifies the missionary activity of the Triune God to His believers. House church can be a place for the visible act of worship. For this purpose, as we see above, it seems that research participants considered the traditional church in the initial stage of their church planting. In other words, they thought of a house church as the alternative model in the beginning stage of church planting because of certain reasons.

Meanwhile, Schulz warns against the paternalistic approach to church planting (especially for a foreign missionary). As seen above, the idea of the 'dependence model' for church planting is not proper for planting a church. Therefore, this idea may not appear in the present or future models in the data.

Chapter 7

# Research Finding 3: House Church and Worldview Change

This section deals with the data regarding what ways house churches transform the worldview of the migrants as well as locals who hold the Hindu worldview in order to evangelize and catechize them in the city.

## 1. The Understanding of the House Church Pastor for the Factors of Worldview Change that Migrants and Locals faced

Under the research question 3, operational question 1 was as follows: In what ways do economic migration and urban environment affect migrants to change their religious and cultural understanding? In what ways does the change of urban environment affect locals to change their religious and cultural understanding? In order to answer these questions, I categorized the expressions of the research participants into four nodes. As seen in the diagram: Economical aspect, Spiritual aspect, Psychological aspect, and socio-cultural aspect.

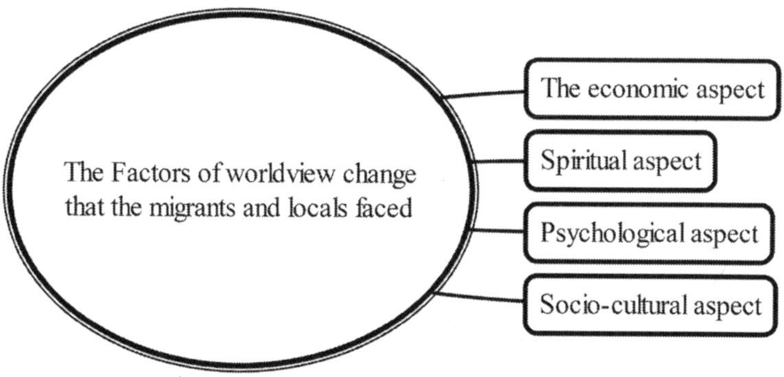


**Figure 17.** The Factors of worldview change that migrants and locals faced

The Factors of Worldview Change in the Economic Aspect

As RP02 stated, "As a means of survival, it (migration) changes their religious and cultural understanding." The sub-theme, the factors of worldview change in the economical aspect, has two nodes: economic urban environment and economic failure. The urban migrants and locals experienced both economic urban environment and failure. In other word, these experiences cause their worldview to change.

### *Economic and urban environment*

RP12 expressed that the economic and urban environment influenced the migrants' and locals' worldview change in positive way.

> Certainly it affects to the migrants in a positive way, when they grow up in economic and urban environment. For example, many village girls (migrants from rural) have no chance to go school and study or self-determination, due to their religious and cultural settings. But when they start to attend urban house church, their thinking also changes.

Meanwhile, as RP12 stated, the house church provides space and preparation to the migrants and locals in order to adjust the urban new life. RP31 also mention, "Therefore, they come to church in order to identify with the civilized modern people." In this point, the house church has a role as a gate for migrants to enter the city life.

### *Environment of Economic hardship and failure*

Many research participants expressed that migrants and locals have experienced their worldview change when economic failure of the migrants and the locals lead them to the house church. In other words, migrants and locals experience their worldview change when they are in economic failure and difficulty.

RP01 and RP31 expressed that being poor is a factor of worldview change that migrants faced. RP01, "Migrants from the rural are lonely. They are in poor and danger. They face transformation in physiological aspect because of environment change. This transformation can be an opportunity to deliver the gospel to them." RP31, "Poverty, life status and quarrels push the migrants to seek for rich, good status of life and peace. Therefore, they come to church in order to identify with the civilized modern people." RP32 also stated that the experience of economic adversity challenges the migrants and locals to change their worldview. "People have more world desires. The locals are addicted to drinking habits. So, it makes them poor. When they come to church, they are delivered from these bad habits. Therefore, the money is saved. Now they are happy, the economy and their life style have changed. Now they feel that they are in the right track."

RP34, RP17 and RP20 also expressed that financial crisis is a cause of worldview change for migrants and locals, and it leads them to the house church.

RP34, "The migrants face lots of problem financially as they need to survive and settle. The place where we have planted a church is a backward area like slum." RP17, "When there is no solution to their problem of financial crisis, sickness, they seek for God and come to house church." RP20, "People who have debt, diseases are pushed to seek God. We as house church deal with his issues."

RP15 expressed that migrants and locals come to the house church because they want to solve their economic difficulties and to fulfill their desire to change. "Failure in economic status in society will motivate them to come upto house church. Migrant expect financial blessings to come up in life. They need change in their life and livelihood."

RP25 described how a house church leads the migrants and locals to change their worldview with the gospel.

> The gospel of Christ impacts the mindset of all the people that what they believe, how they believe because of the power of the gospel and salvation. We changes culture of the believer which is not the biblical. They come to the city for the economics purpose that earning money. Money is not everything; God is everything, also to learn to not pursue the money as the rule of Christ. Christ is the answer for life. We change their economic view differently.

RP10 spoke of the economic disadvantage for the migrants and locals when their conversion results in worldview change.

> When schedule caste's children convert to the Christian, they lose the government's support. Therefore, the percentage of Christian in India is not increasing. Most People are not honest those are from the schedule caste and low caste because they lose their benefit from the government when they convert to the Christianity. God will guide you, lead you, the pastor should teach in this way. We should change our value from previous Hindu background. Not only physical but also spiritual.

### The Factors of Worldview Change in the Spiritual Aspect

Urban migrants and locals experience both the change of spiritual identity and concern for spiritual matters. RP06 stated that when they come to the house church, they realized the differences between Christianity and Hinduism. "People understand and see the difference between Jesus Christ and the gods they worshipped." These experiences cause their worldview change.

First, one factor of worldview change that the migrants and locals face in their spiritual aspect is the change of spiritual identity. RP30 expressed that the migrants and locals could not leave their previous religion (Hinduism). "For the migrants intuition levels on spirituality would be less comparatively to an urban person. The migrants would not easily give up their ancestral religion. That is sacred for them but if one family converts there will be a possibility for the other family to convert." This reveals that family is more important than religion for them to change their spiritual identity.

RP27 and RP23, however, stated that it is the gospel that influences their change of spiritual identity from Hinduism to Christianity. RP27, "Even though there is social and economic change and its environment does not much affect to the locals and the migrants, the gospel impact to these people." RP23, "Through sharing gospel, they come to know truth from diseases and sinful life." Meanwhile, RP14 depicted the power encounter that the migrants and locals experienced that influenced them to spiritual change. "Mostly, Roman Catholics (Christians) come to my house church after they know the truth and the unbiblical practice of Catholic Church. Demonic powers attack the people. So the locals come to house church to seek the great power."

Second, one of the factors of worldview change that the migrants and locals faced in the spiritual aspect is interest for spiritual matters. RP21 and RP18 stated that when people pursue spiritual matters, the opportunity of spiritual change is opened.

RP21, "People see the genuine love of our lives. When they see the enmity, fight, injustice in the society, they find true love and fellowship in our churches, which motivate them to change their worldview and follow Christ." RP18, "People come to house church to hear God's word. Since India is a devote country and the people are more spirituals, people show interest anything related to God." The migrants and locals faced their spiritual change when they have met the Word of God.

### The Factors of Worldview Change in the Psychological Aspect

The urban migrants and locals experienced both anxiety and conflict in the psychological aspect. These experiences cause their worldview to change.

First, anxiety is one of the factors of worldview change for the migrants and locals. RP29 expressed that insecurity influenced the worldview change of the migrants and locals.

> Insecurity is the main problem of migrants within the country, even moving from rural to Urban, because they leave their comfort zone and venturing into new area. They cannot continue to hold to their own system which does not work in new areas or they are considered primitives due to influence of modern technology and media.

RP23 stated that the factors of anxiety like diseases and sinful life influenced the people's psychological aspect and causes a worldview change of the people. RP13 stated that when the people meet anxiety factors like pressure in the city, they come to the house church. "As the church is in an urban set up, the church is generous, so there is no pressure on individuals."

Like RP13, RP28 and RP16 portray people move into a house church because they want to find a safety zone from anxiety.

> RP28: First of all as people migrate from one place to another, they have to leave back their cultural pride because they go to new areas where the cultural values differ and therefore, they feel more insecure, so they need some acceptance and therefore are willing to be a part of some community to have urban identity. In that situation Christianity attracts them; they see someone caring for them in kind of foreign setup for them. This helps them to come to Christ.

RP16 also said, "People come with different reasons. Most of the time, the middle class comes to church for social security, the poor comes to get rid of economic issues. People come not just to seek God but to find love and acceptance." This reveals their physical status of anxiety. Thus, this experience of anxiety influences people's worldview change.

Second, one of the factors for worldview change that the migrants and locals face is the conflict. RP11 expressed that there is conflict between their previous worldview and new worldview. "It is very difficult to come out from previous traditions. We support them with word of God. Then they may grow according to God's words, with that they may overcome their tradition." This not only has a spiritual aspect but also a psychological aspect. RP29 also stated that when their previous culture conflicts with a new culture, their worldview is influenced. "They cannot continue to hold to their own system which does not work in new areas or they are considered primitives due to influence of modern technology and media."

RP30 stated that culture shock, a conflict in a new urban environment, influenced people's worldview change. "There would certainly be a drastic change in the economy of the migrant as the cost of living in the urban set up would be high and there would also be some cultural shocks for them in the urban area. I personally feel that wouldn't be a hindrance for embracing a new religion."

### Factors of Worldview Change in the Socio-Cultural Aspect

The urban migrants and locals experienced both persecution, new relationships and a new environment in a psychological aspect. These experiences cause their worldview to change.

First, persecution of the migrants and locals is one of the factors for worldview change that the migrants and locals face in the psychological aspect. RP19 expressed the migrants and locals as a persecuted community. "House church is attraction mostly for the downtrodden community and the abandoned people. We welcome those to our home. House church provides care. It also supports a few families who are in need." RP13 saw that the migrants and locals are under pressure. "as the church is in an urban set up, the church is generous, so there is no pressure on individuals." This experience of alienation and pressure influenced the migrants and locals' worldview change.

Second, new relationship and new environments are one of the factors of worldview change that the migrants and locals faced in the psychological aspect. RP26 and RP29 stated that new social environments (like culture, languages and religions, new areas, technology and media) influenced the people's worldview change. RP26, "We gives them (migrants) an understanding there are different culture, languages and religions that are part of society since most of them lived in homogenous environment." RP29, "Insecurity is the main problem of migrants within the country, even moving from rural to urban, because they leave their comfort zone and venturing into new area. They cannot continue to hold to their own system which does not work in new areas or they are considered primitives due to influence of modern technology and media."

Meanwhile, RP33 and RP22 expressed that new relationships in the new environment influenced the migrants and locals' worldview change. RP33, "When people are in their native places, the social stigma is very high. When people move our Chennai city from villages, they become a nuclear family, self-supported economy. Therefore, they are able to come to church and make their own decision." This socio-cultural change influenced the individual's worldview.

RP22 expressed that the migrants want to have new relationship in their new environment. Their desire for new relationships influenced their worldview change regarding social position and role:

> There is more openness among people who are migrated from other area. But people move one place to other place to searching the job, when they come to urban sector, they aware of their family. In India, there is great family bond. Where this people come to urban place, they are apart from their family. They are looking forward new relationship. When they coming touch us as Christian group, there is more open us among them toward the gospel. They are more receptive. If we suppose to share the gospel them in the whole place and whole town, they will not respond. They will not even want to listen. Now because they are in the city, we have some church members that somebody can get touch with them. They slowly open up. The chance is being more receptive to the gospel.

## 2. Evangelism of House Church to the Hindu Migrants and Locals

Under research question 3, operational question 2 was as follows: In what ways does your house church communicate with Hindu people in order to deliver the gospel and transform their worldview? In order to analyze research participants responses, I categorized them under six nodes under the theme, Evangelism of house church to the Hindu migrants and locals (see diagram: Figure 18): Evangelism through helping with the peoples' problem and their change, Evangelism through contextualization, Evangelism through personal relationship, Evangelism through various meetings, Traditional evangelism, and The attitude and approach to other cultures and religions for evangelism.

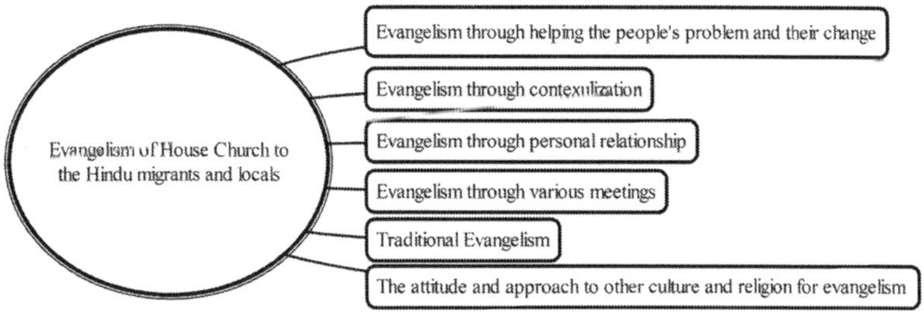


**Figure 18.** Evangelism of House Church to the Hindu migrants and locals

Evangelism through Helping with the People's Problem and their Change

According to data, it was found that a house church helps the Hindu migrants and locals that face worldview change. It also creates the point of contact for people to deliver the gospel through helping with people's problems.

First, research participants expressed how a house church helps Hindu migrants and locals for their worldview change in order to evangelize them. RP01 explained, "They face transformation in physiological aspect because of environment change. This transformation can be an opportunity to deliver the gospel to them." His expression can be interpreted that if the house church can help the Hindu migrant's change, the gospel can reach them through this help to change.

RP11 and RP30 also expressed how the house church helps the Hindu migrants and locals from their previous Hindu tradition, worldview and cultural identity. RP11, "I believe that they will come out from their previous religion and culture by the word of God." RP30,

> It would take some time for a new convert to give up some of the Hindu practices instantly. But gradually they would learn the biblical culture and follow it. We don't condemn them for having a Bindu (Ladies normally have it on their forehead) or Sindur, but teach them gradually. In the initial stage we mostly stress the Gospel and tell them How Christ is the Way, the Truth and Life. We will be in constant touch motivating and encouraging them.

Second, participants depicted how a house church helps people's problems and need for the Gospel. RP34 said, "We need to allow them to express their problems or whatever they want to express." RP33 stated that the house church needs to grasp the present problems of the people, and should suggest proper answers for it with the gospel. "We do issue based ministry. Gospel is the answer to their present issues."

RP27 stated that house church should take care of Hindu migrants and locals who are confronted with illness, family problems or spiritual problems.

> Hindu migrants or locals are coming to the house church because of (1) their sickness. (2) Second is their family problem. (3) Spiritually they are coming for demon possession. They also come because of psychological problem. Sometime people do not distinguish between demon possession and psychological problem. Therefore, before they come to church, the already practice (Black magic, Mantra) some Hindu practice to solve that problem. My concern, I pray for them. I use to lead them in this way. I asked them to come to him for three week regularly. It is not for making them to come to the church, but I asked them to come to understand what/ who they are. Since Hindu people who come to me do not know what is the Christianity, they think the Christianity is one of the Hinduism. They asked me to practice Black magic and Mantra. I said I am not magician. I request him or her to come to me for 3 weeks. I am using in Hindu's idea. If Hindu people have some problem, they come to magician or priest for Three weeks continuously to get solution. In that way I am using for teaching the gospel. I also asked them to come to me three week and I teaching the gospel for 3 weeks (about law and gospel). During that time I teach not only gospel but also pray for them. My wife also worked with me in this matter. In the cultural way, I bring the oil and water to put it to the people. People thinks that they get something through the weeks. This method is not about spiritual aspect but physiological treatment. People bring some medicine to pray before they use. I bring some water to make them drink with that medicine. They think I brought prayer water. This is psychological treatment.

RP20 stated the need for caring of their economic problems and illnesses. "People who have debt, diseases are pushed to seek God. We as house church deal with their issues." RP32 expressed that the need to help for urban poor migrants and locals. "Our method is soup, soap, salvation. We feed the hungry, and then share the gospel since they are urban slum dwellers. We show our love in action."

Evangelism though Contextualization

Research participants RP04, RP05 and RP17 described how they work on evangelism through contextualization as a way to deliver the gospel to the Hindu migrants and locals.

RP04: "We go with the local people culture and deliver the gospel message in their (migrants and locals) bowl (culture)." RP05,

> More than 90% of my house church members are from Hindu background. We try to contextualize. I was talking about sacrifice

> before. Hindu religion still keeps on offering sacrifice after sacrifice after sacrifice. But according to the Bible, Jesus was the sacrifice, is the sacrifice, and sacrifice all time. So, we don't have to offer sacrifice any more. This is one of the main tools that we use.

RP17, "I analyze the person's context and share the gospel. I introduce Jesus as a liberator and redeemer. We contextualize the gospel to some level at least."

As such, a house church delivers the gospel through discovering the point of contact in the context of Hindu migrants and locals.

Evangelism through Personal Relationship

Participants expressed that evangelism through personal relationships is a way of delivering the gospel to the urban migrants and locals. The house church creates the point of contact for people to deliver the gospel through personal relationships and testimonies.

First, research participants RP08 and RP09 expressed evangelizing through personal testimony. RP08 "It (house church) is primarily by means of personal evangelism. We share our own testimony of how we encountered the power of God." RP09, "We share the Gospel personally to our neighbor by sharing our testimonies of how the Lord has done miracles in our lives."

Second, participants found evangelism through people's demand for spiritual need. Research participants RP02, RP03 and RP06 described that they deliver the gospel to the Hindu migrants and locals when they come and ask about it. RP02, "I do deliver the gospel to the Hindu immigrants or the Hindu locals who join the house church." RP03, "We witness to non-Christian first, when they come to us as seekers; they come and ask so many questions." RP06, "We present the Gospel in simple everyday language and the recipient requests prayer."

Third, research participants described evangelism through making a good relationship. As RP13 said that the house church is opened to everyone. "The Gospel in its (house church) simple form opens to all peoples. None in particular since it (house church) is a multi-cultural group" RP10 also stated that people come to a house church for making good relationships.

As such, research participants RP10, RP12 and RP22 spoke of evangelism through making good relationships. RP12,

> The best way of deliver the gospel is to build good relationship with them, without having proper relationship it's very difficult to deliver the gospel. And we should not criticize their believers and their own worldview, but through the word of God, we must try to change their world view.
>
> As an example, RP10 said,
>
> Some Hindu people come to house church before they are converting. They bring sweets and fruits to distribute to the believers in Hindu

> festival time. They want us to eat them. Dasehra festival, we are sitting there, they bring the food to us to eat. I pray and eat. The Hindu people happy, and they are convert to the Christian and I baptized them. We cannot share the gospel to them when we reject their culture, step by step, slowly.

RP22 explained that how making a good relationship with people impacts to evangelism, giving an example.

> It is more of friendship evangelism. What we encourage our church members is you try to getting touch with them. Getting touch people around you, build up friendship with them... Example, one our believer invited one Muslim man. After coming here, he felt Christian community is so loving, they are so caring, and he wanted to come back. After about 6 months, he started attend the church regularly.

> RP28 expressed evangelism in an equal relationship with Hindu people.

> Since India is predominantly Hindu country with lot of caste and sub-caste system, and in that situation whoever comes to them asks about their Hindu caste and culture and treats them accordingly. But when we go we never ask them their caste and creed but accept them as they are and they see the difference between their own people and the Christian. That leads them to Christ.

RP29 states how a house church treats the people regardless of the peoples' culture and belief by providing a sense of security for evangelism.

> The house church provides them the sense of security because they experience the acceptance regardless of creed and culture. They feel that our own religious people do not accept us but these bunch of people welcome us into their houses and treat us well and do not mistreat us. That brings them to house church one after another Sunday. They hear things they had never heard and that surprises them.

Thus, a house church delivers the gospel through the point of contact of personal relationships with Hindu migrants and locals.

### Evangelism through Various Meetings

Research participants expressed that they organize various meetings (Bible study and prayer meetings, cultural programs, revival and youth group meetings, etc.) as a point of contact to Hindu migrants and locals for evangelism. RP01, "There are few Hindu migrant in our house church. We deliver the gospel to them through the regular bible study and prayer meeting. Especially we emphasis on the bible study and prayer." RP07, "We organize Bible Study for them to know Jesus better." RP24, "The local Hindu immigrants did not join us ... However;

there are many ways to deliver the gospel... organizing revival meeting & youth meeting to invite them help us to share the good news." RP22,

> We invite them our Christian program, sometimes, ... we have cultural program, when they come here, and they are see we are different, all other different there...Our church members invite them to the church program, and they come to the church again and again. In the process, they are able to listen to the gospel; slowly they can attract toward the gospel.

As such, a house church delivers the gospel through various meetings as a point of contact for Hindu migrants and locals.

### Traditional Evangelism

Participants expressed that house churches deliver the gospel in a traditional way to the migrants and locals. RP14, "We are use traditional evangelism. How Jesus started his mission? The same way, we preach repent and Kingdom of God is near." RP16 described that a house church delivers the essentials of the gospel to the people as a traditional way. "We tell people about the purpose God to come and die on the cross. We also tell what you get because of the resurrection of Jesus. Prosperity is also important for our people, but don't emphasize often."

RP18, RP21, and RP25 stated that they emphasized the nature of God when they deliver the gospel as a traditional way. RP18, "Our focus is God's love and then we explain about heaven and hell. We are doing just like other doing. Only Holy Spirit is to work further in bringing people to our house churches." RP21, "It (evangelism) is purely on the traditional but practical way. We show love to Hindus. Jesus is introduced to them as the God of Love, Healer, and Redeemer." RP25,

> Few believers are from other state in rural area. They are from Hindu background. The gospel of Christ impacts the mindset of all the people that what they believe, how they believe because of the power of the gospel and salvation. We changes culture of the believer which is not the biblical ... Christ is the answer for life. We change their view differently.

Thus, a house church delivers the gospel through direct way as a point of contact for Hindu migrants and locals.

### The Attitude and Approach to Other Cultures and Religions for Evangelism

First of all, research participants (RP12, RP15, and RP34) stated that a house church should not criticize a people's worldview. RP12, "The best way of deliver the gospel is to build good relationship with them, without having proper relationship it's very difficult to deliver the gospel. And we should not criticize their believers and their own worldview, but through the word of God, we must try to change their world view." RP15, "Without offending their beliefs, we give importance to culture based gospel."

RP34 described that when delivering the gospel to the migrants and locals, one should not condemn their religion and culture:

> It would take some time for a new convert to give up some of the Hindu practices instantly. But gradually they would learn the biblical culture and follow. We don't condemn them for having a Bindu (Ladies normally have it on their fore hear) or Sindur but teach them gradually. In the initial stage we mostly stress on the Gospel and tell them how Christ is the Way, the Truth and Life. We will be in constant touch motivating and encouraging them. Delivering gospel right away when they came may cause us to lose them. We need to allow them to express their problems or whatever they want to express.

Second, participants stated that we need to understand another's religion and culture so that we can inform them of the differences between Christianity and their religion and culture. "By referring to their Hindu Vedas, we inject the gospel. Talking about the local people gods and Hindu doctrines, we say that how Christianity is a fulfillment of those. Therefore, we should know Hindu doctrines" (RP31). "When I teach the bible to the believer, I compare the Bible to Bhagavad Gita and Ramayana. I tell them what difference between them is. Jesus is savior who comes to us" (RP10).

RP25 also expressed the importance of explaning differences between God and Hindu gods, when he delivers the gospel to the migrants and locals.

> Hinduism is pluralistic religion. Hindu believes many gods. Your gods are not concreted, and we focus on very much moral standard. Let them believe God is departing from universe and human being, he is not part of universe, and he is not part of human being. Hinduism believes that god is a part of creation and a person become a god in the future; we have to first of all let them understand who is God actually. It is important that let them understand whose God is qualification of God and also telling them the nature of the human being who is sinful. Because of this sin, Jesus Christ came to the world for saving us. When we tell who is God, we can tell them who they are, we are sinners, every person without Jesus are no forgiven their sin, then they are go to the hell. They have to learn that there is only one God, and Jesus is only savior of the whole world. These things are still very difficult to present people to accept.

Thus, we understand how a house church takes its attitude and response to the Hindu migrants and locals' culture and religions.

## 3. House Church Programs and Activities that Provide Spiritual Needs for Migrants and Locals

This part deals with data regarding in what ways Hindu migrants and locals experienced their worldview transformation after they had been converted. Under this research question 3 above, protocol question 3 was as follow: how does the house church lead the migrants and locals in the spiritual aspect? What kinds of programs does your house church have in order to support spiritual needs of migrants and locals?

In order to analyze responses to these questions, I categorized the kinds of programs the house church has in order to support spiritual needs of migrants and locals. As seen in the diagram below, four nodes were categorized under the theme, House church programs and activities that provide spiritual needs for the migrants and the locals: Education and training, prayer (worship, revival) meetings, various fellowship meetings, and evangelism and local social services.

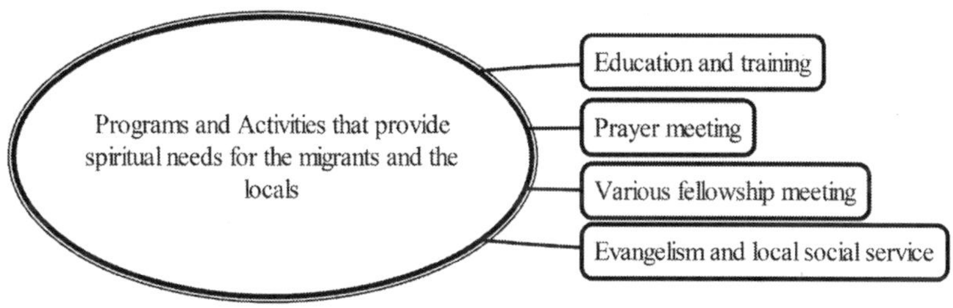


**Figure 19.** Programs and Activities that provide spiritual needs for migrants and locals

RP03 emphasized the established spiritual identity of the migrants and locals. RP05 stated that a house church needs to stress equality in worldview change of the migrants and locals. As a house church of believers who live in a culture of hierarchal relationships, the people in the house church need to change to horizontal relationships.

According to data, 41.8% of participants responded that prayer (worship, revival) meetings were activities of spiritual support for the migrants and locals. Especially, the data demonstrated 29.1% of research participants counted 'understanding Christians belief' (RP26), 'Life of Christ-center and life applied the Bible' (RP12), and 'endeavor for worldview change' (RP05) as the contents of a Christian worldview education.

Besides, research showed that 20% of research participants responded that they met spiritual needs of people through various meetings like small groups, and 9.1% of research participants responded that they filled the spiritual needs of the migrants and locals by encouraging them to evangelize locally and do local social service.

Thus, house churches attempt in various ways to fill the needs of the migrants and locals by using practical programs and activities.

**Table 7.** The Practical Programs and Activities 1

| Division | No. of response | Percentage |
|---|---|---|
| Education and training | 16 | 29.1% |
| Prayer meeting | 23 | 41.8% |
| Various fellowship meeting | 11 | 20% |
| Evangelism and local social service | 5 | 9.1% |
| Total | 55 | 100% |

As we confirmed above, according to the data, prayer (worship, revival) meetings (41.8%) as a program activity of spiritual support for the migrants and locals is very higher than other activities. Then, education and training is the second higher percentage of activity. On the other hand, although evangelism and local social service activities is at a lower percentage, it has missiological meaning in that it supports meeting the spiritual needs of the migrants and locals. This revealed centrifugal aspects while other categories of activities appeared as centripetal aspects in missions.

The following is a sample table. It demonstrates the table title and table source styles.

**Table 8.** The Practical Programs and Activities 2

| | | | |
|---|---|---|---|
| Education and training | Bible study | 10 | 13.5% |
| | Vocational Bible school | 4 | 5.4% |
| | Disciple training | 2 | 2.7% |
| | Seminar | 3 | 4.05% |
| | Christian Worldview education | 3 | 4.05% |
| Prayer meeting | Prayer meeting | 13 | 17.6% |
| | Fasting prayer | 15 | 20.3% |
| | Revival meeting | 2 | 2.7% |
| Various fellowship meeting | Small group | 4 | 5.4% |
| | House visitation | 8 | 10.8% |
| | Fellowship meeting | 3 | 4.05% |
| | Counseling | 2 | 2.7% |
| Evangelism and local social service | Local evangelism | 2 | 2.7% |
| | Local social service | 3 | 4.05% |
| Total | | 74 | 100% |

## 4. The Elements of Hinduism in the House Churches

"Whereas Hinduism is a religion, anything that has religion aspect, that is not a culture. It is a religious practice" (RP02).

This part continuously deals with the data regarding in what ways Hindu migrants and locals experienced their worldview transform after they were converted. Under research question 3 above, protocol question 4 was as follows: What kinds of cultural elements from Hinduism does your house church have? How does the congregation in your house church respond to the elements of Hinduism in their lives? What do the congregations of the house church do on the Hindu festival? In addition, what do you think about Yoga?

In order to respond to these questions, I categorized concepts that research participants counted as elements of Hinduism in the house churches. As seen in the diagram below four nodes were categorized under the theme of The elements of Hinduism in the house churches: Ritual, Myth and Belief, Worship, and Idol and Festival.

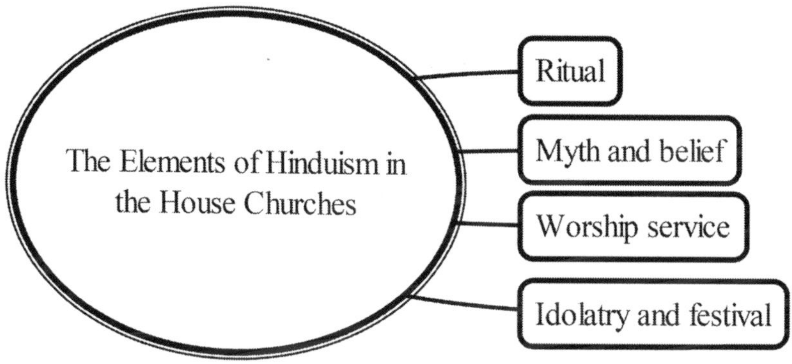


**Figure 20.** The Elements of Hinduism in the House Churches

Ritual

Research participants explained the elements of Hinduism within wedding, funeral and coming-of-age ceremonies. They also expressed responses from house churches toward Hindu ritual.

First, research participants expressed an element of Hinduism in the wedding ceremony of the house churches.

> During marriage bride get 'Manggal sutra' as a sign of married lady. It is not Indian culture but a religious practice of Hindu women. It has religious meaning and importance in Hinduism. And the church at large in India is greatly affected by Hindu religious practices such as during marriage putting turmeric to the couple, throwing rice on the couple. There is problem of dowry in the wedding" (RP02).

RP02 and RP22 mentioned that putting Bindiya on the forehead of a lady. RP26 stated that Christians followed the Hindus style of a wedding in the house church. RP33 said, "Respecting auspicious day is still in the practice...," this appears in the wedding as RP23 stated, as the believers are "fixing marriage in a good day while seeing the calendar."

Second, research participants described an element of Hinduism in the funeral ceremonies of the house churches. "After the death of a person, people are going to the graveyard for the third day to touch feet of the elders and even the dead ones" (RP02). RP23 says, "Celebrating a day for the dead people" as a Hindu element in the house church. "If husband dies, wife keeps the photo of the husband and worship in the house church" (RP14). Besides, RP33 depicted Hinduism elements for a coming-of-age in the house church; "Age attending ceremony of a mature girl are still in practice."

Third, research participants portrayed how house churches responded to the cultural and religious elements of Hinduism found in the ritual of a house church. RP10 stated that the house church accepted the elements of Hinduism. "Some they have, they remove most of them. But they have some. Like house dedication, they ask me to pray for that. Cutting the coconut, banana is there. Cultural matter is still there." On the other hand, RP24 rejects the elements of Hinduism. "In my fellowship we do not encourage cultural elements from Hinduism. In future, believe our members do not Hindu festivals. This is totally against our God. There is only one God we serve and powerful..."

Thus, the elements of Hinduism are founded in the various rituals in the house churches. House churches tried to escape from this and remove it (RP24). But, we can confirm it is not all removed. It seems hard to distinguish what the house church should remove or accept.

### Myth and Belief

Participants explained about the elements of Hinduism regarding myth and belief. They also expressed responses from house churches toward Hindu myth and belief.

First, RP02 expressed that there is 'belief in superstition' in the house church. As an example, RP04 said, "most of the Hindu myths are followed. Believers don't give or take money at nights. Not giving white clothes at nights. Not booming at nights." RP10 and RP21 also noted Hindu myth in the house church. "Superstition they have. Hindu people believe that when the people died, people can be a demon" (RP10). "They also use the *Thayathu*, (It means a sacred thread tied in the right hand in order to protect them from evil spirits)" (RP21).

Second, research participants RP10 and RP31 expressed that the wrong knowledge of God in the house church is because of Hindu belief. "Since they were grown up in the Hindu traditional family background, they have wrong idea about God" (RP 10).

As example of Hindu belief, RP31 said, "Generally, Hindus fear more for God, the same habit continues when they come to house church." RP12 and RP02 also stated examples of it, "The Hinduisms who attend my church they believe in Re-incarnation (the birth of a soul in another body), and Moksha (liberation of the soul from the cycle of life and death)" (RP12). "Insisting on male boy child in the family, less value to the female child in the family" (RP02).

Third, participants expressed that the house church needs to teach about both Hinduism and the Bible in order to change people's worldview. RP28 stated the need of explaning Hinduism. "It took long time to explain them the meaning and forms of Hinduism. Some of the practices are so much rooted that it took several years to take them out like participating in Hindu festivals, fasting in certain days, so on."

Meanwhile, research participants RP10, RP12 stated that the house church needs to teach the Bible to the believers to change their worldview. "Since they were in idolatry worship, personally guide them to know the Christian worship. Share the knowledge about Christ to their life slowly. The pastor gives right direction about the truth of the Bible for changing the Hindu idea" (RP10). "House church uses to respond them through the word of God and try to transform their worldview" (RP12).

Thus, many believers of house churches do not change their Hindu beliefs to Christian faith since they do not know enough of biblical teachings. The house church needs to help them to establish Christian beliefs in order to remove their Hindu false beliefs.

### The Elements of Hinduism in the Worship Service

First, research participants (RP19, RP31 and RP27) expressed the element of Hinduism in worship and its form. "People want sit on the floor as they sit in Hindu temples. They don't want to cover the head and close the eyes as Christians do" (RP19). "They take bath before come to Church and worship the Lord" (RP31).

RP 27 stated the worship of Bahkti style in the house church.

> Singing the song is a program of the house church. Clapping hand and beating the drum and singing the song make them feel more devotion. Hindu people they have their own way to devotion called Bahkti. Bahkti means a way of devotion. We use that devotional manner of the Hindu for our worship with singing song. (2) We are giving the message not in the Hindu way, but evangelical way. (3) prayer: I prayer for them by calling each person's name. They are considering they themselves are important in the house church. Laying hand on the head, pray for the water and oil.

Second, research participants expressed the elements of Hinduism in the Sacrament.

RP5 expressed the element of Hinduism in the Lord's Supper as an example of contextualization.

> We regard to the spiritual elements very careful we are not bringing in any previous religious and cultural elements. But if we talk about the culture in general, it will be a way of sitting. When we take the Lord's Supper, I just use clean water. I don't use color water or wine, I use plain water (contextualization), because water is most general and usual refreshment drink that give it to one another. So, that aspect of cultural thing bring into the church. Hindu think water has divine quality to wash the sin.

PR 27 stated the element of Hinduism in baptisms at a house church.

> Other culture change is about dress. For the baptism church ask locals who have converted to wear the white sari. But white sari in Hinduism means she is widow. Church wants to balance the culture. Some are wearing white sari in the baptism, some are hesitate to wear the white sari. So church allows choosing what they want to wear in the baptism.

Third, research participants (RP05, RP10) compared Christian mediation to Hindu meditation. "If we talk about the meditation, we as Christian also need meditation. But we need to meditate the word of God" (RP05). "Hindus have meditation time in the morning. But we are reading the Bible and praying in the morning" (RP10).

Fourth, RP03 expressed that house is not a holy place for worship in the light of Hinduism. Therefore, a house is not a comfortable place for worship. "You invite people from various faith where never worship god at their home. Hindu people always believe to go for the worship at sacred place to do worship god. For people from the Hindu background, it is hard to understand to worship God at their own house. They may think house is not being a holy place." RP03, however, also continuously described how he teaches about this matter to the believers.

> You can have access to God anywhere, wherever you are. God exists everywhere. He can reach up to anybody, anybody reach up to God any time. With this guide, they can worship comfortably. I found initially people do not feel comfortable to worship at the house. They do not find the any comfortable worship at the house. Although someone pray to God and teach the Word to the believers, they think they worship God in the sacred place. We do not need to tell them you need to go to the sacred place, you can make it sacred. Tell them you are the temple of God, God wants you to become a place where God

> dwell in. That is possible when you accept God. It is only presence. We can make them to understand place is not important.

Meanwhile, RP21 stated that "new believers remove their sandals and worship in house church as they do in Hindu temples." Although the house is a not holy place, believers take off their shoes for the worship.

Idolatry and Festival

Participants see the idolatry and Hindu festivals as elements of Hinduism in the house church, and they also state the reaction of the house church to these Hindu elements.

First, participants expressed how the believers in the house church treat idolatry and its influence. Some believers in the house church did not remove their previous religious habit. "Idol worship occasionally continued if they (the believers) go to some pilgrimages" (RP20). However, some believers did follow the customs of Hinduism because of persecution. RP31 said, "Converted Christians still pay the tax to idols in order to stop the persecution from Hindus. Since, we don't have an own place for ministry, we compromise with the Hindus in some area. Our life is filled with adjustment."

Research participants stated the believers reveal their veneration to the pastor like they do a Hindu idol or guru. "They fall down in the feet of the pastor while praying as they usually fall in front of the idols" (RP21). "Moreover, they also honor their pastors like a guru (Master)" (RP31).

Second, RP03 criticized some mainline churches that celebrate Hindu festivals in their church. "In cultural aspect, mainline church in India they celebrate Hindu harvest festival. I am not talking about the house fellowship. Some people from the mainline church worship Hindu god and goddess trap into churches." Also, PR23 noted, "During Hindu festivals, they (Hindu people) are forced to invite Christian friends."

Response of House church to the Hindu Elements

Participants described the responses of house churches to Hindu elements of the believers. First of all, some participants RP16, RP17 and RP20 pointed out the problem of some believers attending the festival. "Though people say, they don't worship idols, when they go out; they try to some worship to Hindu goddesses" (RP16). "Sometime they go and participate on Hindu festivals" (RP17). "Some attend Hindu festivals also without its knowledge" (RP20).

Second, many research participants (RP06, RP07, RP08, and RP09) reject Hindu elements in the house church and reject attending the Hindu festivals. "We don't have any Hindu elements and don't participate in the Hindu festivals" (RP06). "We don't attend any Hindu festivals" (RP09). RP11 said, "They do not have any Hindu elements. When they become Christians, they removed all Hindu things. They crashed all the idols in their house. They removed all."

Research participants RP01, RP10, and RP12 expressed that they remove Hindu elements using the Bible. "We remove Hindu elements through the Bible" (RP01). "We explain them with the Bible. Idol must forgettable, need to remove. Most of them follow what I teach about it. They try to remove the element of it. It is not easy to Hindu element immediately, but slowly removes" (RP10). "The Hinduisms who attend my church they believe in Re-incarnation (the birth of a soul in another body), and Moksha (liberation of the soul from the cycle of life and death), and church use to respond them through the word of God and try to transform their worldview" (RP12).

RP01 and RP27 say they refuse to attend Hindu festivals because of the danger of syncretism and accommodating Hindu culture. "We encourage the members of our house church not to attend the Hindu festival. We strictly guide them not to go to the syncretism" (RP01).

RP27,

> In Indian church, whatever they are the house church or main church, any denomination, We do not allow accommodating any Hindu culture. Though the people are from the Hinduism, India Christian tells them to avoid the Hindu culture. Roman Catholic Church allows some element (like Bindi) of Hindu culture, but we are not. Hindu festivals need to be avoiding for Christian.

RP02 also guides his believers not to attend the festival. "Some of the Indian Christians do not feel wrong in celebrating Hindu Festivals such as Holi, Deepavali etc. But as for me I have been taught since my childhood not to part take in such festivals. I also teach the house church not to part take in Hindu Festivals."

Meanwhile, RP10 and RP22 guided their believers to remove Hindu elements slowly, not immediately. "We explain them with the Bible. Idol must forgettable, need to remove. Most of them follow what I teach about it. They try to remove the element of it. It is not easy to remove Hindu element immediately, but slowly removes" (RP10).

PR22,

> As spend time with us, they understand who Jesus Christ is. And slowly slowly slowly they themselves remove it. We don't even try to tell. Then they start to commitment. Because many church members are coming from Hindu background, they understand how skill it is. They are able to understand each other.

RP28 said, "But now they have understood the futility of Hindu festivals and other things and therefore, they have left everything. They tell boldly that they will not participate in any kind of festivals."

Third, as a response to the Hindu elements, participants proposed the need of an alternative plan in the house church for the believers during a Hindu festival. RP11 said, "When the Hindu festival has come, we call the members in the house, and we pray for each family member. We share the God's word in that day." RP34 said, "We have meeting like Cottage Meetings, Bible Studies, Fasting Prayers, Women's fellowship, Youth Meetings, Sunday school programs, House Visiting, Any other occasional meeting in the Hindu Festival."

RP03 expressed that they educate the believers to realize the real meaning of festival in the Christian view, comparing Christian to Hinduism.

> We tell them not to worship them to the festivals. The festivals have some meaning. In harvest festival, Hindus offers sacrifices to the idols that are gods and goddesses. We still have harvest festival. But we can thank God and pray. Bless the people and bless the farmers. We bless the food that God help us to have. We don't have strong strategy, but there is confusion to concerning certain festivals. Emerging groups like us try to make people understanding the meaning rather than follow the tradition which may be not a Christian thing, maybe unchristian.

RP05 guides the believer not to attend the festival. He suggests opening the relationship with Hindu neighbors to deliver the gospel.

> In our church members, when they become Christian they removed their previous religious elements. One of the Hindu festivals is Diwali. Although I did not tell them, they know about story behind that festival. After knowing Jesus, they personally do not do anymore. In the Hindu community, someone say, after you become a Christian, you are not participating the festival. But they cannot object very strong manner. They cannot force them. I encourage the believers to go and greet to the neighbors and say happy Diwali, because this will be acted open up a way for us to present true light the Son of God to our neighbors. Make friendship with their neighbors, but not follow their worldview.

RP05 interpreted Diwali in a Christian way to make a friendship with in Hindu neighbor. Unlike RP05, RP27 objected against the possibility of interpreting Hindu elements in a Christian way.

> Hindu festivals need to be avoiding for Christian. Christians go to the Deepavali. They interpret it as Christian way. I don't agree with those kinds of interpretation. Christian family have invited to the Hindu festival by Hindu community. Sometime the festival conducts in the house not the temple. I encourage visiting to the house for that. But do not go to the temple for that.

Pastors' Understanding of Yoga

In this part, I questioned the pastors about Yoga in order to reconfirm their responses regarding Hindu elements. I categorized their responses as seen in the diagram below into three nodes under the theme, Pastors' understanding of Yoga: Acceptable attitude, Negative response, and Nonresponse or Indifference.

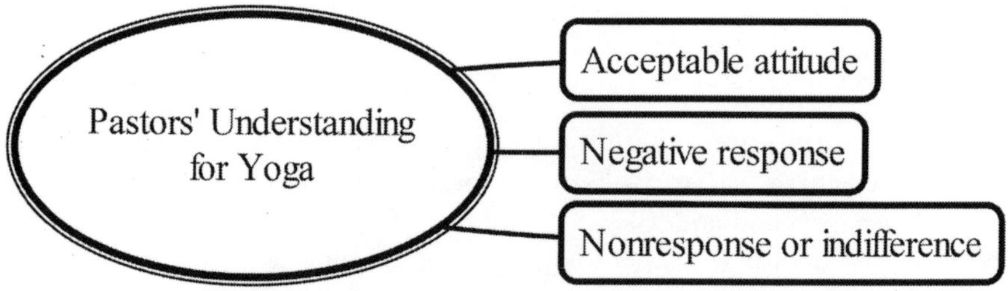


**Figure 21.** Pastors' Understanding of Yoga

First, some research participants expressed their positive response to Yoga for physical health. "There is two meaning of Yoga. Yoga as a sport and yoga as a Hindu ritual. We accept the Yoga as a sport" (RP01). "Yoga is simply an exercise, which is what I think" (RP16). "Exercise yoga without any religious philosophy is good for health" (RP26). "Yoga is very good physical & mental exercise" (RP31). "Yoga is good for body. It physically keeps someone fit. Idol mind is devil's workshop. Yoga keeps someone busy physically and mentally" (RP32). "Yoga - we should think about this scientifically. It makes to fit one's body" (RP17). "Yoga simply helps people to be fit & sound, not in terms of religion, but heals us" (RP04). "Yoga - it is a very good income generating program for high caste Indians to suck the money from Western countries" (RP33).

Second, participants expressed their negative responses for the Yoga as an element of Hinduism. Some research participants above saw positively Yoga as sport. But RP29 considered it as luxurious sports in negative response. "Yoga is business of rich people where they in comfort zone try to bring healing to their body which is not possible for migrants or people who have no time to do all these things" (RP29).

Although RP26 recognized Yoga as a Hindu element, he encouraged it as sport. "Yoga in religious philosophical sense creates spiritual vacuum in hearts so I do not encourage. But exercise yoga without any religious philosophy is good for health" (RP 26).

Unlike RP26, these three (RP15, RP10 and RP19) did not encourage it as sport. "Yoga is completely Hindu spirituality. No spirituality. It is not for Christians. Outside looks like exercise & fitness, inside is union with Brahma (Hindu god)" (RP15). "A ways of Hindu people's meditation is Yoga. But we are reading the Bible and praying in the morning. I don't encourage people to conduct the Yoga. Some Guru practice Yoga like sport, but I don't like it" (RP10). "Yoga is a Hindu meditation. We should not talk about that as a good exercise" (RP19).

Many research participants have their own definitions of Yoga. They understand the purpose and definition of Yoga, and they object it.

RP12,

> The word, yoga comes from Sanskrit an ancient Indian language, which means yoking. This is often interpreted as meaning union. Yoga is said to be for the purpose of uniting the mind, body, and spirit which including breath control, simple meditation, and the adoption of specific bodily postures is widely practiced for health and relaxation.

"Yoga is nothing to do for the Christianity. Yoga is about control the five senses. Christianity teaches we cannot control the five senses. No one can control it. We are not encouraged to practice yoga" (RP27). "But we reject the yoga as a Hindu element. We remove Hindu elements through the Bible" (RP1).

RP02, RP03 and RP05 describe Yoga as a part of Hinduism as ritual and practice of Hindu theology. "According to me Yoga is a Hindu religious practice to take care of the body. It has nothing a cultural value than a religion. If I do Yoga, then I am following Hinduism and its practices" (RP02).

RP03,

> As far as my understanding of the concern, Yoga is basically different formation, even though they call it some kinds of exercise, each position you worship gods and goddesses. This is my understanding of Yoga. As a Christian leader, I may not support the Yoga. But in India, they are going to bring it every educational institute as a compulsory exercise. The school do not force to student to worship the Hindu gods, so far they respect to student's religion. But, there is changing of political scenario. These are the things impact to educational institute and schools.

"Yoga as I see it is something empties the mind. The Bible never tells about the emptiness of the mind. Rather we suppose to fill our mind with the Word of God. I encourage every Christian not to practice Yoga because even its position at all comes out of Hindu theology" (RP05).

RP22 realizes Yoga is the practice of Hinduism.

> Yoga has physical aspect to do it. Yoga is come out from Hinduism. I have been to attend the Yoga class, so I have seen what they are doing in Yoga. Before they do yoga, they do breathing exercise, and they say Oh-m. Actually Oh is a part of Hindu god. Yoga has got to deep Hindu root. Yoga is good for maintain the body, but they have deep

> root in Hinduism. After yoga, they bow down to the master. Surya Namaskara mean you are greeting (bow down) of god's son. All the exercise of Yoga has meaning to depend the aspects of god. People think practice of Yoga as an exercise is good to keep for health, but it has deep root of Hinduism. People do not understand it. I think if the person understands the root of Yoga, they will keep away from it.

Like RP22, RP14, RP18 and RP25 also state that Yoga is the practice of Hinduism.

> Yoga is one of the exercise Hindus follow. We should get rid of all mantras" (RP14). "Yoga belongs to Hindus. We are not here to practice those, as the Americans (the West) are foolishly practicing" (RP18). "Yoga is Hindu concept, although they exercise in physical purpose, but their ultimate purpose is not exercise. It has very much connected to the spiritual world, and it is very dangerous. I found it is not a way to encourage believers" (RP25). In addition, RP23 says, "Yoga is welcoming the devil.

Third, seven research participants (RP06, RP07, RP08, RP09, RP11, RP21, RP24, and RP30) did not express their idea about Yoga. But, in the previous questions, when we looked at how the persons dealt with Hindu elements in the house church, research participants responded on the need to escape from the Hindu elements. Therefore, even though they did not respond about Yoga, we can assume that they may have negative responses toward Yoga if they know it is a Hindu element. Two more participants, RP20 and RP34 expressed indifference for Yoga. "Yoga is not practiced by people of my own. No idea about that" (RP20). "In our locality even Hindus also don't have any idea about yoga" (RP34).

## 5. Application of Theoretical Premise for Research Question 3

Many previous research works dealt with worldview theory as an approach to other cultural and religious contexts for missions. As we have seen in the literature review, many scholars (like Charles H. Kraft, Sherwood G. Lingenfelter, Paul G. Hiebert, Charles E. Van Engen, Louis J. Luzbetak, John R. W. Stott, and Ruth Tucker ) contributed to the understanding of worldview change in the mission context. Therefore, the finding from research question 3 can be defined by theoretical premise of various scholars mentioned above.

According to Charles H. Kraft's theoretical premise, there is no single Christian worldview. If there were, Christians would need to have a single approach, both to things like moral values and to things like time, space, and categorization. Christ's worldview consisted of His Kingdom perspectives integrated into His first-century Hebrew worldview. Therefore, our task is to follow His example by integrating those same perspectives into Hindu cultural worldview. Paul G.

Hiebert, in the literature review, believed that worldview can be transformed. The core contents of worldview transforming are repentance and discipleship.

According to Charles Van Engen, millions of rural-to-urban migrants were ripe for new ideas (transforming the worldview), including religious teaching. The finding from research question 3 is that research participants stated the factors for worldview change in the economic aspect: urban economic environment and economic failure. Then, it also is found that other factors for worldview change in the spiritual aspect (change of spiritual identity), psychological aspect (anxiety and conflict) and socio-cultural aspect (persecution, new relationship and new environment). In the literature review, Engen proposed the need of church programs focusing on those aspects to the migrants and locals. Urban church planting is needed in the slums for the poor and for the working class. Church programs are needed for the working class. A house church needs to model itself for these challenges among migrants, the local poor, and the working class. Therefore, house churches need to provide some programs for helping migrants and locals who face those aspects of the worldview change.

In light of Kraft's theoretical premise, the migrants and locals who have a Hindu worldview can be integrated into an urban environment that has various worldviews (perspective). The task of a house church is to lead them into the Gospel, existing as His Kingdom perspective in the cities. Research participants expressed how they approach the migrants and locals to help them. In the house churches' approach for evangelism, another finding from research question 3 can be defined by some theoretical premise of various scholars already mentioned above.

First, the house church approach to the migrants and locals should help with their changes in the economic and spiritual aspects. Especially, a house church can approach the migrants and locals who are transforming their spiritual identity through contextualization. According to Louis J. Luzbetak's contextualization theory, contextualization is the process by which a local house church integrates its understanding of the Gospel with the local culture and worldview. For this, a house church should find a biblically faithful way to integrate the biblical perspective and the local worldview.

Second, as seen in Engen's proposal for a program among the migrants and locals, research participants described how they deliver the gospel through personal relationships and various meetings. It looks effective because these approaches are fitting to the migrants and locals who experienced urban environment in psychological and socio-cultural aspect

On the other hand, although some scholars (Harvie M. Conn, Klaus Detlev Schulz and Charles van Engen) emphasized church ministry of public areas in the city, only three research participants employed local social service as a program for evangelism. Ministerial concern for the public area is needed in the house churches.

Third, as we have seen in the literature review, according to Pierre Babin and M. Iannone's theoretical premise, some elements of worldview on religious life (such as the way of beauty), the symbolic way remains although one converts to another religion. Ruth Tucker's transplanted Hinduism shows us how Hinduism can influence other religions. It means Christianity in India has elements that borrow from Hinduism.

Fourth, as we have seen in the literature review, in order to overcome obstacles evangelizing to other religions in the practical aspect, some scholars propose dialogue with other religions. According to Lesslie Newbigin, Christians need to go to meet their neighbor of another religion on the basis of his commitments to Jesus Christ. According to John R. W. Stott, dialogue is a useful tool for understanding the Hindu people's worldview in order to deliver the gospel.

For example, from research question 3, many research participants responded to the Hindu elements in the house church with critical viewpoints, especially for attending Hindu festivals. Although many research participants did not encourage their believers to participate in a Hindu festival, they encourage communicating with Hindu neighbors to deliver the Gospel. Thus, it has significant missiological meaning: a house church should remove their Hindu elements, while opening dialogue with Hindu neighbors.

Chapter 8

# Research Finding 4: Obstacles in the House Churches

This section deals with data regarding the kinds of obstacles house churches confront when they evangelize and catechize migrants and locals into God's family.

## 1. Inner Difficulties

Under research question 4, difficulties in the house churches, operational question 1 was as follows: What kinds of inner obstacles does your house church have when it evangelizes and catechizes the migrants and locals into God's family in the city? In what ways does the house church overcome these obstacles? What elements of the house church help it to overcome?

In order to respond to these questions, I categorized the concepts research participants counted as inner difficulties in the house churches that the migrants and locals faced. As seen in the diagram below four nodes were categorized under the theme, Inner difficulties: Pastors' difficulties, Leadership problems, Theological issue, and Conflicts in the house churches.

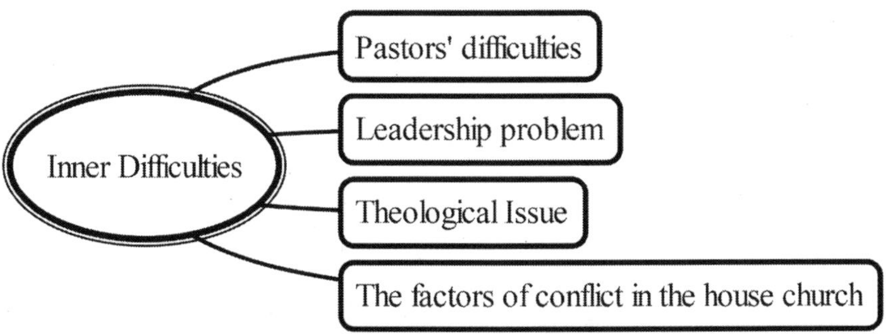


**Figure 22.** Inner Difficulties

### Pastors' Difficulties

The difficulties that the pastors face are due to three factors: Conflicts and misunderstanding between the pastor and the believers' family, a sense of failure, and the problem of financial support.

Research participants expressed conflicts and misunderstanding between the pastor and the believers' family as a pastor's difficulty. While RP10 described the conflicts that the believers experienced at their home, other research participants depicted the problem of the believer's husband and how to respond to them.

First, RP10 stated the conflict of the believers' husband and their relatives: "Wife and children comes to the house church for the prayer meeting and worship. But most husbands do not like to come. This is problem." For these husbands, RP10 responded as follow.

> Wife bring husband once in a while to the house church, then I talk to them. Husband never objects attending the house church. One lady need to baptism. But I asked to bring her husband to come to the church. Then I asked them it is better to have baptism together. After two years, they have baptism together. I encourage her to wait for baptism with her husband, even though our house church recognize her faith, her dedication to the Lord, for her family and husband, it is better to have baptism with her husband. The practice of Baptism itself is not important, but saving her husband is more important. So I asked her to wait till her husband gets a faith by the grace of God. Baptism is one of command of the Christ, but it is not the condition of salvation, it is not the condition to go to the heaven.

RP10 also described the conflict with the relatives. "Wife and children are coming to the house church, but her mother and sisters go to the Hindu temple. They visit to the Hindu Gurus to get know about their future. Some believers visit to the Gurus with their relatives." For response of this conflict, RP10 said, "I teach them our future is in only God's hand not a Guru's hand."

Other research participants stated conflicts between the pastor and the believers' family. RP03 expressed that such conflicts are because of misunderstandings about the pastors. "Once you get the believers from other faith, their family and relatives or friends come and challenge you. Sometimes even spouses come and challenge you. They said how you do this to my family?" (RP03).

As a response for the believers' family, RP03 said,

> We need to tell them that we are not to try to change your spouse's religion. He just come and prays for his request. We are not interest in somebody's religion change instead change in heart. He just got the need; we pray over him, he receives the miracle. He wants us to pray for him. So, anybody is welcome.

RP27 also stated how he deals with conflict between the pastor and the believer's family. "In thanksgiving, the pastor visit to the member's house. When the pastor conflict relatives of members, the pastor respect their idea and request to pray in Christian way. Then most of them allow praying in Christian way."

RP05 gave an example of the conflict from the family, RP05 said,

> Some believers were not yet to take water baptism. One of believers comes from Hindu background. He stays with his father. His father is also against Christians and anyone converting from the family. So it becomes hindrance kinds of thing when the church would like to go to their house for fellowship. We will pray and wait for this particular family.

Second, RP03 expressed that the sense of failure in their calling as a pastor is a difficulty.

> Pastor nurture only few people like ten to fifteen. Are you willing to spend your time for only few people? As long as you are convinced, this is your calling; you are going to really train this people to nurture other believers, then you feel that is work doing this. In the house church, you don't have many people. You have small people. Suppose in a holiday, summer holiday, most believers left to other place for their holiday. You felt that you are a failure. In the small group, you can easily misunderstand others like there is a problem with one man, sometimes the wife come and share it with you. We need to deal it careful in individuals. Two or three families are there, if we do not handle the families care, that family influence to other family also. What happens? You lose your church believers all the sudden.

Although only RP03 depicted the sense of failure as a difficulty, it is a meaningful statement that other research participants may have experienced.

Third, RP22 stated the financial difficulty of a house church because of the increasing house rental fee. "Sometimes at the house where we conduct the house church, rent is too high; it is small group of people, so you are not able to raise so much support the rent."

Research participants expressed that it is difficult to maintain and support not only the house church, but also pastors. Research participants (RP30, RP03, RP15, RP26, RP28 and RP24) expressed financial difficulties for supporting the pastors in the house churches. RP30,

> In our church we mainly have the financial constraints in supporting the pastor. Since it is a small group it would be difficult to support a pastor and his family especially in the urban areas. We set a monthly salary for a pastor and if the church gets enough offerings we pay him

> that amount if we do not get. We add the rest of the amount in the next month's salary.

"We have financial problem to support pastor, when the house church is grow, if there are increased to give their tithe, offering to support the pastor, it can be a support" (RP03). RP15 said, "Financial support of pastors is difficult in our house church." "There are difficulties in pastor finance. Believers love to give vegetables and share some crops but financially not adequate" (RP26). "Lack of support from the members when it is required financial difficulty to the leader to run his family. All these things were overcome with God's wisdom and consistent grace upon me" (RP24).

RP28 depicted the difficulties of the pastors' livelihood and their bi-vocational situation.

> There are difficulties of the pastors and leaders' livelihood. This one of the major issue of Indian Churches. Even the so called established Churches' pastors are under paid and deprived of many monitory benefits, so by all means house churches suffer with this issue. When we talk about House Churches of course they are less number, and many a time it depends on the size of your house. Majority house churches are by default in the slum of poor areas, so even the members are poor. Though they are taught to tithe and they are faithful in giving it regularly, pastor cannot survive on the meager amount, so daily wages in only solution to meet your financial needs, so most of us are bi-vocational.

### Leadership Problems

The difficulties that the pastor's leadership faces are categorized by three factors: The Problem of Women leadership, Conflicts among leaders, and the Problem of leadership qualification.

First, RP30 stated that women leadership is not encouraged in the house church. Research participants described that the house church limited women leadership because of cultural reason. RP01, "We had experience to give leadership to the women. Finally, we did not give leadership to the women because of cultural reason. We solve the theological questions from minors through explanation of Christian cultural tradition." RP28,

> The limitation of women leadership and its cultural reason, Indian culture does not permit to take leadership over the men, therefore, it was difficult to handle this matter, so we decided to make turns of every women where other men's wives got chance to come into leadership for a while, and we asked other people to find out what are the positive points to appreciate.

Thus, women leadership in house churches of India is restricted by a cultural reason.

Second, research participants (RP01 and RP12) expressed conflicts among leaders. "There was some conflict among the leaders. Although leaders have conflicts in their discussion, we try to overcome through the prayer" (RP01). "There are some inner difficulties in a house church like divisions. Some believers and some pastors they don't like other minster come to their own area and have some prayer meeting, they reject other meetings in homes" (RP12). Thus, the conflict between leaders in the house churches lead to division and are hindrance for evangelism.

Third, the problem of leadership qualification in the house churches arose from the absence of theological education training and of ordained pastors. RP29, RP07 and RP08 stated the absence of theological education training among the leaders in the house churches. "No theologically trained leader. They only attend shot term Bible/Leadership training" (RP07). The problem of leadership qualification is "Lack of trained leaders. There is a need of theologically trained leader. Provision has been made to have a trained leader" (RP08). "Due to less education and poor living condition there is always the lack of theological training. Due to poverty, no funds to buy books and though the English books are available but most of the leaders are semi-illiterates" (RP29).

Meanwhile, RP06 expressed the need of an ordained minister. "Ordained minister is invited to conduct ceremonies in the house church." "Being from Baptist background, I am not ordained and I cannot fulfill the expectation of the members in the matters of baptism and sacrament. We invite an ordained Baptist minister for such official purposes" (RP09).

### Theological Issue

The absence of theological training for the pastors in the house church connect to the theological problems that take place in the house churches. The absence of pastors having a theological education causes the absence of theological education in the house church. This absence is connected to false teaching and the lack of understanding for ecclesiology.

The difficulties arising from theological issues in the house church are categorized by four factors: The absence of Theological education for the leaders and the believers, lack of understanding for ecclesiology, false teaching, and difficulty of overcoming previous religious and cultural tradition.

First of all, RP26 and RP29 portrayed the absence of theological education for the leaders and the believers. "Difficulties in achieving theological education due to illiteracy of members. It's not impossible but very difficult (RP26). Lack of biblical resources-printed materials in vernacular is lacking or unaffordable to buy. Printed materials are useful only for youth and school going children. For the adult, illustrated books in story forms and video would be great help to teach through the bible" (RP26). "Due to less education and poor living condition there is always the lack of theological training. Due to poverty, no funds to buy books and though the English books are available but most of the leaders are semi-illiterates" (RP29).

Second, some believers do not think of a house church as a church because of the absence of theological education for them. In other word, they do not have an understanding of ecclesiology. RP05 and RP16 described how people consider the house church. "When we talk about Christians we talk about church, we think of big building. This is one of thing which I deal with, which I have to let them understand that church is not living in the building, but it is about believers coming together. This is one of obstacles we faced" (RP05). "People take advantage of pastor by visiting him without informing in his residence. We cannot worship freely in house church. People also think only traditional church is holy where God lives" (RP16).

Third, false teachers and their teaching are widely prevalent because of the absence of theological education in the house church. RP01 said, "Some theological questions from minors in the house church make trouble (for example, Christmas is not December 25). There was false teacher's teaching in our house church. But through this experience, we recognized the importance of sound biblical doctrine."

RP04, RP12 and RP34 uttered the danger of a false teacher. "False teachers were diverting our believers. We had to arrange special bible study to deal with heresies" (RP04). "There is a chances to follow the heresy teachings, and follow the false-leadership, these things can be overcome only through proper theology, proper church government" (RP12). "Few are attracted to prosperity gospel but we are teaching them sound doctrine. Frequent Bible studies will protect such believers" (RP34).

Fourth, the theological education in the house church is essential for the believers for changing their previous worldview to a Christian worldview. Research participants (RP11 and RP02) stated their difficulties to overcome their previous tradition and religion. These described the reason why theological education is needed in the house churches. "It is very difficult to come out from previous traditions. We support them with word of God. Then they may grow according to God's words, with that they may overcome their tradition" (RP11).

RP02,

> The aspect of sin, life after death, good karma, etc were the inner difficulties to deal in the house church. I had to teach the church through the word of God. The impact of the other religious practices upon the church. I had to teach the church what is the understanding of the Bible about such practices.

The Conflicts in the House Church: What are the Factors of Conflict?

Research participants expressed various factors of conflict in the house church. First, research participants expressed that interrelationship problems among the believers are a cause of conflict in the house church. RP24 expressed that the cause of conflicts in the house church is the lack of understanding and support among the believers. "Lack of understanding between members is a cause of conflict among the believers. However, this problem did not create much misunderstanding. Lack of support from the members when it is required is another cause of conflict among the believers."

RP25 and RP33 stated that interrelationship problem is occurred when the weakness is exposed each other.

> One of difficulties is to find the personal problem. The problem when they come close to each other, in small community church, a lot of weakness will expose. In the early church of the New Testament, people love one another; forgive one another, so they all depended on their church. Interpersonal problem, and family problem, and relationship also challenge in our house church. So we have to teach them loving one another, forgiving one another (RP25).

"Since it is a smaller group, believers know each other's weaknesses. Too much of personal inference and abuses are happening. Further, it leads to judgmental attitude" (RP33).

RP32 and RP27 described the interpersonal problem among the believers in the house church. "To bring the people in oneness is a big challenge. Moreover, when we compare with other churches, sometime we feel lonely. Some believers are abuse others and take advantage of others. It makes me sad and I feel bad" (RP32). "Another problem is that someone says we don't want come to this house." I have a personal problem with that lady. Therefore, we rent another house, but it is too long distance for him. Second problem is relationship problem. This lady does not like that lady. This thing affect to the house church" (RP27).

Second, research participants depicted some rules in the houses as a cause of conflict in the house church. "Some rules in house" is a factor of conflict among the believers (RP15) and "House rules hurt the individuals" (RP16). "Some rules in the house are not accepted by all. So they destroy the house atmosphere at least once in a week" (RP31). "Not cooperating to keep the house church as clean" (RP21).

Third, RP05 and RP27 noted that the believers hesitated to provide their house for worship place. "In the beginning they did not open their own house for the worship. They hesitate because their neighbor would come for complain. It was difficulty for the house church worship" (RP05).

> People don't want to give their house for worship. Every village, every colony they have Hindu people are there. Hindu people come to the house owner to tell not to give the house for the Christian worship.

> Hindu people warn the house owner that our god will angry with you because of this matter. e.g. one lady asked us to use her hall for worship. But afterward her mother was sick. So one Hindu man come to her house and said, your mother is sick because of you. You allow Christian people to come and worship in your house. So, our god become angry and they made your mother sick. Then she cancels and she asked us to rent some other houses. This is real difficulties in the village for the house church (RP27).

They also stated how they dealt with this problem. "But now, we meet at different believer's house every week. Now they are opening their house for the weekly service. They say coming week we will meet my place. They will say furthering week we will meet my place" (RP05). RP27 expected to find the common place and to have their own house.

Fourth, research participants portrayed the problem of caste among the believers as a cause of conflict in the house church. "Even though the house church is open to all caste-based society, it is impossible for different casts to come together. It brings trouble to both the host and the guests" (RP26). Caste issue is severe. If we start church in Low caste area, high castes don't come. Vice versa" (RP23).

> Some of them do want and don't feel to come to someone's house, so we divided the house church in different place so that people can come to the house church in their convenience. For example, when the low caste people gather in the house, high caste people do not come to that house. Therefore, we were deciding to separate and rent the house for worship. Now we have six house churches in separate place for worship. In the beginning, although we divided the house churches in different place according to their cultural and social status, I put my effort to teach them in biblical way in order to overcome their cultural and social differences. There is no caste system in the bible, and let them know the biblical realities for them. Once the house church is growing, it is better to get separate place for the worship effectively. Since we are starting high caste community, low caste people do not come to this house church. I also lead house church for the low caste people. So, I can bring them together to have fellowship sometimes (RP10).

Fifth, research participants stated the problem of money trading among believers as a cause of conflict in the house church. RP08, RP20, RP23 and RP31 expressed instances of believers not returning money borrowed from the house church. "Obstacles come in the form of financial matters. Some members were provided loan from the church fund but the same wasn't returned. Some would ask for financial assistance without genuine reason. It has been resolved that the church fund will not be used for loan anymore" (RP08). "Believer borrowed money from other believer. Later, they disappeared. Finally, I have to pay from my pocket. Issues are there" (RP20). "Borrowing money and running away from church" (RP23). "One believer borrowing money from others is an issue. Moreover, believers are given their money for interest from other believers" (RP31).

Sixth, research participants described distractions during worship as a cause of conflict in the house church. RP14 and RP19 expressed some believers distract the worship service in the house church. "People eat, drink during worship services which distract the worship mood" (RP14). "Baby cries, asks for food from home, simply moving around the house. We politely said to take care and plan ahead" (RP19).

Seventh, research participants expressed their difficulties arose from various demands from the believers in the house churches. RP04, RP13 and RP15 depicted that the believers demand larger space. "Space was an issue as the members were increasing. People want space and garden to go around praying" (RP04). "Space is a challenge; need to find a bigger place" (RP13). "One of inner difficulties is space for worship, some want bigger building" (RP15).

RP30 expressed believers in the house church revealed their preference for the mega church. "Some of the church members are influenced by the mega church and expects the house church to follow that model. We teach them that the Church's structure doesn't matter but our hearts and the brotherly love that we have as a family matters." RP27 revealed his difficulty arose from the believer's demand specifics about the worship place. "Having common place is inner difficulties. Recently, I rent two houses for the house church. Some people say the place that rent house is too long distance from our house. It is problem. However, we encourage to them come to the house church."

## 2. Outer Difficulties

Under research question 4, operational question 2 was as follows: What kinds of outer obstacles does your house church have when she evangelizes and catechizes migrants and locals into God's family in the city? In what ways has the house church overcome these obstacles? What elements of the house church help her to overcome these obstacles? In order to respond these questions, I categorized the concepts that research participants counted as outer difficulties in house churches that the migrants and locals faced. As seen in the diagram below four nodes were categorized under the theme, Outer difficulties: Threaten from false teachers, Negative recognition of traditional church toward the house churches, Conflict with neighbors, and Threaten from local community and political group.

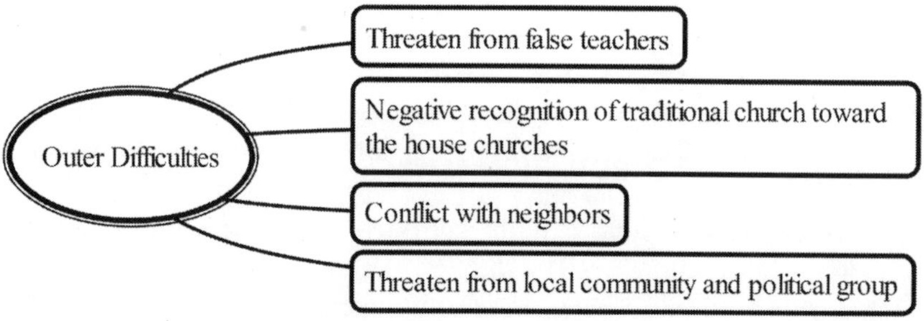


**Figure 23.** Outer Difficulties

Threats from False Teachers

RP01, RP4 and RP12 already stated about threats from false teachers in a house church in the previous section, Inner difficulties. Some inner difficulties could originates from the outer environment. For example, "There was false teacher's teaching in our house church. But through this experience, we recognized the importance of sound biblical doctrine" (RP01). "False teachers were diverting our believers. We had to arrange special bible study to deal with heresies" (RP04). "There is a chances to follow the heresy teachings, and follow the false-leadership, these things can be overcome only through proper theology, proper church government" (RP12). These threats from false teachers in the house church are from an outer environment.

Other participants (RP15, RP29, and RP34) also expressed false teaching around their house church. "There is a threat from heresy. By teaching and patience, we overcome it" (RP15). "There are many prosperity preachers around the church. Few preachers are reaching the homes of congregation through media-TV/Radio. But we are teaching them sound doctrine to avoid such teachings" (RP34).

RP29,

> House Churches are vulnerable to false teaching and heresy because leaders are not educated enough. There is no proper guide of faith on which they can cling to. Many time new things are just accepted without any investigation or consultation. Sometime whatever is attractive, it accepted without any questions. So, there is great measure of threat of false teaching and heresy. We invite well educated bible teacher to teach us the basic doctrine or the creed having them explained to us.

Negative Recognition from Traditional Churches toward the House Churches

Research participants stated negative recognition from traditional churches toward house churches as a difficulty in the house church. "Some church leaders oppose. Church leaders are appraised about the house church in negative way (RP06)." "Other pastors look house church very negative. So it is hindrance" (RP15). "Since there is another church nearby, wanted to stop our fellowship" (RP19).

Research participants described that traditional churches and their pastors do not welcome the house churches, because they consider the house church as thieves of their sheep (RP01), or not having any order and system church (RP28), and a no-building church (RP26).

> Traditional church also does not welcome the house church. Dominant leadership in the traditional church make hard to communicate to the house church. They treat our house church as inferior church since our church members are in poor and uneducated. Some tradition churches recognize the house church as a sheep thief that steals the members of the traditional church. But, we try to contact to them through various communication way to change their recognition on the house church (RP01).

"Main churches or those have built church building look down upon the house churches claiming that this is a mockery of the church and therefore, they should join the main churches. They are criticized for simple form of worship, no much glamour etc." (RP28). "Mainline churches alienates pastors of house church or small churches especially run by lay-pastors. The reason they say is that there is no order and system in the ministry or church" (RP26).

### Conflicts with Neighbors

Research participants stated conflicts with neighbors in the house churches can be an difficulty that the house church faces. The conflicts that a house church faces with neighbors are conflicts with a house owner, parking problems and noise problems. Research participants expressed that neighbors and house owners demand the house church to move to another place. "There is continuous opposition to gather for worship in our rented houses. Neighbors complained to vacate the house. They informed to Hindu militant to threaten us" (RP20). RP22 also mentioned it as follows.

> When we have worship go on the house rented by other house in India, house is very close. There are no much distance between one house and another house. When you worship is going in the house church, we have people neighborhood place opposition who want us to vacant. We had this problem one house church, so we moved from there. There are always these problems. To solve this problem, we kindly ask to the neighbor we have worship once a week or twice a week. We try to music low, we don't do too much song, we try to keep the windows close, and we try to adjust to it.

RP21, RP16, and RP18 described conflicts with house owners.

"Since we were in a rented building, it happened to move. Believers did not allow us though the owner asked us to vacate" (RP21). "Local people are opposing. Rent houses are facing a threat to vacate" (RP16). "Neighbors are not allowing placing the name board of our house church. Also they oppose to keep a cross over the terrace building" (RP18).

As an example of conflicts with neighbors, research participants spoke of parking and noise problems. "Vehicle parking within the believers was an issue" (RP21). "Parking is another issue, as it is making problem for the neighbors on Sunday" (RP16). As another example of conflicts with neighbors, research participants expressed noise problems. "Songs are not allowed to sing loudly" (RP17).

RP25,

> Sometimes our neighborhood have problem with us because they hear the noise when we gathered together in the church. Within the community, because of noise also some people create problem, but other is okay. We don't have serious issues within the church, but we have many minor problems that can be managed.

### Threats from the Local Community and Political Groups

"Persecution is not somewhere in a far state or country but it is next door" (RP30). RP12, "When I think of outer difficulties mainly I face almost all the house churches face the pressure from the locality or pressure from the some fundamental people and the attacks from the religious people and from the political leaders."

Participants stated threats and interruptions that house churches face from the outside are a difficulty faced. The factors that threaten a house church are categorized by two: Threaten from the local Hindu community, and political and religious threats.

First, research participants stated threats and attacks from the outside are caused by difficult relationships with the local Hindu community. RP25, "There is rejection from the community." RP13, "The outer difficulties are based on people's response to a church that engages with culture. It's more of an image (image of the church) issue." It means the local community does not have a good image of the house church. RP33 also described the absence of relations between the house church and the local community. "House church is not approved by government and the community… This is a great challenge." For this reason, RP11 portrayed that the neighbors in the local community misunderstand house churches. RP20 said, "They (neighbor) informed to Hindu militant to threaten us." RP26, "Pressure comes from the community in which the house church exists. According to them, coming to Christ means changing one's caste and identity. Some Hindu-extremist groups give trouble to pastors." RP27 illustrated how Hindu groups interrupt the worship of the house church.

> Hindu people, they will disturb indirectly. When we start worship in the house, they start shouting and crying. They disturb our worship. Although we are inviting to the other's house, if other member of that family not allow coming into the house we cannot enter in. Hindu youth disturb our house church worship with shouting. Then, we close the window for worship. We never react for it toward them. Some area they did not allow to come in their place, now they allow coming in their community. But still not allow visiting door to door.

Other participants also expressed their experience of threats from outsiders (local Hindu people) to the house churches. RP14, "Earlier they (outsiders) shouted, now they are toleration. Police comes sometime to protect us on Christmas and Easter days." RP20, "There is continuous opposition to gather for worship in our rented houses." RP21, "Stones were thrown while we worship the Lord occasionally." RP17, "They criticized for conversion."

Participants (RP17, RP32 and RP23) stated that there is verbal abuse from outsiders toward the house church. "Verbal abuse takes place" (RP17). RP23, "Verbal abuse is very high. Outsiders think that we are converting. Wives are willing to come but husband don't allow them fully" (RP32). "When people come to house church, others criticize their past personal life. When people come to house church, others criticize their past personal life." For these reasons, RP09 expressed, "There is a threat to anyone seeking to embrace Christianity. Baptism, therefore, is conducted secretly." RP25 explained that they overcome difficulties from the local community by encouraging each other. "There is rejection from the community. So we as a church encourage all together getting comfort."

Second, participants said that threats and attacks from the outside are caused by political and religious groups. RP01, "Hindu BJP (political party) watches our house church. So, we always look out for their attack." RP12, "Attack toward pastor, attack towards church and believers. Mainly persecutions from the non-Christians, especially from some community like BJP, RSS, Bhajarangddal. These difficulties can be overcome only through prayer."

RP10 and RP15 also depicted some difficulties from the government. RP10,

> Cooperation, street leader, government leader object us not to make people convert. When someone converts to the Christian, others report to the police station. We did not force them to convert to the Christian, but the police warn us not to do. We need to keep our morality to the Hindu people. We are not force them to be a convertor.

Especially, participants (RP15 and RP30) described the difficulty as a "response to Hindu government authority" (RP15). RP30, "BJP rule is provoking all the Hindus to revolt against Christians and they are softly doing it. Things are not the same as it was before open for the Gospel."

While RP12 and RP25 explained house churches overcome this political threaten with prayer, RP05 expressed how he educates his believers about citizen rights in the constitution in order to encourage them to overcome their difficult situation.

> I anticipate our neighbor will notice us and might appeal uncomfortable their feeling for us. Currently in India, BJP government which is very pro-Hindu political party they are in power. In order to deal with this kinds of I am educating member by telling them about constitutional right that we have Article no. 25. I think where each of the citizens given the right to choice to follow religion of own choice. That is one of the fundamental rights of each one of the citizens of India. I am telling them about that.

## 3. Practical Meaning of the House Church in Obstacles

Under research question 4, difficulties in the house churches, protocol question 4 was as follows: In your opinion, how do you describe the house church as a mission tool of evangelism during persecution? In order to respond to these questions, I categorized the concepts that research participants counted as the practical meaning of the house churches in difficulties. As seen in the diagram below four nodes were categorized under the theme, Practical meaning of the house churches: House church as independent church, house church as an invisible church established in the persecution, house church as missional springboard for outreach and evangelism, and house church as local church that lead to change.

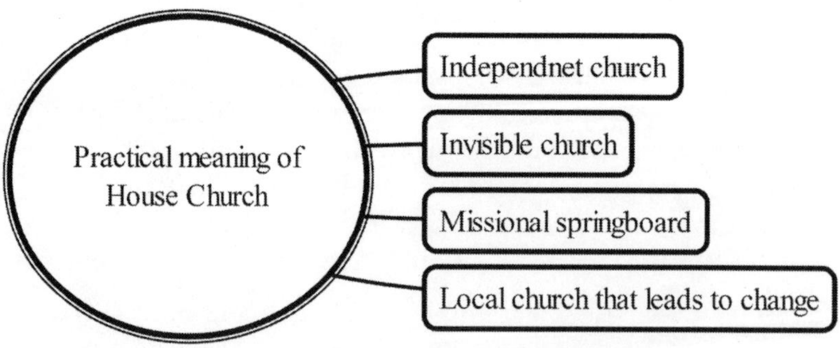


**Figure 24.** Practical meaning of House Church

House Church as Independent Church

Research participants saw the house churches as independent churches. "After all, the house church is independent. Those inner and outer difficulties in the house church need to overcome through the three self-principles and sound theological doctrine for the deliver the gospel" (RP01). "House church order should be different from other mainline church. Need to be careful about order of service. Running pattern should be different. House church should not religious, not socialize. If not, it will give tension. House churches transform the culture & incarnate the word" (RP15). In other words, it means that house churches have their own independent order and pattern.

RP22 described the independent features of the house church as follow.

> Running house church is not cost, you don't need big music system, you don't need big light, and you can save a lot of money. It becomes more economic. It is very strong church in term of quality of the believer that is training them in house church. It comes to the spirituality of the believers. One side some people who go to the large church because of the number, but the spirituality if you look at the spiritual life, they don't apt to the standard. But in the house church you can easily make up. If one or two believer missing we can recognize them easily find them to contact them if there is any problem to encourage. That makes much stronger relationship and stronger spiritual investment in their lives.

House Churches are an Invisible Church Established in the Persecution

Participants state that house churches faced persecution. "House churches are under more threat. Local people are informing to Hindu militant. We are also equally facing problem" (RP14). "Every house churches have to face the issue. We can't escape for persecution" (RP32). Participants (RP03, RP05, and RP12) described the house churches as invisible churches in the persecution.

> RP03,
>
> In Delhi, nobody can see the existence of the house church in Delhi. What's happen, some groups sent someone to the specific area to find out the church that is growing one part of India. They came and search big building to find the churches, but they did not get any prove thousands people convert to the Christian and the growth of churches in that area. Then, they concluded that no church is growing in this part of India. If we are going to have challenge by militant religious group, if we are going to worship inside of houses like the New Testament, nobody will get to know how many people really come to the Lord.

RP12 emphasized the house church needs to take care of evangelism during the persecution, since it is another opportunity for delivering the gospel.

> In my opinion, the best way to describe is (Acts 8:4) in this verse we can see those who had been scattered preached the word wherever they

> gone. According to this verse and according to my opinion, sometime God allows the persecution to spread the gospel and to do His work effectively in this world. But, during the persecutions house church must be wise enough to preach the gospel.

RP03 and RP05 expressed how a house church can be an evangelism tool in the persecution.

> If people are come to bother you, if they are going to trouble with you, this is the best way escape from the persecution I believe. You gather in the believer's home, you quietly do whatever you want to do, and you are going to evangelize all of the country like Gospel always work silently without making much noise. It can break heart and heart. That is possibility for us to silent work penetrate into hard regions and hard soil. Nobody will get to know, persecution is not even know where this people are gathering (RP03)

> Right now in India, Delhi, capital of India there has been attacked the church. Physical church can be seen by people, physical church can be attacked. But no matter how much might be persecution, house church can always be stay in underground like China. As we stay in underground, we can always reach people with the gospel. Because where the house church, we don't have to worry about protect the building. I see house church is very effective mean for evangelism even in the times of persecution (RP05).

RP24 and RP29 stated that the importance of evangelism for the house churches in the persecution.

> RP24,

> Christians are encouraged to open their homes to share the Gospel message with friends, family, colleagues, and neighbors using one of several new evangelistic programs featuring life-changing testimonies and powerful messages. I feel better way to reach the people to build house fellowship in the persecution.

"Personal Evangelism of house church is great tool in times of persecution. Where once you gain the confidence of an individual, you can share the gospel very well and he can continue to hold fast to his faith" (RP29). Indeed, the house churches are a mission tool for an era of persecution. "It is a perfect model of New Testament church. It helps to spread out to the people during the time of persecution. Each one in the congregation gets involved in the mission of the church. It is more vibrant in persecution" (RP02). "House Church is a small group congregation and I feel to an extent it would be a great mission tool in the times of persecution" (RP30). "House Church is a powerful tool as India is facing persecution" (RP04).

Research participants compared a traditional church building to a house church in times of persecution. As RP05 mentioned, "we (house church) don't have to worry about protect the building." Participant RP25 and RP28 expressed their comparison between a (traditional) church building and house church: "In north India, church building had broken down when I see, the house church is a good model in the place of persecution. They can gather in house and just be security church or underground church which don't appear in publicly." RP28, "House Church is a house of a person where Church gathers to worship the Lord. House Church is not the building where people will go and vandalize it. So the house owner is host and Church is the guest, during the persecution anyone can enter into the house without any objection."

RP09, RP16, RP18, and RP22 compared traditional (visible) church building to the (invisible) house church during persecution. "House church being without a traditional church building stays discreet and hence doesn't attract threat as much as the traditional church does. So, it has advantage" (RP09).

> Many people don't recognize the house churches. They don't consider the houses as a being place of the worship. Hindu thinks of the church as a building. They think of structural building. They don't think of as small group of believer that they meet in the house. So, most people have different understanding of the house church. Most time they attacked and burnt the church building, church structure (RP22).

RP18, "Where there is a persecution, we are peacefully sat inside the house church and pray. This cannot be done with the regular churches" (RP16). "It (the house church) is less persecuted church than the bigger church buildings." On the other hand, RP19 and RP20 expressed that there is no difference between a church building and a house church in persecution. "House churches also fall equally into the hands of persecutors. So house church cannot be something a special one" (RP19). "Traditional churches are protected by police. Sadly, house churches are persecuted continuously" (RP20).

House Church as a Missional Springboard for Outreach and Evangelism

Research participants (RP07, RP08, RP13, and RP21) see house churches as springboards for missions and evangelism: "It (house church) becomes a place for believer to seek refuge and also to organize themselves for future activity" (RP07). "It (house church) becomes a succor and a springboard to move ahead for the people" (RP08). Thus, "as a mission tool, house church is a place where people can find care and comfort for them to rely on the host as well as the Word of God" (RP13).

RP21 also described the house church in the aspect of centripetal mission. "Apart from persecution, it is also financially not burdened anyone. Traditional

Church does not attract Hindus, but the house church. I highly recommend the house church aspect very much to become a powerful tool for evangelism." As an example, RP27 expressed that the Hindu people did not think house churches gave a negative influence to them, rather they think house church contribute to narrow social gaps between the people.

> Although there is hinder of Hindu people to the house church, once the house church has started, we regularly are gathering the house for worship and fellowship. The Hindu thinks that these figures of the house church do not give any bad influence. I am not directly preaching the gospel to the Hindu people. House church member approach to the people, then they invites the people to the house church. Then I teach the gospel to them. The teaching and fellowship take place in the house church. This is not open evangelism, but we evangelized them in the house church. House church concept is good. In my personal experience, house church is best strategy model for unreached people area. The house church makes people or locals to recognize church is near to them not located in long distance from their house. The contribution of the house church is break social inferiority. It makes people (low caste) to come out to the society. It reduce social gap between high caste (class) and low caste (class).

Research participants rejoiced in the house church's outreach to the mission field. They noted the believers' life testimonies (RP26) and outreach activities for evangelism (RP10). "People around us see our lives and character in the house church. Through godly disciplines, not only lives but living standard also positively changes for the believers so no mater even in persecution believers witness is powerful" (RP26). "We visit to the many villages to preaching the gospel. We visited to the 110 places/villages. We were gathering house to house every day. Every house prepares different activities and programs" (RP10).

Research participants speak of the house church as a mission tool for fulfilling the Great Commandment. "Surely, house church is a mission tool" (RP23). "It (house church) is a powerful tool to evangelism and pioneering work and to plant churches" (RP17)

RP34,

> For a few people it's too long to attend at one place. And regularly gathering at one place we may not reach many people. But if we establish as many house churches as we can, then we can reach many people. The number of the members may not be visible to all (we may not show them at one place) but it will certainly please God. We can fulfill God's Command: The great Commission.

House Church as a Local Church that leads to Change

Research participants see house churches as the local church that leads to change. RP27 mentioned this.

> Although there is hinder of Hindu people to the house church, once the house church has started, we regularly are gathering the house for worship and fellowship. The Hindu thinks that these figures of the house church do not give any bad influence. I am not directly preaching the gospel to the Hindu people. House church member approach to the people, then they invites the people to the house church... The contribution of the house church is break social inferiority.

RP01 described how his local community recognizes his house church as a local church. "Since I am pastoring in my born town, my community recognize me as a Christian and pastor of the house church. They won't make problem with me." RP31 stated that "house church model will solve some problems that the believers faced." It means the house church leads the transformation for the believers. As an example, RP11 said, "I believe that they (believers) will come out from their previous religion and culture by the word of God." In other words, house churches help the believers to overcome (transform) their previous worldview.

Research participants expressed that the house church is leading not only the transformation of the believers (RP26) but also a social change (RP27). "People around us see our lives and character. Through godly disciplines, not only lives but living standard also positively changes for the believers so no mater even in persecution believers witness is powerful" (RP26). "The contribution of the house church is break social inferiority. It makes people (low caste) to come out to the society. It reduce social gap between high caste (class) and low caste (class)" (RP27).

## 4. Application of Theoretical Premise for Research Question 4

Previous research dealt with difficulties that house churches face from inside and outside. As we have seen in the literature review, many scholars contributed to the understanding of difficulties for a house church in each context. Therefore, the finding from research question 4 can be defined by some theoretical premises of various scholars mentioned in the literature review.

The research participants described some of the inner difficulties of house churches. First of all, participants experienced financial difficulties for renting a house and supporting their family. In the light of Robert Lee Turner's theory, the house church multiplication occurs with leaders who get little or no financial compensation for developing leaders within their respective network. He says that most leaders that are trained have families and full time jobs while leading the various aspects of house churches.

Second, participants expressed the problem of women leadership and the conflict among the leadership. According to Paul Yonggi Cho's theory for women leadership, men are offended by women leading Bible study and small groups because of cultural reasons in some countries like Korea. Craig Ott and Gene Wilson's theory is that although women have important leadership roles for church planting, there are inequities in the church because of certain cultural reasons. Furthermore, according to Clyde Reid's theory, leadership competition is one of a small group's problems.

Third, research participants expressed the lack of theological education in the house church. According to Prosperly Bell Lyngdoh's theory, the lack of lay leadership training is a serious handicap for the house church planting ministry.

Fourth, participants spoke of the various difficulties in the house churches: interrelationship problems among the believers, difficulties arising from the believers' demands, lack of desire to open their own house, the caste problem, and money trading among the believers. Clyde Reid's theory explained interrelationship problems in the small group as follows: In the two groups of small groups, while one group dominates an issue, the other has apathy on that issue. Individuals attempt to dominate a group. Schaeffer's theory is that some people prefer maller settings and some people prefer the anonymity of a large church. Another theory of Schaeffer is that the house church is not for everyone. This means that some people desire privacy and the opportunity to choose who they want to get close to. In the literature review, according to Younggi Cho, a cultural problem in a small group of the church is cultural relationships among individuals. In some cultures, borrowing money from other church member sometimes becomes a great obstacle for the small group ministry.

Research participants described some outer difficulties for house churches. First, they described difficulties that were experienced by false teacher. In order to overcome a false teacher, according to David Adeney, the most important need is for biblical materials and pastor-teachers who can lead new believers into the knowledge of the truth. According to Schaeffer's theory, in order to counter the impact of false doctrines, there needs to be high context communication in the house churches so that cohesion and uniformity in the group are developed.

Second, research participants portrayed the critical and negative recognition of the traditional church towards the house church. According to Alan Munden's critical viewpoint for the house church, one should notice how others dealt with house churches, and also re-evaluate one's own position without totally condemning the house churches. From the literature review, although Prosperly Bell Lyngdoh maintained that house churches are not counter parts of the institutional and structural church, Victor Choudrie's theory is that traditional and organizational church are counterparts of the house church.

The research participants defined a practical meaning of a house church in persecution. Rodney Stark argues that the effect of a social network and its contribution was that the church grows through the social network in the persecution period. In light of his theory, the researcher questioned the research participants for practical meaning of the house church in the difficulties (including persecution) of today, especially in India. As a result, the practical meaning of a house church in today's difficulties is that it is an independent, invisible church in the persecution, it is a missional springboard for outreach and evangelism, and it is a local church that leads to change.

Chapter 9

# Research Conclusions

In this chapter, I conclude my research to assess how the house church in urban settings evangelize and catechize migrants and locals into God's family. I have verified four themes that impact and influence to the house churches to evangelize and catechize migrants and locals.

Here, the research questions have been summarized in light of some of the major theories in order to confirm and determine the hypothesis of this study, and concluded that the house church in an urban setting is an effective means for evangelizing and catechizing migrants and locals into God's family. The sub-hypotheses as follow are under the hypothesis of this study: *the house church in an urban settings is an effective means for evangelizing and catechizing migrants and locals into God's family.*

## Sub-hypothesis 1

*The positive results of leadership in interdependent relationships influence the house church to evangelize and catechize migrants and locals in the city.*

In terms of collected data, there were different expressions for the relationship between the pastors and the believers: leader and followers, father and children, spiritual caregiver, and friend. Especially, spiritual dimension has emphasized on their interdependent relationship. The key core words in their relationships are trust, partnership and efforts for solving problems.

Interdependent relationships and leadership in the house church brought positive results. The house church stands firmly as an independent church in financial stability and her ministry has been strengthened because of her strong unity.

These factors influenced the believers to do evangelism voluntarily, motivating them to penetrate the local society. Thus, the roles of the pastors and believers in interdependent relationships encourage their house church's approach to the migrants and locals in order to evangelize and catechize them into God's family.

Therefore, the house church can be defined in the practical aspects as a preparation place for missional expansion, as a local church adjusts to local needs with Christ's love, and as a small church that is a local worship community.

## Sub-hypothesis 2

*There exist various house church models for evangelizing and catechizing migrants and locals in the cities.*

Models for house churches exist, not just one, but various. On the basis of the findings, the participants had various ideas for house church models. House church models can be defined according to motivation, purpose, and context.

In the cultural aspect, particularly within an India context, house church is a transition process from the house to traditional church. Pastors and believers desire to move to the traditional church, since a house is not 'a holy place'. A house church needs more space because of her growth. Some house churches consider moving into a church building because of conflict with a homeowner or neighbors.

The house church model is the easiest model. It is an initiate model for church planting, an initiate stage for approaching neighbors and a local community. Since a house church understands the natural process of church planting and growth, the house church understands the process towards a large scale church. Trust and team ministry between the pastor and the believers make possible this model, a house church planting mission model. Thus, the house church is a good place to practice evangelism and for training for evangelism. Especially, a house church planting mission model is a proper model in an environment of persecution and economic weakness. This model includes the house church as a subsidiary church of a traditional church. An independent subsidiary church can be established in a place remote from the mother church. As a missional church model, the house church becomes a place of centripetal and centrifugal mission work.

Meanwhile, the house church is recognized as an alternative church for a traditional church. The experience of failure and weakness of a traditional church leads the church planters to start a house church as the alternative model for it.

Although a house church is often treated as a competitor of a traditional church and as being threatened by the large scale church, yet the house church is recognized as equal to other traditional or institutional churches. In actuality, often the house church is better than traditional churches in the aspects of intimacy and relationship, and it has a higher economic efficiency than a traditional church.

Notably, a house church model with an ecclesiological aspect was pursued. The house church model is proposed that emphasizes an identity with the church community. The starting point of a house church is not a visible building, but people. Therefore, the house church model that focuses on the people proposes a church model that centers on the needs of people.

## Sub-hypothesis 3

*The efforts of a house church toward transforming the world of the migrants as well as locals who hold a Hindu worldview influences them to evangelize and catechize.*

On the basis of the findings, the migrants and locals have experienced their worldview change in economic, spiritual, psychological, and sociocultural aspects. The efforts of the house church to help them confront this experience of worldview change is in order to evangelize and catechize them.

Urban and economic environments of migrants and locals are a setting for their worldview change. Especially, economic failure and crisis of migrants and locals provide an opportunity for their worldview change. In the new environment, like a house church, migrants and locals who hold to a religious mind have interest in spiritual matters.

With regards to psychological aspect, the dissatisfaction and conflicts in the urban environment that migrants and locals have experienced are main factors for worldview change. In the sociocultural aspect, new relationships and environment, and persecution from the outside towards the house church, influence migrants and locals' worldview change.

The house church evangelizes and catechizes migrants and locals through helping them with their problems and assisting them in a worldview change. The house church delivers the gospel by using contextualization through the migrants and locals' religious understanding.

In order to deliver the gospel, syncretism needs to be overcome. It is important to confirm the spiritual status of the believers in the house church because they were previously holding to the Hindu culture and its worldview. The pastoral leadership role is to confirm how the believers can remove their Hindu factors and whether the believers can deliver the gospel in order to evangelize and catechize the migrants and locals.

Although some pastors have a generous attitude towards some Hindu factors in the house church, many pastors recognize the Hindu factors that exist in the house church. The task is, how can they remove the Hindu factors in the house church through the Bible and how can they deliver the gospel to the Hindu neighbor without compromising the faith.

For this, house church pastors need two kinds of effort. One is that they need to put their effort to remove Hindu elements in the believers with the Bible completely, and the other is that they need to put their effort on how to approach the Hindu neighbors with understanding of their worldview as well as how to deliver the gospel in their context. By doing so, the house church can evangelize and catechize migrants and locals in their worldview change.

## Sub-hypothesis 4

*House church is a mission means to evangelize and catechize migrants and locals in difficult circumstances that are not easily overcome.*

In terms of difficulties of a house church, there exist a lot of obstacles inside and outside of a house church. These obstacles make for difficulties in the house church to evangelize and catechize migrants and locals. Practically, there is only a few ways to overcome these difficulties of a house church, except through prayer. Participants express that it is hard to overcome their difficulties in the house church. A house church faces inner obstacles like difficulties of pastors, absence of theological education, and various conflicts that are experienced when they deliver the gospel.

There exists the threat of false teachers, of negative recognition by the traditional church, as well as conflict with neighbors, political menace, and threats from the local community. Despite all the negative recognition by the traditional church, the house church is an independent church. She endures political threats and menace from the local community. The reason why she can deliver the gospel is that she is an 'invisible church.'

Despite the various problems in the house church, she is effective as a missional spring board to deliver the gospel in the mission field. She is the church that brings transformation by preaching the gospel in the difficult situations.

In summary, my qualitative research hypothesis is that *the house church in an urban settings is an effective means for evangelizing and catechizing migrants and locals into God's family.* Its sub-hypotheses are as follow.

First, the positive results of leadership by interdependent relationships influence the house church to evangelize and catechize migrants and locals in the city. Second, there exist various house church models for evangelizing and catechizing migrants and locals in the cities. Third, the efforts of a house church toward transforming the world of the migrants, as well as locals who hold to the Hindu worldview influence them in order to evangelize and catechize. Fourth, a house church is a mission means to evangelize and catechize migrants and locals in the difficult circumstances that are not easily overcome.

## Missiological Implication and Recommendations for Future Study

A variety of missiological research of the house church model has already been done. It has already been studied in biblical, historical, and archeological aspects, and also in social network theory. The researcher used social interdependent theory and qualitative methodology in order to do missiological research of house churches that exist in a unique area and context, and the researcher especially focused on the missiological role of house churches. As a result of that, the researcher drew the hypothesis as above.

The hypothesis could be applied to India and similar contexts in other countries; however, one should evaluate and examine its hypothesis through a quantitative research method, and should confirm this hypothesis in order to get a clearer missiological implications.

For future study, one can undertake the roles of house churches in various mission fields. As a result of that study, it would be interesting to find the differences by comparing its hypothesis with the present one.

The researcher believes that God's prior dealings in the mission context using house churches leads the house church to become a means of *missio Dei.* For His mission, the researcher hopes many research works arise to support house churches around the world in order to help her do her mission for delivering the gospel.

Appendix 1

# An Initial Interview Protocol

## Interdependent relationship and leadership in the house church

1. In your house church, what are contents of interdependent relationship among congregations? What are the factors that promote their interdependent relationship among congregations?
2. In your house church, what are contents of interdependent relationship between congregation and leader (pastor)?
3. How do you describe the benefits received from the role of interdependent relationship among congregations?
4. How do you describe the benefits received from the role of interdependent relationship between congregation and leader (pastor)?
5. In your opinion, how the interdependent relationships among congregation influence the house church to reach migrants or locals to evangelize?
6. In your opinion, how the interdependent relationships between congregation and leader (pastor) influence the house church to reach migrants or locals to evangelize?
7. In your opinion, what is the practical meaning of house church in light of the interdependent relationship between congregation and leadership (pastor)?

## House church planting model in the city

1. Before you planted your house church, what was your idea about house church?

   At that time, what kinds of house church did you plan to establish?
2. After you planted your house church, did you change your idea about house church? Why did you change the definition of house church?
3. In what way can you describe your house church model in the present? What are differences before and after you planted your house church?

4. What is your future plan for your house church? In your opinion, what is an ideal model for house church?

## Worldview Change

1. In what way economic migration and urban environment affect to migrants to change their previous religious and cultural understanding?
   In what way the change of urban environment affect to locals to change their previous religious and cultural understanding?
2. How do you deliver the gospel to the Hindu migrants or Hindu locals who join your house church?
3. How house church leads the migrants or locals in the spiritual aspect?
4. What kinds of programs does your house church have in order to support spiritual need of migrants or locals?
5. What kinds of cultural elements from Hinduism does your house church have?
   How do congregations in the house church respond to the elements of Hinduism in their life? What do you think about Yoga? What do the congregations of the house church do on the Hindu festivals?

**Obstacles:** You can use "possible examples" in appendix for your response in each question.

1. What were the inner difficulties in your house church? How did you overcome?
2. What were the outer difficulties in your house church? How did you overcome?
3. What kinds of inner difficulties in your house church you did not overcome? What kinds of countermeasure for these difficulties?
4. What kinds of outer difficulties in your house church you did not overcome? What kinds of countermeasure for these difficulties?
5. In what way these difficulties impact to establish the house church and deliver the gospel?

Appendix 2

# Follow-up Interview Protocol

## Theme One: Understanding of Interdependent relationship and leadership

1. The Definition of Interdependent Relationship and Its contents
   a. In what way can you describe the interdependent relationship between the pastor (leader) and congregations?
   b. In your house church, what are contents of interdependent relationship between the pastor (leader) and congregations? In other words, what are the factors that promote their interdependent relationship in your house church?
2. The Benefits of Interdependent Relationship
   c. In your opinion, what are the benefits of interdependent relationship between pastor (leader) and congregations?
3. Interdependent Relationship and Evangelism
   d. In your opinion, how is the interdependent relationship between the pastor (leader) and congregation influence the house church members to reach migrants or locals in order to evangelize?
4. Interdependent Relationship and the Practical meaning of House Church
   e. In your opinion, what is the practical meaning of house church in light of the interdependent relationship between the pastor (leader) and congregation?

## Theme Two: The House Church Planting Model

1. Motivation of Planting House Church and Its Understanding
   a. Before you planted your house church, what was your idea about house church?
   At that time, what kinds of house church had you planned to establish?

b. After you planted your house church, did you change your idea about house church? If yes, what made you change your idea about house church?

2. House church Model in the Present

c. In what way can you describe your house church model in the present? What are the notable differences before and after the house church plant?

3. House church Model in the Future

d. What is your future plan for your house church? What is your future model for house church?

## Theme Three: Worldview Change

1. Environmental and Worldview Change

a. In what ways does the economic migration and urban environment affect the migrants or the locals to change their previous religious and cultural understanding?

2. Worldview Change and Evangelism

b. How do you deliver the gospel to the Hindu immigrants or the Hindu locals who join your house church?

3. Support for Worldview Change

c. How does the house church lead the migrants or locals in the spiritual aspect? What kinds of programs does your house church have in order to support spiritual needs of immigrants or locals?

4. Response toward Other Religion

d. What kinds of cultural elements from Hinduism does your house church have?

How does the congregation in your house church respond to the elements of Hinduism in their lives? What do you think about Yoga? What do the congregations of the house church do on the Hindu festivals?

## Theme Four: Obstacles of the House Church

You can use "possible examples" in appendix three for your response in each question.

1. Inner Obstacles

a. What were the inner difficulties in your house church? How did you overcome (deal with) them?

2. Outer Obstacles

b. What were the outer difficulties in your house church? How did you overcome (deal with) them?

3. Obstacles and Evangelism

c. In your opinion, how do you describe the house church as a mission tool evangelism during persecution?

Appendix 3

# "Possible Examples" for Inner and Outer Difficulties in the House Church

**You can use the followings for Theme Four.**

**Inner Obstacles**

- The limitation of women leadership and its cultural reason
- The difficulties in the interdependence (e.g. borrowing money from other in the house church)
- The difference of opinion and issue on the leadership and authority
- Difficulties from some rules in the house church that hurt the congregations or individuals.
- Issue on a clique
- Difficulties of the pastors and leaders' livelihood
- Difficulties of the financial support to pastors and leaders
- Deficiency of the space (size) of house church for worship.
- Some are favor unique environment. Are there any individuals want 'building' rather than 'house' for worship?
- Complains of congregation toward the pastors and leaders.
- Are there individuals who had attended other church (not house church) before? What were the difficulties they had experienced in previous church? Then now what they feel difficulties in the house church?
- Absence of theological education or training in the house church
- Lack of Biblical resources
- Is there any limitation to join to the house church? Is house church open to anyone?

- Lack of interaction with other Christians. Do you have house church network with other house church? In what way does the house church interact with other house church?
- Is there any Baptism issue in the house church?
- What kinds of negative impact on the leadership

## Outer Obstacles

- Threat from heresy or false teaching
- Hindu people take for granted that Hindu priests lead special function in the temple. In this point, is there any difficult for lay leaders when they administer baptism.
- How the house church responds to the Hindu government' authority
- How pastors and leaders' view from other church (not house church) toward the house church? Negative? Positive?

Appendix 4

# Demographic Attributes of Research Participants

## The Thirty-Four Research Participants: Tables 8 and 9

Table 9. The Thirty-Four Research Participants 1

| Respondents No. & Their Place | Age | Birth State | Mother tongue | Educational Background | Job |
|---|---|---|---|---|---|
| RP01, Gujarat | 60 | Maharashtra | Marathi | B.A. | Manager |
| RP02, Maharashtra | 40 | Maharashtra | Marathi | 12th grade | None |
| RP03, Delhi | 50 | Tamil Nadu | Tamil | 12th grade | N.G.O |
| RP04, West Bengal | 28 | West Bengal | Nepali | 12th grade | Teacher |
| RP05, Assam | 38 | Assam | Assamese | B.A. | None |
| RP06, Assam | 35 | Assam | Assamese | Higher Secondary | Office Assistant |
| RP07, Assam | 32 | Assam | Assamese | 10th grade | Auto Rickshaw Driver |
| RP08, Assam | 42 | Assam | Assamese | 10th grade | House wife |
| RP09, Assam | 43 | Assam | Assamese | 10th grade | Farmer |
| RP10, Karnataka | 47 | Andhra Pradesh | Telugu | B.A. | None |
| RP11, Karnataka | 49 | Andhra Pradesh | Telugu | B.A. | Part Time Job |
| RP12, Karnataka | 28 | Karnataka | Kannada | M.Div | None |

| | | | | | |
|---|---|---|---|---|---|
| RP13, Karnataka | 35 | Karnataka | Kannada | $12^{th}$ grade | Coffee shop |
| RP14, Karnataka | 50 | Tamil Nadu | Tamil | B.E. | Engineer |
| RP15, Karnataka | 30 | Tamil Nadu | Tamil | $12^{th}$ grade | Researcher |
| RP16, Karnataka | 34 | Karnataka | Tamil | $7^{th}$ std | None |
| RP17, Karnataka | 32 | Karnataka | Telugu | $10^{th}$ std | Warden |
| RP18, Karnataka | 45 | Tamil Nadu | Tamil | $4^{th}$ grade | Painter |
| RP19, Karnataka | 37 | Karnataka | Tamil | $12^{th}$ grade | None |
| RP20, Karnataka | 54 | Karnataka | Tamil | $10^{th}$ grade | Driver |
| RP21, Karnataka | 61 | Karnataka | Tamil | $12^{th}$ grade | None |
| RP22, Andhra Pradesh | 37 | Andhra Pradesh | Telugu | $12^{th}$ grade | None |
| RP23, Andhra Pradesh | 37 | Tamil Nadu | Tamil | $12^{th}$ grade | None |
| RP24, Andhra Pradesh | 30 | Andhra Pradesh | Telugu | B.com | None |
| RP25, Andhra Pradesh | 39 | Andhra Pradesh | Telugu | $12^{th}$ grade | None |
| RP26, Tamil Nadu | 33 | Tamil Nadu | Tamil | M.A. in English | Instructor |
| RP27, Tamil Nadu | 43 | Tamil Nadu | Tamil | M.A. | None |
| RP28, Maharashtra | 40 | Jalgaon | Pavari | $12^{th}$ grade | Full Time |
| RP29, Maharashtra | 30 | Jalgaon | Pavari | $4^{th}$ grade | None |
| RP30, Andhra Pradesh | 61 | Andhra Pradesh | Telugu | BTH | None |
| RP31, Andhra Pradesh | 25 | Andhra Pradesh | Tamil | MBA | College Lecturer |
| RP32, Karnataka | 48 | Karnataka | Konkani | BTH | Business man |
| RP33, Tamil Nadu | 40 | Tamil Nadu | Tamil | M.Div | Full time |
| RP34, Andhra Pradesh | 55 | Andhra Pradesh | Telugu | SSC | None |

**Table 10.** The Thirty-Four Research Participants 2

| Respondents No. & Their Place | Denomination | Theological background | Established Year | No. of HC | No. of Members | |
|---|---|---|---|---|---|---|
| | | | | | Adults | Children |
| RP01, Gujarat | C&MA | M.Div. | 2009 | 2 | | - |
| RP02, Maharashtra | The Nazarene | M.Div. | 2003 | 1 | 35 | 20 |
| RP03, Delhi | Interdenominational | M. Th. | 2012 | 1 | - | - |
| RP04, West Bengal | Pentecostal | M. Th. | 2006 | 1 | 10 | 15 |
| RP05, Assam | Assembly of God | M.A | 2014 | 1 | 8 | - |
| RP06, Assam | Baptist | Lay leader | 2012 | 1 | 22 | 9 |
| RP07, Assam | Nondenominational | Lay leader | 2013 | 4 | 25 | - |
| RP08, Assam | Independent | Lay leader | 2012 | 20 | 120 | 20 |
| RP09, Assam | Baptist | Lay leader | 2013 | 2 | 8 | - |
| RP10, Karnataka | Baptist | M.Div | 2000 | 7 | 7-12 each | - |
| RP11, Karnataka | Baptist | M.Div | 2008 | 3 | 7-8 each | - |
| RP12, Karnataka | Presbyterian | M.Div | 2010 | 2 | 22 | 20 |
| RP13, Karnataka | Presbyterian | M.A. | 2011 | 4 | 70 | 17 |
| RP14, Karnataka | Pentecostal | M.Div. | 2006 | 1 | 40 | 20 |
| RP15, Karnataka | Pentecostal | B.Th. | 2011 | 8 | 50 | 20 |
| RP16, Karnataka | Pentecostal | B.Th. | 1996 | 2 | 40 | 10 |
| RP17, Karnataka | Interdenominational | B.Th. | 2006 | 1 | 45 | 35 |
| RP18, Karnataka | Pentecostal | C.Th. | 2012 | 1 | 25 | 8 |
| RP19, Karnataka | Pentecostal | D.Th. | 2009 | 1 | 25 | 10 |
| RP20, Karnataka | Pentecostal | C.Th. | 2009 | 1 | 50 | 10 |
| RP21, Karnataka | Pentecostal | C.Th. | 1996 | 1 | 4 | - |
| RP22, Andhra Pradesh | Independent | M.Th. | 2006 | 1 | 35 | 15 |
| RP23, Andhra Pradesh | Pentecostal | D.Th. | 2008 | 4 | 15 | 6 |
| RP24, Andhra Pradesh | Independent | Short-term training | 2014 | 1 | 5 | 2 |
| RP25, Andhra Pradesh | NTRF/ Mission agency | Lay leader | 2009 | 1 | - | - |
| RP26, Tamil Nadu | Independent | M.Th. | 2012 | 1 | 8 | 2 |
| RP27, Tamil Nadu | Lutheran Confessional | B.D. | 2007 | 5 | 15 | 25 |
| RP28, Maharashtra | Independent | C.Th. | 2003 | 5 | 70 | 50 |
| RP29, Maharashtra | Independent | D.Th. | 2008 | 5 | 50 | 20 |
| RP30, Andhra Pradesh | Independent | B.Th | - | 3 | 70 | 30 |
| RP31, Andhra Pradesh | Pentecostal | M.Div | 2006 | 5 | 40 | 12 |
| RP32, Karnataka | Pentecostal | B.Th | 1995 | 4 | 75 | 40 |
| RP33, Tamil Nadu | Pentecostal | M.Div | 2004 | 4 | 100 | 45 |
| RP34, Andhra Pradesh | Independent | SSC | - | 2 | 65 | 45 |

## Living Areas of Research Participants

Research participants in the study are mainly from different cities of eight states of India. The researcher selected research participants from three parts (North, Northeast and South) of India for the test: North (Delhi, Gujarat, Maharashtra and West Bengal); Northeast (Assam); and South (Andhra Pradesh, Karnataka and Tamil Nadu).

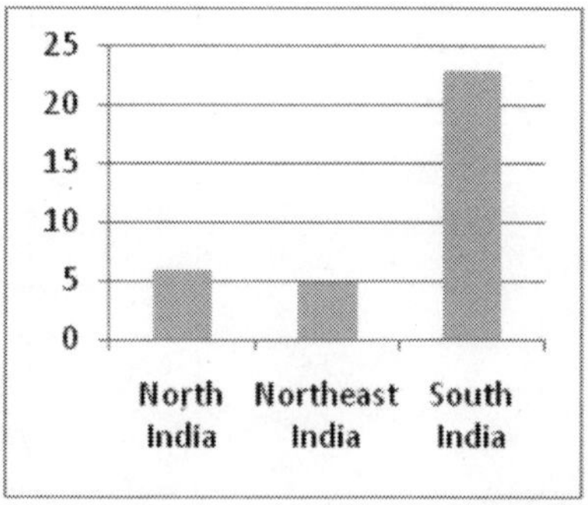


**Figure 25.** Living Areas of Research Participants

Among the thirty four research participants, six are from North India. One research participant live in Delhi (03Delhi), one live in Gujarat (01Gujarat), three live in Maharashtra (02Maharashtra, 28Maharashtra and 29Maharashtra), and one from West Bengal (04WestBengal). Five research participants are from Northeast India. They live in Assam (05Assam, 06Assam, 07Assam, 08Assam, 09Assam).

Another twenty three research participants are from South India. Seven research participants live in Andhra Pradesh (22AndhraPradesh, 23AndhraPradesh, 24AndhraPradesh, 25AndhraPradesh, 30AndhraPradesh, 31AndhraPradesh, 34AndhraPradesh), thirteen live in Karnataka (10Karnataka, 11Karnataka, 12 Karnataka, 13Karnataka, 14Karnataka, 15Karnataka, 16Karnataka, 17Karnataka, 18Karnataka, 19Karnataka, 20Karnataka, 21Karnataka, 32Karnataka), and three live in Tamil Nadu (26TamilNadu, 27TamilNadu, 33TamiNadu). (See Figure 26 and 27)

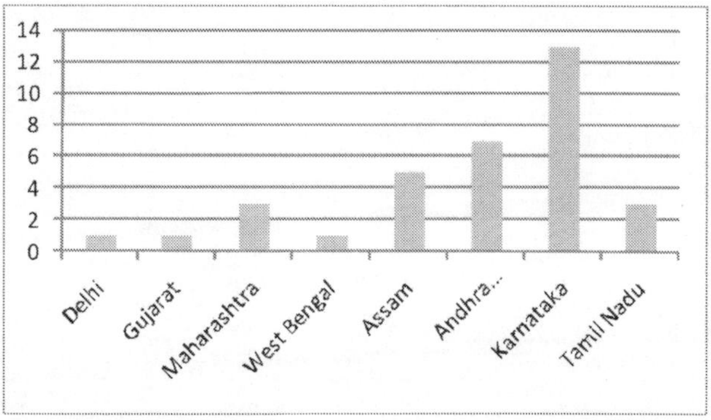


**Figure 26.** The Name of Cities in Living Area

**Figure 27**. The Map of India: Living Places of Research Participants (Not to be Scaled)

## Age Range of Research Participants

The age range of research participants is from 25 to 61: three 20's (25-28), fourteen 30's (30-39), ten 40's (40-49), four 50's (50-55), and three 60's (60-61). (See Figure 28). Among the thirty four research participants, there are thirty three males and one female (08 Assam). Two research participants themselves are second generation of migrants from another state to the present state that are leading the house churches (04WestBengal born in West Bengal and mother tongue is Nepali, and 17Karnataka born in Karnataka and his mother tongue is Telugu). (See table 8)

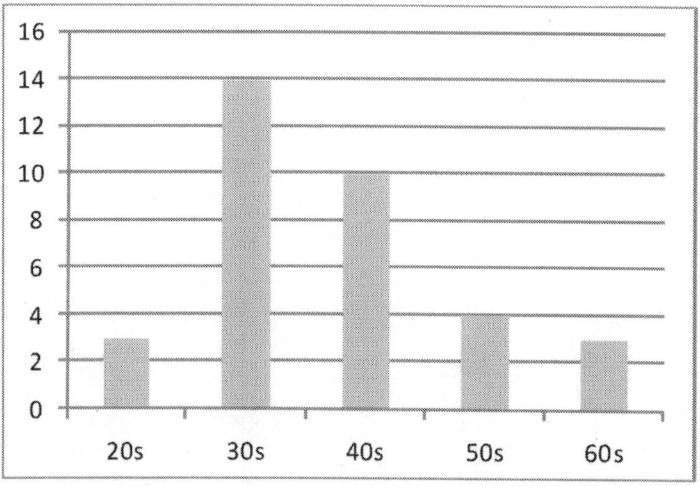


**Figure 28.** Age Range of Research Participants

## Bi-vocational Ministry and Full Time Ministry

Sixteen research participants are in bi-vocational ministry (01 Gujarat, 03 Delhi, 04 West Bengal, 06 Assam, 07 Assam, 09 Assam, 11 Karnataka, 13 Karnataka, 14 Karnataka, 15 Karnataka, 17 Karnataka, 18 Karnataka, 20 Karnataka, 26 Tamil Nadu, 31 Andhra Pradesh, 32 Karnataka). Other eighteen are in full time ministry (02 Maharashtra, 05 Assam, 08 Assam, 10 Karnataka, 12 Karnataka, 16 Karnataka, 19 Karnataka, 21 Karnataka, 22 Andhra Pradesh, 23 Andhra Pradesh, 24 Andhra Pradesh, 25 Andhra Pradesh, 27 Tamil Nadu, 28 Maharashtra, 29 Maharashtra, 30 Andhra Pradesh, 33 Tami Nadu, 34 Andhra Pradesh). (See Figure 29 and Table 10)

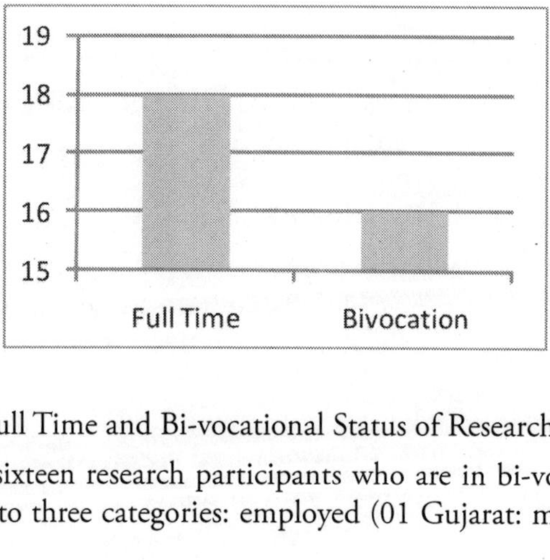


**Figure 29.** Full Time and Bi-vocational Status of Research Participants

Job area of sixteen research participants who are in bi-vocational ministry mainly divided into three categories: employed (01 Gujarat: manager, 03 Delhi:

NGO, 06 Assam: Office Assistant, 07 Assam: Auto Rickshaw Driver, 11 Karnataka: Part Time Job, 14 Karnataka: Engineer, 17 Karnataka: Warden, 20 Karnataka: Driver), education (04 West Bengal: Teacher, 15 Karnataka: Researcher, 26 Tamil Nadu: Instructor, 31 Andhra Pradesh: College Lecturer) and business (09 Assam: Farmer, 13 Karnataka: Coffee shop, 18 Karnataka: Painting Contractor, 32 Karnataka: Business man) (See Figure 30).

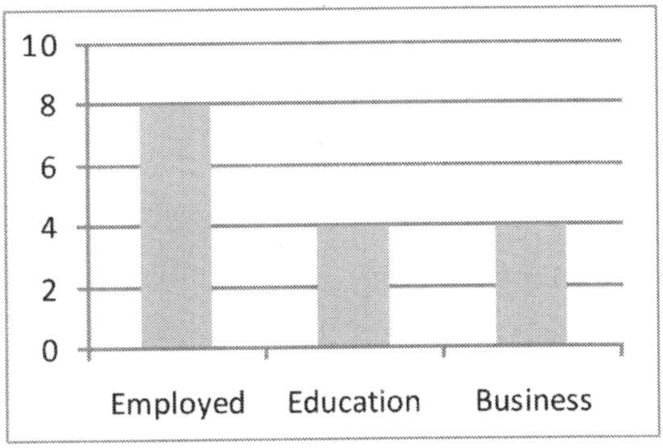


**Figure 30.** Job Area of Bi-Vocational Research Participants

Research participants have various denominational backgrounds. This sometimes reveals their theological identities toward a house church ministry. Therefore, it is important to know their denominational background. Among thirty four research participants, twelve are Pentecostal (04 West Bengal, 14 Karnataka, 15 Karnataka, 16 Karnataka, 18 Karnataka, 19 Karnataka, 20 Karnataka, 21 Karnataka, 23 Andhra Pradesh, 31Andhra Pradesh, 32 Karnataka, 33 Tamil Nadu), and eight are Independent (08 Assam, 34 Andhra Pradesh, 24 Andhra Pradesh, 26 Tamil Nadu, 28 Maharashtra, 29 Maharashtra, 30 Andhra Pradesh, 22 Andhra Pradesh). Four are Baptist (06 Assam, 09 Assam, 10 Karnataka, 11 Karnataka) and two are Presbyterian (12 Karnataka and 13 Karnataka). 01 Gujarat is in C&MA, 02 Maharashtra is in Nazarene, 25 Andhra Pradesh belongs to house church mission agency called NTRF, 27 Tamil Nadu is a Lutheran Confessional, 05 Assam is in Assembly of God, 17 Karnataka and 03 Delhi are Interdenominational and 07 Assam is Nondenominational. Indeed, house churches have various denominational backgrounds (See Figure 31).

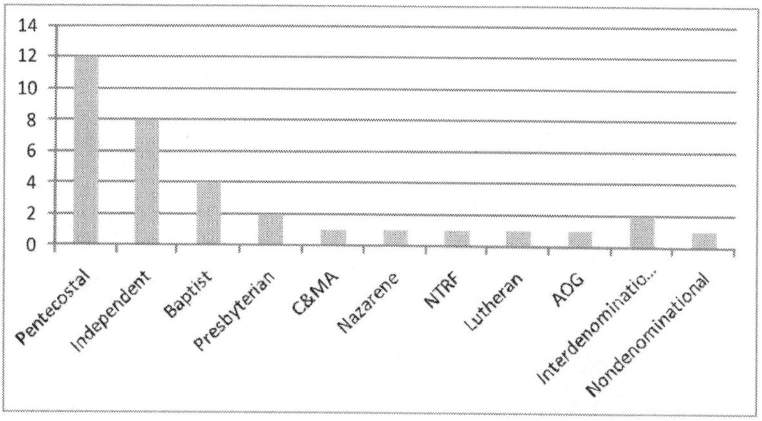


**Figure 31.** Denominational Background of Research Participants

## Theological Education of Research Participants

It was reported that twenty seven research participants out of thirty four took theological education and hold theological degrees from a seminary. Four research participants hold a M.Th degree (03 Delhi, 04 West Bengal, 22 Andhra Pradesh, 25 Andhra Pradesh), eight have a M. Div. (01 Gujarat, 02 Maharashtra, 10 Karnataka, 11 Karnataka, 12 Karnataka, 14 Karnataka, 31 Andhra Pradesh, 33 Tami Nadu), and two hold M.A degree (13 Karnataka and 05 Assam). Another five hold a B.Th. (32 Karnataka, 30 Andhra Pradesh, 15 Karnataka, 16 Karnataka and 17 Karnataka), one has B.D. (27 Tamil Nadu), three hold a Dip.Th degree (19 Karnataka, 29 Maharashtra, 23 Andhra Pradesh), and four have a C.Th. (28 Maharashtra, 20 Karnataka, 18 Karnataka, 21 Karnataka). Another six research participants had not taken any theological education. Among them, 24 Andhra Pradesh had taken short-term training for leading a house church (See Figure 32).

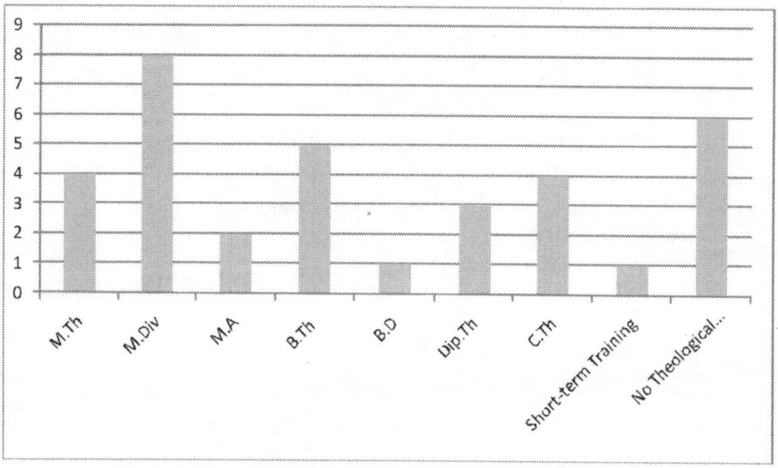


**Figure 32.** Final Theological Education of Research Participants

## The Church's Age

As seen in the data, there are various house church ages. The distribution of house church ages are presented in the graph as follows. See Figure 33 below. It was reported that twelve research participants' house church are within 5 years of age (03 Delhi, 05 Assam, 06 Assam, 07 Assam, 08 Assam, 09 Assam, 12 Karnataka, 13 Karnataka, 15 Karnataka, 18 Karnataka, 24 Andhra Pradesh and 26 Tamil Nadu), thirteen are 6 to 10 years old (01 Gujarat, 04 West Bengal, 11 Karnataka, 14 Karnataka, 17 Karnataka, 19 Karnataka, 20 Karnataka, 22 Andhra Pradesh, 23 Andhra Pradesh, 31 Andhra Pradesh, 27 Tamil Nadu, 29 Maharashtra and 25 Andhra Pradesh), four are 11 to 15 years old (02 Maharashtra, 10 Karnataka, 28 Maharashtra, 32 Karnataka and 33 Tamil Nadu), and three are 26 to 30 years old (16 Karnataka, 21 Karnataka and 32 Karnataka). One research participant did not respond with his house church's age (See Figure 33).

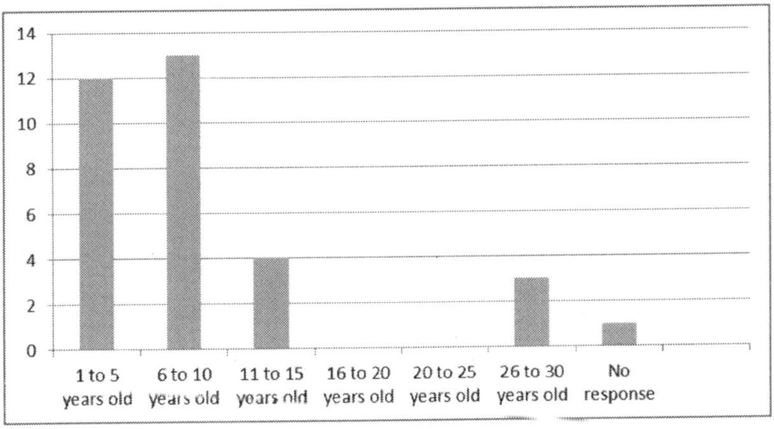


**Figure 33.** The Church's Age

## Numbers of House Churches

Fifteen research participants (02 Maharashtra, 03 Delhi, 04 West Bengal, 05 Assam, 06 Assam, 14 Karnataka, 24 Andhra Pradesh, 25 Andhra Pradesh, 26 Tamil Nadu, 17 Karnataka, 18 Karnataka, 19 Karnataka, 20 Karnataka, 21 Karnataka, 22 Andhra Pradesh) are leading one house church, while others are leading more than one. Five research participants are leading two house churches (01 Gujarat, 09 Assam, 12 Karnataka, 16 Karnataka, and 34 Andhra Pradesh), and two are leading three house churches (30 Andhra Pradesh and 11 Karnataka). Another five research participants are leading four house churches (07 Assam, 13 Karnataka, 23 Andhra Pradesh, and 32 Karnataka, 33 Tamil Nadu), and four are leading five house churches (31 Andhra Pradesh, 27 Tamil Nadu, 28 Maharashtra, and 29 Maharashtra). Research participant, 10 Karnataka is leading seven house churches, and 15 Karnataka is leading ei ght house churches. One woman leader, 08Assam is leading twenty house churches (See Figure 34).

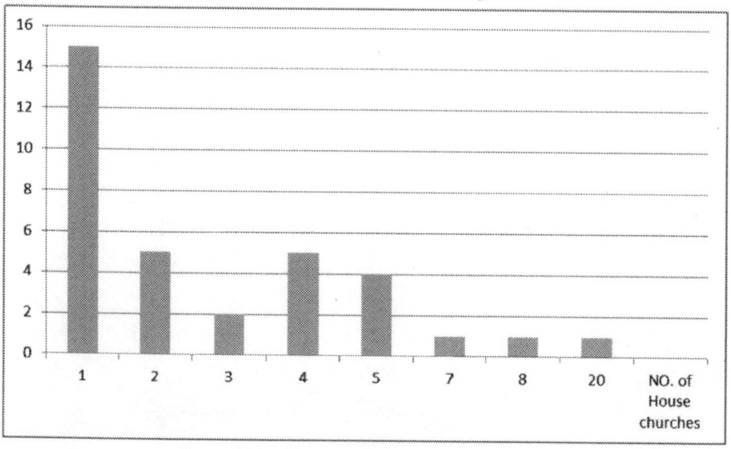


**Figure 34.** Numbers of House Churches that Research Participants are leading

## Numbers of believers in the House Churches

Seven research participants (04 West Bengal, 05 Assam, 09 Assam, 26 Tamil Nadu, 21 Karnataka, 24 Andhra Pradesh, 15 Karnataka) responded there are four to ten believers in their house churches. 09 Assam leads two churches, while six of them are leading one house church. Another seven research participants (06 Assam, 07 Assam, 12 Karnataka, 27 Tamil Nadu, 23 Andhra Pradesh, 18 Karnataka, 19 Karnataka) responded there are fifteen to twenty five believers in their house churches. Three of them (06 Assam, 18 Karnataka and 19 Karnataka) lead one house church, one of them (12 Karnataka) leads two house churches, two of them (07 Assam and 23 Andhra Pradesh) lead four house churches, and one of them (27 Tamil Nadu) lead five house churches (See Figure 35).

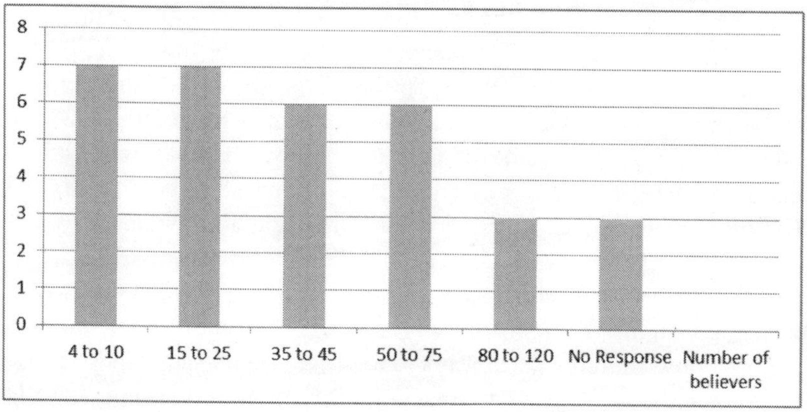


**Figure 35.** Numbers of believers in the House Churches

# Bibliography

Adeney, David. "Springtime for the Church in China." *Christianity Today*, June 18, 1982, 30.

Aghamkar, Atul Y. "Mission and Ministry of House Churches." *Class Lecture at SAIACS*, January 22, 2005.

——. *God So Loves the City,* ed. by Charles Van Engen & Jude Tiersma, Monrovia: MARC, 1994.

——. *Insights into Openness: Encouraging Urban Mission,* Bangalore: SAIACS, 2000.

Alexander, Gary. "House Churches : Your Hope for the Future? " *Christian Life*, January, 1982.

Allen, Roland. *Missionary Methods: St. Paul's or Ours,* London: Robert Scott Press, 1962.

——. *The Spontaneous Expansion of the Church,* Grand Rapids: Eerdmans, 1984.

Anderson, Philip and Phoebe Anderson, *The House Church,* Nashville, TN: Abingdon Press, 1975.

Ann S. Michaelsen. "Interactive teaching methods double learning." Accessed October 30, 2014. http://annmichaelsen.com/2011/06/01/interactive-teaching-methods-double-learning.

Atkerson, Steve. et al., *House Church: Simple, Strategic, Scriptural,* Atlanta, GA: NTRF Publishing, 2008.

Augsberger, David W. *Pastoral Counseling Across Cultures,* Philadelphia, PA: Westminster Press, 1986.

Babin, Pierre, and M. Iannone. *The New Era in Religious Communication,* Minneapolis: Fortress Press, 1991.

Banks, Robert. *Paul's Idea of Community: The Early House Churches in their Cultural Setting*, Peabody: Hendrickson Publishers, 2007.

Barrett, David. *Cosmos, Chaos and Gospel: A Chronology of World Evangelization from Creation to New Creation,* Birmingham, Ala.: New Hope, 1987.

Barth, Markus. *Ephesians 4-6.* The Anchor Bible Commentary. New York, NY: Doubleday Publishing, 1960.

Barton, Stephen C. "Paul's Sense of Place: An Anthropological Approach to Community Formation in Corinth." *New Testament Studies* 32, no. 2 (April 1986): 232.

Beesley, Mark B. "At the Boundary of Place: Rethinking the Provenance of Early Christian Architecture." PhD diss., The University of St. Andrews, 2010.

Berkhof, Louis. *Systematic Theology*, Grand Rapids, MI: William B. Eerdmans Publishing Company, 1941.

Best, Ernest. *Ephesians*. International Critical Commentary. Dorset, England: T & T Clark Publishing, 2001.

Billings, Bradley S. "From House Church to Tenement Church: Domestic Space and the Development of Early Urban Christianity." Master's thesis, The University of Melbourne, 2010.

Bird, Warren. "The Great Small-Group Takeover." *Christianity Today*, Febuary 7, 1994.

Birkey, Del. "The House Church: A Missiological Model." *Misssiology: An International Review,* Vol. XIX, No.1 (1991): 69.

——. *The House Church,* Scottdale, PA: Herald Press, 1987.

Blue, Bradley. "Acts and the House Church," in *The Book of Acts in its First Century Setting, Vol.2, Greaco-Roman Setting*, ed. by David W. J. Gill and Conrad Gempf, Grand Rapids, MI: William B. Eerdmans Publishing Company, 1994.

Bob Munson. "Dependence, Independence, and Interdependence." Accessed September 20, 2014. http://www.bukallife.org/articles/Interdependence.pdf.

Bock, Darrell L. *Acts*. Baker Exegetical Commentary on the New Testament. Grand Rapids, MI: Baker Academic, 2007.

Branick, Vincent. "The house Church in the Writing of Paul" in *Zacchaeus Studies: New Testament*, ed. by Mary Ann Getty, Wilmington, DE: Michael Glazier Publishing, 1989.

Bruce, F. F. *The Epistles to the Colossians, to Philemon, and to the Ephesians*. The New International Commentary on the New Testament. Grand Rapids, MI: William B. Eerdmans Publishing Company, 1984.

Bunkowske Model. "The Golden Circle." accessed November 19, 2014. http://gregandmeg.net/wp-content/uploads/2013/05/Bunkowske-model.jpg.

Bunkowske, Eugene W., and Richard French, *Receptor-Oriented Gospel Communication,* Fullerton, CA: The Great Commission Resource Library, 1989.

Cababiss, Allen. *Pattern in Early Christian Worship*. Macon, GA: Mercer University Press, 1989.

Cho, Paul Yonggi. *Successful Home Cell Groups,* Plainfield, Logos International, 1981.

Choudhrie, Victor. *The Church in Your House* (English Edition, 2006).

City Population. "Major Agglomerations of the World: All agglomerations of the world with a population of 1 million inhabitants or more." Accessed November 17, 2014. http://www.citypopulation.de/world/Agglomerations.html.

Clarke, Andrew D. "Serve the Community of the Church: Christians as Leaders and Ministers," in *First-Century Christians in the Graeco-Roman World*, ed. by Andrew D. Clarke, Grand Rapids: Eerdmans, 2000.

Clowney, Edmund P. *The Church: Contours of Christian Theology*, Downers Grove, IL: InterVarsity Press, 1995.

Cole, Neil. *Organic Church: Growing Faith where Life Happens,* San Francisco, CA: Jossey-Bass, 2005.

Conn, Harvie M. & Manuel Ortiz. *Urban Ministry : The Kingdom, the City & the People of God,* Downer Grove: InterVarsity Press, 2001.

Crouch, Andy. *Culture Making: Recovering our Creative Calling,* Downers Grove, IL: InterVarsity Press, 2008.

Deiss, Lucien. *Springtime of the Liturgy: Liturgical Texts of the First Four Centuries,* Collegeville, MN: The Liturgical Press, 1979.

Deutsch, M. "A Theory of Cooperation and Competition." *Human Relations*, no. 2 (1949), 129-152.

——. "Cooperation and Trust: Some Theoretical Notes," in *Nebraska Symposium on Motivation*, ed. by Marshall. et al. Jones, vol. 10. Lincoln: University of Nebraska Press, 1960.

——. "Field Theory in Social Psychology," in *The Handbook of Social Psychology*, ed. by G. Lindzey & E. Aronson, 2nd ed., Menlo Park, California: Worldcat Libraries, 1968.

Deyoung, Kevin and Ted Kluck, *Why we Love the Church: In Praise of Institutions and Organized Religion,* Chicago, IL: Moody Publishers, 2009.

Dixon, Suzanne. *The Roman Family,* Baltimore: The John Hopkins University Press, 1992.

Dunn, James D. G. *The Epistles to the Colossians and to Philemon.* The New International Greek Testament Commentary. Grand Rapids, MI: William B. Eerdmans Publishing Company, 1996.

Dupont, Florence. *Daily Life in Ancient Rome,* translated by Christopher Woodall, Oxford: Blackwell, 1992. Originally published as a *La vie quotidienne du citoyen romain sous la Republique* (Hachetee, France, 1989).

Elliott, John H. *A Home for the Homeless,* Philadelphia: Fortress Press, 1981.

Ellision, Edgar J. *Home Grown Leaders,* Pasadena, CA: William Carey Library, 1992.

Engen, Charles Edward Van. *Mission on the Way: Issues in Mission Theology,* Grand Rapids, MI: Baker Academic, 1996.

Enroth, Ronald M. *A Guide to New Religious Movements,* Downers Grove: InterVarsity Press, 2005.

Erickson, Millard J. *Introducing Christian Doctrine,* Grand Rapids, MI: Baker Academic, 2001.

*Evangelical Dictionary of World Missions* (2000), s.v. "Strategy in Mission."

Feddes, David J. "Caring for God's Household." *Calvin Theological Journal* 45 (2008), 285.

Fee, Gordon D. *The First Epistle to the Corinthians.* The New International Commentary on the New Testament. Grand Rapids, MI: William B. Eerdmans Publishing Company, 1987.

Filson, Floyd V. "The Significance of the Early House Churches." *Journal of Biblical Literature* 58 (1939): 109-112.

Fitts, Robert. *The Church in the House: A Return to Simplicity,* Salem, OR: Preparing The Way Publishers, 2001.

Foster, Arthur L. "Dimensions of House Church Experiencing," in *The House Church Evolving,* ed. by Arthur Foster, Chicago, IL: Exploration Press, 1976.

Francisco, Adam. "Being A Hindu." *The Lutheran Witness,* September 2014.

Frost, Michael and Alan Hirsch, *The Shaping of Things to Come: Innovation and Mission for the 21st Century Church,* Peabody, MA: Hendrickson Publishing, 2003.

Frykenberg, Robert Eric and Alaine M Low. *Christians and Missionaries in India: Cross-Cultural Communication since 1500,* Grand Rapids & Cambridge: Eerdmans, 2003.

Garrison, David. *Church Planting Movements,* Midlothian, IL: Wigtake Resources, 2004.

Gehring, Roger W. *House Church and Mission,* Peabody, Massachusetts: Hendrickson Publishers, 2004.

George, Carl F. *Prepare Your Church for the Future,* New York: Fleming H. Revell Company, 1991.

Gerrish, Jim. "The Evangelical Triangel." Accessed October 10, 2014. http://www.wordofgodtoday.com/evangelical-triangle.

Gibbs, Eddie. *Churchmorph: How Megatrends are Reshaping Christian Communities,* Grand Rapids, MI: Baker Academic, 2009.

Greeson, Kevin. "Church Planting Movements among Muslim Peoples." Accessed January 15, 2015. http://www.missionfrontiers.org/issue/article/church-planting-movements-among-muslim-peoples

Gregory J. "The House Church: From Acts to Constantine." *Lutheran Theological Journal* 43, no. 2 (August 2009), 97.

Grudem, Wayne. *Systematic Theology,* Grand Rapids, MI: Zondervan, 1994.

Guy, Calvin. *Discipling the City: Theological Reflections on Urban Mission*, ed. by Roger S. Greenway, Grand Rapids: Baker Book House, 1979.

Hadaway, C. Kirk., Francis M. Dubose, and Stuart A. *Wright, Home Cell Groups and House Churches,* Nashville, TN: Broadman Press, 1987.

Hays, Richard B. *The Moral Vision of the New Testament: A Contemporary Introduction to New Testament Ethics,* NY: HarperCollins, 1996.

Hiebert, Paul G. "The Christian Response to Hinduism," in *Missiology for the 21st Century: South Asian Perspectives*, ed. by Hedlund, Roger E., and Paul Joshua. Bhakiaraj, Delhi: ISPCK/MIIS, 2004.

——. *Anthropological Reflections on Missiological Issues,* Grand Rapids, MI: Baker Academic, 1994.

Hiebert, Paul G., R. Daniel Shaw, and Tite Tiénou. *Understanding Folk Religion: A Christian Response to Popular Beliefs and Practices,* Grand Rapids, MI: Baker Academic, 1999.

Hinson, Glenn E. *The Evangelization of the Roman Empire,* Macon, GA: Mercer University Press, 1981.

Hirsch, Alan. *The Forgotten Ways: Reactivating the Missional Church,* Ada, MI: Brazos Press, 2007.

Historymakers: The Fuel of Missions Flame. "5 Countries You Never Knew Were Buddhist." Accessed January 15, 2015. http://www.historymakers.info/blog/5-buddhist-countries-you-never-thought-about.html

Hoehner, Harold W. *Ephesians: An Exegetical Commentary.* Grand Rapids, MI: Baker Academic, 2002.

Horrell, David. "Leadership Patterns and the Development of Ideology," *Sociology of Religion* 58, no. 4 (1997): 323-341.

Hrangkhuma, F., Padmini Chand, and Beulah Wood. *Tribes in Transition: Indian Christians Reflect on the Original Inhabitants of the Land : A SAIACS Consultation,* Bangalore: SAIACS, 2004.

Johnson & Johnson, "Social Interdependence Theory." Accessed October 30, 2014. http://www.ceebl.manchester.ac.uk/events/archive/aligningcollaborativelearning/Johnson_Johnson.pdf.

Johnson, D. W. & R. T. Johnson. *Cooperation and Competition: Theory and Research,* Edina, MN: Interaction Book, 1989.

Johnson, David W. "Social Interdependence Theory." *American Psychologist* (2003): 934.

——. "Social Interdependence: Interrelationships among Theory, Research, and Practice." *American Psychologist* (2003): 939.

Johnson, Luke Timothy. *The Acts of the Apostles,* Sacra Pagina Series, vol. 5. Collegville, MN: The Liturgical Press, 1992.

Jones, E. Stanley. *Christ at the Round Table,* New York: Abingdon Press, 1928.

Kelly, Mark. "Gospel multiplies among India's Lingayat people so much that coordinators may leave." Accessed October 13, 2014. http://www.baptistpress.com/22192/gospel-multiplies-among-indias-people-so-much-that-coordinators-may-leave.

Kim, Daniel. "The Effective Missionary Strategy for the Chinese House Church." *The Chinese Church and Missions* 10 (2001): 93-94.

Klauck, Hans-Josef. *The Religious Context of Early Christianity: A Guide to Graeco-Roman Religions,* Edinburgh: T & T Clark, 2000.

Kraft, Charles H. *Anthropology for Christian Witness,* Maryknoll, NY: Orbis Books, 1996.

Kreider, Larry. *House Church Networks: A Church for a New Generation,* Lititz, PA: House to House Publications, 2001.

Levine, Amy-Jill. "Theological Education, the Bible, and History," in *Early Christian Families in Context: An Interdisciplinary Dialogue*, ed. by David L. Balch and Carolyn Osiek, Religion, Marriage and Family. Grand Rapids, MI: William B. Eerdmans, 2003.

Lincoln, Andrew T. *Ephesians.* World Biblical Commentary. Nashville, TN: Thomas Nelson Publishers, 1990.

Lingenfelter, Sherwood G. *Transforming Culture: A Challenge for Christian Mission,* Grand Rapids, MI: Baker Academic, 1998.

Longenecker, Richard N. *Community Formation in the Early Church and in the Church Today,* Peabody, MA: Hendrickson Publishers, 2002.

Ludden, David. *Contesting the Nation: Religion, Community, and the Politics of Democracy in India*, Philadelphia: University of Pennsylvania Press, 1996.

Luzbetak, Louis J. *The Church and Cultures: New Perspectives in Missiological Anthropology,* Maryknoll, NY: Orbis Books, 1988.

Lyngdoh, Prosperly Bell. "Church-Based Training for Lay Church Planters in India." PhD diss., The Southern Baptist Theological Seminary, 2004.

MacMullen, Ramsay. *Paganism in the Roman Empire,* New Haven and London: Yale University Press, 1981.

Malherbe, Abraham J. *Social Aspects of Early Christianity.* Baton Rouge, LA: Louisiana State University Press, 1977.

Mandryk, Jason. *Operation World,* Downers Grove, IL: InterVarsity Press, 2010.

Manual. "Best Practices Institute." Accessed October 13, 2014..

Marshall, I.H. *Luke: Historian and Theologian,* Downers Grove, Ill.: InterVarsity, 1988.

Mastsui, T., T. Kakuyma & M. Onglatoco, "Effects of Goals and Feedback on Performance in Groups." *Journal of Applied Psychology* 72 (1987): 407-415.

Mattson, Daniel L. "Church Planting through Leadership Formation." *Missio Apostolica* 3 (1995): 80.

Meeks, Wayne. *The First Urban Christians: The Social World of the Apostle Paul,* New Haven, CT: Yale University Press, 2003.

Mengsteab, Yohannes A. "Effective Urban Congregations: A Study of Ministry Factors that Contribute to the Effectiveness of a Lutheran Church –Missouri Synod Urban Congregation." Ph.D. diss., Concordia Theological Seminary, 2008.

Miller, Paul M. *Leading the Family of God,* Scottdale: Pennsylvania, 1981.

Moo, Douglas. *The Epistle to the Romans.* The New International Commentary on the New Testament. Grand Rapids, MI: William B. Eerdmans Publishing Company, 1996.

Moody, James & Douglas R. White, "Structural Cohesion and Embeddedness: A Hierarchical Concept of Social Groups." *American Sociological Review* 68 (2003): 103-127.

Moorman, Donald. *Harvest Waiting,* St. Louis: Concordia Publishing House, 1993.

Moreau, A. Scott. "Paul G. Hiebert's Legacy of Worldview." *Trinity Journal* 30NS (2009): 229.

Morris, Leon. *The Gospel According to John, The New International Commentary on the New Testament.* Grand Rapids, MI: Eerdmans, 1971.

Morton Deutscch. "Field Theory in Social Psychology," Accessed October 30, 2014. http://www.institutovenezolanodegestalt.com.ve/Gestalteca_Articulos/Field%20Theory%20in%20Social%20Psychology%20-%20Deutsch%20Morton.pdf.

——. "Field Theory in Social Psychology." Accessed October 30, 2014, http://www.institutovenezolanodegestalt.com.ve/Gestalteca_Articulos/Field%20Theory%20in%20Social%20Psychology%20-%20Deutsch%20Morton.pdf.

Munden, Alan. "Encountering the House Church Movement: A Different Kind of Christianity." *Anvil* 1 (1984): 213.

Narayan, K. Laxmi. "India's Massive Migration Crisis." Accessed January 10, 2015.

Neighbor, Ralph W. *Where Do We Go From Here? A Guide Book for the Cell Group Church,* Houston: Touch Publication, 2000.

Nelson, Reed E. "Five Principles of Indigenous Church Organizations: Lessons from a Brazilian Pentecostal Church." *Missiology: An International Review,* Vol. 17, No. 1 (1989): 50.

Newbigin, Lesslie. *The Open Secret: An Introduction to the Theology of Mission,* Grand Rapids, MI: William B. Eerdmans, 1995.

O'Brien, Peter T. *Colossians, Philemon.* World Biblical Commentary.Waco, TX: Word Books, 1982.

Oetting, Walter. *The Church of the Catacombs,* St.Louis: Concordia Publishing House, 1964.

Ott, Craig and Gene Wilson. *Global Church Planting: Biblical Principles and Best Practices for Multiplication,* Grand Rapids, Michigan: Baker Academic, 2011.

Pocock, Michael, Rheenen Gailyn Van, and Douglas McConnell. *The Changing Face of World Missions: Engaging Contemporary Issues and Trends,* Grand Rapids, MI: Baker Academic, 2005.

Polhill, John B. *Acts.* The New American Commentary. Nashville, TN: Broadman Press, 1992.

Praveen Bose. "Population Boom: At 46.68%, Bangalore Tops Urban Districts," accessed September 25, 2014. http://www.businessstandard.com/india/news/population-boom-at-4668-bangalore-tops-urban-districts/431302.

Rad, Zdero. "Launching House Church Movements." Accessed April 10, 2014, http://www.missionfrontiers.org/issue/article/launching-house-church-movements.

Ramachandra, Vinoth. *Faiths in Conflict?,* Secunderabad, India: OM, 1999.

Reid, Clyde. *Group Alive-Church Alive: The Effective Use of Small Groups in the Local Church,* New York: Harper and Row, 1969.

Rutz, James and Victor Choudhrie, "House Church Explosion in India." *House-2-House Magazine*, Issue 2, 2002, accessed April 10, 2014, http://www.house2house.com/files/MAG_issue_2.pdf.

Schaeffer, Glenn Earl. "A Study of the House Church and Its Relevance for Planting Churches in the Greater Toronto Area." PhD diss., Concordia Theological Seminary, 1996.

Schreiner, Thomas. *Romans.* Baker Exegetical Commentary on the New Testament. Grand Rapid, MI: Baker Books, 1998.

Schulz, Klaus Detlev. "Toward a Missionary Church for the City" in *Missio Apostolica,* Vol. XI, No. 1 (May 2003): 5.

——. *Mission from the Cross: The Lutheran Theology of Mission,* St. Louis: Concordia Publishing House, 2009.

Schwarz, Chrsitian A. *Natural Church Development: A Guide to Eight Essential Qualities of Healthy Churches,* Carol Stream, IL: Church Smart Resources, 1996.

Shaw, R. Daniel. and Charles E. Van Engen, *Communicating God's Word in a Complex World: God's Truth or Hocus Pocus?* Lanham, Maryland: Rowman & Littlefield Publishers, 2003.

Shenk, Wilbert R. (1981). "Rufus Anderson and Henry Venn: A Special Relationship?" *International Bulletin of Missionary Research* 5 (4): 168–172.

Simson, Wolfgang. *House that Change the World: The Return of the House Churches,* Wayneboro, GA: Authentic, 1998.

Stanne, M., D. W. Johnson & R. T. Johnson, "Social Interdependence and Motor Performance: A Meta-Analysis." *Psychological Bulletin*, no. 125 (1999), 133-154.

Stark, Rodney. "Epidemics, Networks, and the Rise of Christianity." *Semeia* 56 (1992): 159-175.

Stark, Rodney and William Sims Bainbridge, "Networks of Faith: Interpersonal Bonds and Recruitment to Cults and Sects." *American Journal of Sociology* 85 (1980), 1397.

Stegemann, Ekkehard W. and Wolfgan Steggemann, *The Jesus Movement: A Social History of Its First Century.* Translated by O. C. Dean, Jr. Minneapolis, Fortress Press, 1999. Originally published as an *Urchristliche Sozialgeschichte: Die Anfänge im Judentum und die Christusgemeinden in der mediterranen Welt* (Stuttgart, Germany: Verlag W. Kohlhammer, 1995).

Stott, John R. W. *Christian Mission in the Modern World,* Mumbai: F.C. Durham for Gospel Literature Service, 1978.

——. *The Spirit, the Church, and the World: The Message of Acts,* Downers Grove, IL: InterVarsity Press, 1990.

Susan, Bordenkircher. "Outstretched in Yoga Worship: A Christian Approach to Yoga." Accessed October 10, 2014. www.christianyoga.us.

Tangence. "Hirsch #3: Third Places." Accessed Octorber 30, 2014. http://tangence.wordpress.com/2008/07/02/hirsch-3-third-places.

Tennent, Timothy C. *Christianity at the Religious Roundtable: Evangelicalism in Conversation with Hinduism, Buddhism, and Islam,* Grand Rapids, MI: Baker Academic, 2002.

Terry, John Mark, Ebbie C. Smith, and Justice Anderson. *Missiology: An Introduction to the Foundations, History, and Strategies of World Missions,* Nashville, TN: Broadman & Holman, 1998.

Thiselton, Anthony C. *The First Epistle to the Corinthians.* The New International Greek Testament Commnetary. Grand Rapids, MI: William B. Eerdmans Publishing Company, 2000.

Tucker, Ruth. *Another Gospel: Cults, Alternative Religions, and the New Age Movement,* Grand Rapids: Zondervan, 2004.

Turner, Robert Lee. "Leadership Development Process of Select House Church Network in North America: A Case Study." PhD diss, The Southern Baptist Theological Seminary, 2010.

Verner, David C. *The Household of God: The Social World of the Pastoral Epistle,* Chicago, Calif.: Scholars Press, 1983.

Viola, Frank. *From Eternity to Here: Rediscovering the Ageless Purpose of God,* Colorado Springs, CO: David C. Cook Publishers, 2009.

Wagner, C. Peter. *Church Planting for a Greater Harvest,* Ventura, CA: Regal, 1990.

White, L. Michael. "Social Networks in the Early Christian Environment: Issues and Methods for Social History." *Semia* 56 (1992): 23.

——. "Adolf Harnack and the Expansion of Early Christianity: A Reappraisal of Social History." *The Second Century* 5 (1985): 115-117.

——. "Domus Ecclesiae-Domus Dei: Adaptation and Development in the Setting for Early Christian Assembly." PhD diss., Yale University, 1982.

——. "Social Networks: Theoretical Orientation and Historical Applications," *Semeia* 56 (1992): 32.

——. "The Social Origins of Christian Architecture," in *Texts and Monuments for the Christian Domus Ecclesiae in its Environment,* Vol. 2. Valley Forge, PA: Trinity Press, 1997.

——. *Building God's House in the Roman World: Architectural Adaptation among Pagans, Jews and Christians,* Baltimore: John Hopkins University Press, 1990.

Witherington, Ben III. *The Acts of the Apostles; A Socio-rhetorical Commentary,* Grand Rapids, MI: William B. Eerdmans Publishing Company, 1998.

Withheld, Name. "Assisting Chinese House Churches to Become Great Commission Churches." PhD diss., The Southern Baptist Theological Seminary, 2012.

Yarnell, Malcolm B. "The Person and Work of the Holy Spirit," in *A Theology for the Church*, ed. by Daniel L. Akin, Nashville, TN: B&H Publishing, 2007.

Yoder, John Howard. "Martin Luther's Forgotten Vision." *The Other Side*, April, 1977.

Yoo, Jong Keol. "Training Chinese House Church Leaders: Factors Influencing Leadership Development Strategies." PhD diss., The Southern Baptist Theological Seminary, 2005.

Young-Sung, "From Temple to House-Church in Luke-Acts: A Lukan Challenge to Korean Christianity." PhD diss., University of St. Andrews, 2000.

Zdero, Rad. *Nexus: The World House Church Reader,* Pasadena, CA: William Carey Library, 2007.

——. *The Global House Church Movement,* Pasadena, CA: William Carey Library, 2004.

# Glossary

High Context. It is culture that places a high value on interpersonal relationship (Donald Moorman, Harvest Waiting, 1993, p. 78).

Hindu Caste. Any of the social divisions into which Hindu society is traditionally divided, each caste having its own privileges and limitations, transferred by inheritance from one generation to the next.

Hinduism. It is a civilizational dynamic incorporating every aspect of life, embracing those who live in or identify with India and its culture. As a religion, it is a pluralistic network of religious beliefs and systems ranging from the philosophical (self-realization), to Vedic-influenced rituals, to popular expression (idols), to village Hinduism (animism, occultism). It absorbs elements of any religion it encounters and is widely regarded as an inclusive religion, one of tolerance and peace. Its global influence is significant through movements such as yoga, Hare Krishna/ISKCON, New Age of Living and others. Many concepts of Hinduism have become part of 21st century postmodern culture – yoga, gurus, karma, dharma, reincarnation and transcendental meditation. (Jason Mandryk, Operation World, 2010, p. 410).

House Church. The term "house church" is, however, not easy to define since there is a general confusion and lack of agreement regarding this term by people who use the term. Nevertheless, house church in the New Testament seem to be best described as a small group of believers who met regularly as a congregation in homes, halls, or some other available place for worship (i.e. study of the Word, prayer, fellowship, and the Lord's Supper, Baptism) under the guidance of pastoral leadership. Glenn E. Schaeffer refers to the house church as "the whole church in *microcosm*." (Schaeffer, "A Study of the House Church and Its Relevance for Planting Churches in the Greater Toronto Area," 1996, p. 21).

Low Context. It is culture that places a high value on the individual and privacy and therefore has a marginal emphasis on interpersonal relationship. (Donald Moorman, Harvest Waiting, p. 78).

Migrants. People who moves from rural area to urban area to get work.

Worldview. A worldview is a fundamental orientation of the heart, that can be expressed as a story or in a set of presuppositions (assumptions which may be true, partially true or entirely false) that we hold (consciously or subconsciously, consistently or inconsistently) about the basic constitution of reality, and that provides the foundation on which we live and move and have our being. The essence of a worldview lies deep in the inner recesses of the human life. A worldview involves the mind, but it is first of all a matter of the soul. It is a spiritual orientation more than it is a matter of mind alone. (James W. Sire, "What is a Worldview?" accessed February 2, 2016. http://www.christianity.com/christian-life/worldview/what-is-a-worldview-11627153.html).